THE BEAUTY OF
SHORT HOPS

THE BEAUTY OF SHORT HOPS

*How Chance and Circumstance
Confound the Moneyball
Approach to Baseball*

Sheldon Hirsch *and*
Alan Hirsch

McFarland & Company, Inc., Publishers

Jefferson, North Carolina, and London

LIBRARY OF CONGRESS CATALOGUING-IN-PUBLICATION DATA

Hirsch, Sheldon, 1955–
    The beauty of short hops : how chance and circumstance
confound the moneyball approach to baseball / Sheldon Hirsch
and Alan Hirsch.
        p.   cm.
    Includes bibliographical references and index.

    ISBN 978-0-7864-6288-9
    softcover : 50# alkaline paper ∞

    1. Baseball — Statistical methods.   2. Baseball — Mathematical
models.   I. Hirsch, Alan, 1959–   II. Title.
    GV877.H57   2011
    796.35702'1— dc22   2010054077

BRITISH LIBRARY CATALOGUING DATA ARE AVAILABLE

Front cover design by David Landis (Shake It Loose Graphics)

Manufactured in the United States of America

*McFarland & Company, Inc., Publishers
    Box 611, Jefferson, North Carolina 28640
    www.mcfarlandpub.com*

Table of Contents

To our parents,
Shula and Martin Hirsch,
who introduced us to baseball
and so much else

Preface

Here's a quirky one-question quiz. What do the following statements by prominent figures in the sports world have in common?

(1) "I mean, who the hell is Bill Russell?"—NBA coach and broadcaster Hubie Brown on the legendary Boston Celtics center Bill Russell

(2) "Players don't win championships. Coaches don't win championships. Organizations win championships."—Chicago Bulls general manager Jerry Krause

(3) "Anything but a World Series championship is unacceptable."—Yankees owner George Steinbrenner

The arrogant ranting of egomaniacs? True enough, but these utterances have something more specific in common. Brown, Krause and Steinbrenner all believe, on some deep level, that athletes are a secondary component of sports. To credit players with a team's success is like crediting pawns for the success of a chess master or cows for the success of a steakhouse.

The idea of a basketball coach condescending to Bill Russell seems remarkable only until you understand Hubie Brown's world view. A sportswriter once speculated that Hubie would prefer the mediocre Rory Sparrow (a workmanlike point guard) to Magic Johnson, because he could control Sparrow, tell him just what plays to run, whereas Johnson liked to improvise. When Hubie serves as color commentator for NBA games, he frequently uses the word "unfortunately," almost invariably in the same context. A play, presumably called by the coach or at least drilled by him in practice, had been run to perfection and led to an easy shot. "Unfortunately," the player missed the shot. In Hubie's world, the players spoil basketball. If only they could be replaced by robots, the best coach would win and the world would be just.

Jerry Krause's suggestion that organizations, rather than players or coaches, win championships, is transparent. Translation: Primary credit for the Bulls' titles belongs not to Michael Jordan or Phil Jackson but to Jerry Krause. Krause, like Hubie Brown, sees the players as merely a component of his master plan. The only difference is that Krause locates the success of a team at general manager rather than coach. And George Steinbrenner, of course, thought sports revolve around the owner. He pitched fits whenever his Yankees didn't dominate because he had spent whatever money his advisers said was needed and, since he had more money than everyone else, that should have been the end of it.

This attitude can reach a comical extreme. Consider an item that ran in a Boston newspaper after a Bruins victory over the Montreal Canadiens in an NHL playoff game a few decades ago. Rene Rancourt, the Bruins' anthem singer, received a note from Rouget Doucet, his Canadiens counterpart, crediting him with the Bruins' victory because his stirring rendition of the American and Canadian anthems inspired the crowd and set the tone for the game.

The tendency of people peripheral to the athletic contest to see themselves as the crucial variable entails seeing the game as essentially decided before it begins. Everyone from the owner on down to the anthem singer sees his pre-game work as decisive. All of them, consciously or not, diminish the role of the people who actually play the game and short-change the spontaneity and unpredictability that make sports so compelling.

Baseball is being hijacked by people with such a mindset. They call themselves "sabermetricians." The name, which combines an acronym for the Society for American Baseball Research with the Latin word for "measurement," was coined by Bill James, the father of a revolution that changed how the game is seen.* Sabermetrics, loosely defined as the search for objective knowledge about baseball through statistical analysis, has inspired a passionate response in opposite directions: followers believe it rescued the national pastime from a tradition of ignorance, while detractors claim

---

*This is no exaggeration. As Jonah Keri wrote in the introduction to a book of essays by sabermetricians published in 2006, "Today there's a whole new way of thinking about baseball that extends from the bleachers to every major league front office."

it damages the sport by drowning it in statistics that deflect attention from what really matters. They are both right.

Traditional Old School baseball featured what might charitably be called an anti-intellectual streak. In *Ball Four*, Jim Bouton's 1970 best-selling book, manager Joe Schultz advises his players, "Boys, it's a round ball and a round bat and you've got to hit it square." *That* passed for baseball wisdom, not some bearded guy with a spreadsheet and formula to measure the effect of a particular ballpark on runs created. That's not to say managers had zero use for numbers. They tracked rudimentary statistics like batting average, home runs, and runs batted in, as well as a pitcher's wins, losses, and earned run average. At least some of them did. At one point in *Ball Four*, when Bouton whips out data to convince Schultz he deserves a start, the manager says, "Aw shit. I don't want to see any statistics. I know what's going on out there just by watching the games."

Sabermetricians err in the opposite direction: they don't need to watch the games. They find the meaning of baseball in something other than the good old-fashioned athletic struggle; for them, it's in the numbers. The players are primarily vehicles for organizing data — names to attach to sets of statistics. Listening to sabermetricians, one gets the feeling that some of them enjoy board games like Strat-O-Matic Baseball more than real live major league games.

One finds this attitude exemplified in *Moneyball*, the best-selling book which announced and accelerated the success of the sabermetrics revolution. The protagonist, Oakland A's manager Billy Beane, grew up a Strat-O-Matic fanatic and can't stand the actual games. Some of *Moneyball's* most revealing moments monitor Beane during an A's game. He won't watch. He goes home or hangs around the weight room inside the clubhouse, sporadically checking the radio to hear what is happening just outside. When the A's went for a historic 20th consecutive victory, and a prospective record crowd jammed the Oakland freeways, Beane intended to drive home against the traffic rather than witness his team's pursuit of glory. Folks urged him to stick around for public relations reasons, and he reluctantly agreed. He still wouldn't watch the game, until the A's jumped out to an 11-run lead. At that point, he allowed Michael Lewis (*Moneyball's* author) to corral him into watching on television from the manager's office. When Lewis describes Beane's response as the game unfolds, we see why Beane finds the game torturous. He can't bear seeing the damn players muck up what should be a perfectly predictable contest.

Beane's attitude echoes that of Brown, Krause, and Steinbrenner. You win by spending the most dollars (Steinbrenner), spending them most efficiently (Krause), or devising the best game plan (Brown). Then the doggone players have to get involved and things go wrong. Even the guys who win for you are really beside the point. "I mean, who the hell is Bill Russell?" "Players don't win championships."

This perspective denigrates the central appeal of the athletic contest: its relentless capacity to surprise. Nothing is decided except by the players on the field of play, regardless of everyone else's best-laid plans. Especially in baseball, the capacity to surprise transcends the element of performance. The game's unpredictability manifests itself in all sorts of oddities that defy categorization — but are captured by this little poem we entered in a "Baseball Poetry" contest years ago:

Bard Game

A Red Sox fell, his foot undone,
rounding base, on a home run.
While he was carried off on cot,
a teammate finished off his trot
to score a broken run.

From time to time two runners come
together at a base, as one.
The fielders tag them both and wait
for puzzled ump to ruminate
on what is to be done.

Once, *three* runners met at third.
All were tagged, but no one stirred
'til Dazzy Vance, the king of cool,
triumphantly recited rule.
"*I'm* entitled to third," he averred.

Grateful for this consultation
from occupant of crowded station,
the men in blue stayed confusion
by embracing Daz' conclusion
to the player's jubilation.

4

> Forget the famous feats of Gods
> recorded on their baseball cards.
> Whimsy, wiles, weird mistakes
> and wondrousness — that's what makes
> baseball the game of bards.

The first stanza refers to Red Sox player Gabe Kapler tearing cartilage as he flew past second base — unnecessarily, as it turns out, because the ball cleared the fence. Kapler was too injured even to walk around the bases, so the Sox sent in a pinch runner *in the middle of the play*. They did so pursuant to a specific provision in the rulebook, Rule 5.10 (c): "If an accident to a runner is such as to prevent him from proceeding to a base to which he is entitled, as on a home run hit out of the playing field ... a substitute runner shall be permitted to complete the play." The very existence of such a rule reflects a sport aware of its own quirkiness.

Amazingly, this rule again came into play just a few years later, under even odder circumstances. In a game in 2008, when the slow-footed Bengie Molina of the Giants singled off the top of the wall, Omar Vizquel was sent in to pinch-run. Meanwhile, the Giants called for replay review, which determined that the ball was actually a home run. This created a problem for Molina, because a player removed from a game may not return. Once again, the situation was salvaged by the rule permitting a pinch-runner to complete a home run trot. Vizquel jogged around the bases and was credited with scoring the run on Molina's home run. (Molina received credit for the home run and RBI.)

Baseball's deliciously improvisational quality can determine outcomes, as when Game 2 of the 2007 American League Division Series between the Yankees and Indians turned on a swarm of insects that chose for refuge the neck of Yankees pitcher Joba Chamberlain. The rookie had been unhittable since joining the club in August, so the Yankees felt good about their chances when he started the eighth inning protecting a one-run lead, with the equally dominant Mariano Rivera poised to pitch the ninth. But the insects undid the rookie, despite repeated sprayings of insecticide by the team trainer. Chamberlain lost control and gave up the lead, a martyr to baseball's uncontrollable and unforeseeable craziness.

If that fate had befallen the Red Sox, an organization obsessed with data, the result would have been a comprehensive study about the risk of insect assault at each ballpark and which pitchers would handle it best. Maybe that's exaggeration. Maybe. Consider that the Red Sox employ a systems engineer to conduct esoteric studies based on mathematical modeling, one of which analyzed 100 years of weather in Boston to explore possible connections between climate and performance. Allegedly, the Red Sox used this material to identify the sort of pitcher who might succeed in Fenway Park in particular months.

It's bad enough that sabermetrics compromises a real appreciation of baseball, but making matters worse, it fails on its own terms. It cannot succeed in doing what its more ambitious adherents openly espouse: reducing baseball to a social science understandable wholly in terms of data. It often fails in the more limited effort to guide player selection and game decisions.

The bulk of this book exposes flaws at the heart of sabermetrics, beginning with a hard-hitting critique of *Moneyball*. Latter chapters present a vibrant vision of baseball that has been occluded by the fixation with numbers. George Will has written that "part of baseball's charm is the illusion it offers that life can be completely reduced to numbers." As we hope to show, Will is bang-on about "illusion" but wrong about "charm." Baseball's charm lies in that which cannot be reduced to numbers.

CHAPTER 1

Where *Moneyball* Went Wrong

Al Gore may not have invented the Internet, but he did something equally remarkable: he turned a PowerPoint presentation on science into a best-selling book and hit movie. That may seem incomprehensible, but Gore actually followed a proven formula. You can attract an audience for *any* material, no matter how arcane, if you make it part of a melodramatic story. Pit good against evil, and you've got a fighting chance. Michael Lewis understood as much when he conceived of *Moneyball*. Lewis encountered skepticism when he announced his intention to write a book about baseball which featured things like the proper relationship between on-base percentage and slugging percentage. But Lewis is a gifted storyteller who knew he could smuggle in esoteric statistical analysis provided it was part of an engaging story in which David whips Goliath. In his version, the geeks triumph over the jocks. What makes the story irresistible is that the geeks best the jocks at the jocks' own game — sports.

The outline of the story begins with a sport shrouded in ignorance. For more than a century, baseball managers made multiple decisions every game (bunt? steal? change pitchers?) without meaningful information. While baseball was celebrated as the sport beloved by intellectuals, those who ran the show proceeded mindlessly, never suspecting that there might be a concrete basis for their decisions. It wasn't just managers who languished in darkness, but also the general managers who assembled teams. What should they look for in players — power? Speed? Defense? For the longest time, most GMs relied on educated guesses at best. Often, there was nothing educated about their guesses. Throughout the history of America's national pastime, most managers and general managers, not to mention media and fans, were pretty much without a clue. That, in a nutshell, is the historical background for Michael Lewis's tale in *Moneyball*.

The good guys in his melodrama rode to the rescue armed only with a thirst for data and the ability to think outside the box. *Moneyball* features two such heroes: Bill James and Billy Beane. James as in Jesse, Billy as in the Kid, baseball outlaws worthy of the names. To be sure, James was hardly the first person to recognize the primitive nature of baseball knowledge. Back in the 1940s, the Brooklyn Dodgers hired a Canadian named Allan Roth to supply what were then considered advanced statistics. But James transformed how the game is seen. His annual *Baseball Abstract*, the first edition of which in 1977 attracted all of 75 buyers (who received a mimeographed collection of eclectic thoughts supported by data few would dream of gathering), eventually became must reading for the many Americans who start each day from April through October poring over box scores. James and his followers developed his approach to baseball into something systematic that he and they call sabermetrics.

As *Moneyball* emphasizes, baseball's managers and general managers were no fans of sabermetrics. Or, if they were, they read the stuff clandestinely, like a teenager sneaking a peek at *Playboy* and stuffing it in a drawer lest his parents find out what kind of boy he really is. To baseball insiders, paying attention to Bill James made as much sense as military generals studying astrology. Sparky Anderson said of James, "This guy has never played baseball. I don't think he knows much about it." Baseball was about spitting tobacco juice and knocking the cover off the ball, not deep thinking. As Joe Garagiola put it during a telecast, "If you want thinkers, go to the library."

Of course, there were exceptions. A few managers like Whitey Herzog, Earl Weaver and Tony La Russa paid more attention to numbers than did their counterparts. But the numbers that interested them were relatively primitive. La Russa earned such a reputation as a sage that three books chronicled his deep thinking. To read these books today is to find his reputation amusing. La Russa's idea of useful data is a comparison of different players' career numbers against the opposing pitcher — which, as Bill James would tell us, is next to meaningless.

Herzog, Weaver and La Russa succeeded because on balance a little knowledge beats complete ignorance. But make no mistake, even these three, and the handful of other thinking man's managers throughout baseball history, did relatively little thinking by the standards of Bill James and had shockingly little acquaintance with the vast reservoir of numbers that can inform questions about baseball that they didn't even think to ask. As James and fellow sabermetricians mined these data and made discoveries that could help major league teams, virtually all the insiders ignored them. An exception was Billy Beane, who became general manager of the Oakland Athletics in 1999, and *Moneyball*'s second hero.

Beane took James's insights seriously, and applied them to the task of assembling a team. At the highest level of generality, James's doctrine comes down to this: baseball decision-makers can't know what they're doing without numbers. There's some truth in that. To take just one example (which James multiplied by dozens every year), throughout baseball history managers have ordered intentional walks to load the bases. It doesn't take a calculator to realize that this is risky business. Pitching with the bases loaded affords no margin for error. The batter can expect pitches to hit, and *very good* pitches to hit if the pitcher falls behind. Yet managers continued to put their pitchers in that situation, just to gain the comparatively small advantage of a force at every base and potential double play. More importantly, for present purposes, they did so with no awareness of whether batters in fact hit better with the bases loaded. It turns out most do.

Or, to take another example, imagine a manager deciding whether to sacrifice bunt. If the play succeeds, you go from a runner on first with no outs to a runner on second with one out. Before bunting, shouldn't you know whether teams score more often in the latter situation than the former? Amazingly, no one thought to ask. And when James amassed the data, he found something that would undercut the assumption underlying the widespread use of the sacrifice bunt; in fact, teams score more with runners on first and nobody out than with runners on second and one out.

But if James's notion that one ignores data at his peril seems self-evident, Billy Beane's corollary is breathtaking: virtually *all you need* is data. If you suspect that's exaggeration, consider Michael Lewis's description of Beane's perspective: "The game can be reduced to a social science.... It is simply a matter of figuring out the odds, and exploiting the laws of probability" because "baseball players follow strikingly predictable patterns." *Moneyball* chronicles Beane's preparation for the annual player draft, where Beane turns on its head the conventional wisdom passed down for decades about how to spot future major leaguers. The traditional idea was to send scouts to watch or find highly-regarded prospects. These scouts, of course, notice the player who slugs home runs or blows batters away, but kids all over America dominate in school or club ball and only a tiny percentage have what it takes to make the Show. Scouts look beyond a player's achievements, focusing on his physique and athleticism. Is he a rare physical specimen with the speed, strength, and reflexes needed to compete at the very highest level? Scouts beat the bushes in search of such athletes.

Billy Beane thought they were wasting their time and his money. Just because you can outrun speeding bullets and leap over tall buildings doesn't mean you possess the set of skills needed to play major league baseball, especially the most crucial yet undervalued skill for batters: mastering the strike zone. Conversely, if you have that skill, you can make the big-time even if you're too slow and out of shape to finish the 100-yard dash without an inhaler. The way to determine whether a player has the necessary skills? His statistics. The player who hits well and walks often —*that's* the guy who catches Beane's attention, and to spot him all you need is *Baseball America* or some other obliging journal that lists the relevant statistics for college players nationwide.

In *Moneyball*, Lewis provides a savvy explanation for how Beane arrived at that view. A former major leaguer himself, Beane had been the kind of player scouts drooled over, a can't-miss star based on his sculpted body and sensational athleticism. But he turned out to be a bust, and his foray into the world of sabermetrics was an attempt to understand why. Beane ended up adopting an explanation for his failure that exonerated himself from blame; he was never much of a prospect to begin with. The blame lay with the misconceptions which led to false expectations. A torso men would kill for and a track star's speed do not predict success at hitting major league pitching.

Beane's inference was correct; world class athleticism doesn't begin to guarantee professional baseball success. The problem is that Beane took his epiphany to an equally silly extreme: forget body, forget athleticism, none of that matters. The flaw in this thinking was embodied by a key character in *Moneyball*, a portly catcher for Arizona State named Jeremy Brown. Scouts who saw Brown play unanimously declared that he had no chance of making the major leagues; he was too slow, fat, and non-athletic. Billy Beane regarded these scouts as if they were using a Ouija board to predict the stock market. He knew from personal experience. If the perfect body and unlimited athleticism did not make Beane a star, why should the absence of a decent body and athleticism stop someone? There was an elementary error of logic there, but logic doesn't matter to people of faith, and Billy Beane worshipped at the altar of on-base percentage. Beane coveted Jeremy Brown despite the catcher's physical shortcomings, because Brown knew how to get on base. He could hit (college pitching at least), and my how he drew walks.

Sabermetricians consider on-base percentage the holy grail.* Dumpy Jeremy Brown had such a great on-base percentage in college that Billy Beane drafted him in the first round. Michael Lewis turns Beane into a hero for such outside-the-box thinking. Lewis closes *Moneyball* with an epilogue centered on Brown's dominance in the A's minor league camp and culminating in his home run in a summer league game. In a critical passage in the epilogue, one of Brown's teammates tries to convince him to ignore his critics. "All that stuff they write in *Baseball America*— that's bullshit. You can play. That's all that matters. You can play. You think Babe Ruth was a stud? Hell no, he was a fat piece of shit." This amusing vignette, coupled with the ending a few pages later featuring Jeremy Brown's magical home run, combine to end *Moneyball* with a bang: the suggestion that Billy Beane has discovered the next Babe Ruth and been greeted with derision from a baseball world still living in yesterday's darkness.

---

*Of course, nothing is new, and in his book *The Numbers Game* Alan Schwarz shows that a healthy (if not excessive) respect for on-base percentage traces back to the nineteenth century and resurfaces, intermittently, throughout baseball history. However, until sabermetricians made on-base percentage a crusade, these moments of lucidity were the exception — the occasional writer or manager or general manager who saw the light — and didn't catch on.

Six years later, Jeremy Brown retired from organized baseball. He made it to the big leagues for a cup of coffee — ten at-bats. It turned out the scouts were right. To compare Jeremy Brown to Babe Ruth because both were fat and walked a lot was like comparing Manute Bol to Wilt Chamberlain because both were tall and blocked shots. Brown was an ungainly, modestly talented catcher who, given his athletic shortcomings, predictably peaked in college. Michael Lewis, caught up in a theory and a story, found their merger in this improbable spectacle. If Jeremy Brown didn't exist, Beane and Lewis would have invented him. In fact, that's exactly what they did.

Beane's apologists respond that the draft is always somewhat of a crap-shoot; Beane took Jeremy Brown with the 35th pick, not the first or second, and it's unfair to single out one flub. Okay, let's look at the seven players who joined Brown on Beane's "definite want" list prior to that 2002 draft: Stephen Stanley, John Baker, Mark Kiger, Shaun Larkin, John McCurdy, Brant Colamarino, and Brian Stavisky. Never heard of them? For good reason. Beane landed several of these players and practically levitated, believing they were undervalued by the benighted scouts and the general managers who rely on scouts. If they had made it big, Beane would have been deservedly hailed as a genius. That they went nowhere cannot be dismissed.

Brant Colamarino provides a comic aspect to the whole thing, but in service of a serious point. In *Moneyball*, after acquiring Colamarino, Beane's sidekick Paul DePodesta "wears an expression of pure bliss" because "no one else in baseball will agree, but Colamarino might be the best hitter in the country." At this point, Lewis can barely contain his admiration for the new baseball paradigm that his book illuminates: because of "how contrary the A's measuring devices were, they were able to draft possibly the best hitter in the country with the 218th pick of the draft." Then Lewis tells a funny anecdote from some months later, only he dumps the punch line on the wrong guys. "When Brant Colamarino removes his shirt for the first time in an A's minor league locker room he inspires his coaches to inform Billy [Beane] that 'Colamarino has tits.' Colamarino, like Jeremy Brown, does not look the way a young baseball player is meant to look. Titties are one of those things that just don't matter in a ballplayer."

12

Those are Lewis's words, but he leaves no doubt that Beane shares the sentiment, again driven by the perverse logic derived from his own experience: If powerful pectoral muscles didn't help Beane hit, then "titties" can't be a problem. We'll never know for sure the significance of Brant Colamarino's ill-shaped body, but we do know that he never made the major leagues. His pedestrian career in the minors culminated in a single season in Triple A, where he hit .243. We shouldn't be too rough on Colamarino. It's not as if he called *himself* the best hitter in baseball. But suffice to say he's done nothing to reverse the reputation of major league wannabes with titties.

Lewis discusses at length how Beane managed to compensate for the loss of star free agents Johnny Damon and Jason Giambi, and the discussion, while meant to laud Beane, actually highlights the same flawed thinking that led to some of Oakland's shakier selections in the 2002 draft. Lewis reports that, to figure out how to replace his departed stars, Beane relied on the "AVM system" (Advanced Value Metrics) for all-out quantification. The AVM folks allegedly plotted every play in every major league game for ten years. Not just the summary result as revealed by a scorebook (single, ground out, etc.) but an actual physical accounting of just where the ball landed and what transpired. One sentence by Lewis should suffice to convey the idea: "In the AVM recording of a baseball game, a line drive double in the left-center gap became a ball hit with a certain force that landed on point #643." Yes, every spot on the diamond was assigned a number. Using such data, DePodesta was able to assess the difference between playing Damon in center field and his likely replacement, Terrence Long. He determined that the total cost was 15 runs. Not 14 or 16. He was not rounding off. After all, precision is AVM's hallmark. "Damon over Long by 15" was a calculation, not an estimation.

Numerical precision of this sort may seem crackpot, but it has a distinguished pedigree with roots in the foundation of western thought. In Plato's *Republic*, Socrates undertakes a series of mathematical calculations which yield the conclusion that the philosopher is 729 times happier than the tyrant. This claim is no dottier than the notion that one can specify how many runs Johnny Damon's defense saved the A's.

To assess defense with such precision, you'd need to measure not only the velocity and arc of every batted ball, but also, among other things, wind resistance, weather (including wind and sun), game situation, and where the fielder was positioned at the start of each play. Paul DePodesta, to his credit, recognizes the latter. "There was still no exact number," Lewis quotes him as saying, "because the system doesn't measure where a player started from. It doesn't tell you how far a guy had to go to catch a ball." That's a nice concession, but the problem DePodesta describes isn't insurmountable. Why *not* look at where the player starts from? (Of course, the fact that players start in different positions may reflect superior ability at positioning, something computers would have a hard time measuring.) If you buy into the Beane/DePodesta program, it's just a matter of time before we can measure precisely how many runs every player is worth — on offense and defense. Indeed, Bill James has produced a formula he calls "Win Shares" to capture each player's value.

In later chapters, we will explain why this effort at total quantification lies somewhere between folly and fantasy. For present purposes, it's easy to see the flaw in the idea that the A's front office calculated with near exactitude how many runs Johnny Damon's defense saved. To know that, you'd need to factor in not only all the situation-specific factors mentioned above, but also the harm from Damon's poor throwing. That, in turn, requires knowing how many runners took an extra base because of his reputation for a weak arm. How would you get such information — by *asking* the players? And then asking whether they would have attempted to run against Terrence Long in the identical situation? You could, of course, see how many players went from first to third on Damon, but that information is meaningless in a vacuum. No two outfielders field the same number of balls, in the same spot, with the same runners on base, in the same game situations.

Moneyball helped accelerate a paradigm shift, resulting in the replacement of one flawed outlook by another. If the traditional view of baseball allowed little room for sophisticated numerical analysis, failing even to scrape the surface of potentially fruitful knowledge, the new paradigm placed too much confidence in numbers of all kinds, such as the on-base percentage of fat college catchers and the number of runs saved by particular outfielders. This isn't surprising, because the very nature of paradigm formation invites error. Stephen Jay Gould wrote an important essay that captures the problem. For good measure, Gould's essay revolves around baseball.

Gould talks about the 1986 World Series — you know, the one where Bill Buckner cost the Red Sox their first championship in 68 years, continuing their curse until it mercifully ended almost two decades later. But wait a minute: did Buckner really cost the Red Sox the Series? If you're like most people, you think that had he handled that routine ground ball off the bat of Mookie Wilson with two outs and the Red Sox leading in the ninth inning of Game 7, the Red Sox would have been world champions. Since he flubbed it, the Mets were crowned instead and Red Sox Nation went into a collective depression.

That widely accepted account is false. The messier reality is that the Mets had already rallied to tie the game by the time Wilson chopped the fateful grounder to first. Had Buckner made the play, the game would have gone into extra innings, where the Red Sox had less than a 50-50 chance of prevailing. (The Mets had the momentum, the home team's advantage of batting last, and a less depleted relief corps.) Moreover, this was Game 6, not Game 7. Thus, even after Buckner's miscue, the Series was tied at three games apiece, with the Red Sox still very much alive. Indeed, in Game 7, they jumped out to a three-run lead. At that point, *post–Buckner*, they were still clear favorites to win the World Series.

How can people get basic facts wrong about one of the most famous games in baseball history? For the same reason, Stephen Jay Gould explained, that we've received an incomplete version of the famous battle at the Alamo in 1836. If Buckner is an exaggerated goat, Jim Bowie may be an exaggerated hero. History teaches that Bowie went down heroically fighting when General Santa Anna's forces massacred him and his badly outnumbered men. According to the legend, Bowie unthinkingly (in the best sense of the word) accepted martyrdom. But a letter by Bowie (and other circumstantial evidence) indicates that he actually sought a diplomatic resolution that would have resulted in a peaceful surrender. If so, Bowie is not quite the unadulterated macho man that folklore suggests. More to the point, Bowie's letter is prominently displayed in the foyer of the Alamo shrine, where visitors can't miss it. Yet historians and laypeople alike walk in imagining Bowie as wholly unwilling to surrender, read the letter suggesting otherwise, and ignore its implications. According to Gould, they do so because the letter complicates a satisfyingly melodramatic story.

Gould shrewdly connects the oversight of Bowie's revealing letter with the mis-recollection of the 1986 World Series. In each case, the tidy version of history handed down feeds a need. We need heroes and goats. Moreover, Red Sox fans and foes liked to think of the team as cursed. How perfect, then, to imagine that the Red Sox had the World Series in their grasp until a tragic muff. The reality, that they might not have won anyway, and could have won regardless, is much less satisfying.

For shorthand, we'll call this tidying-up tendency the Buckner-Bowie, which we have rehearsed because it goes a long way toward explaining the phenomenon of paradigm shifts and resulting errors. Insofar as *Moneyball* more or less announced and affected a paradigm shift, it comes as little surprise that its pages are filled with Buckner-Bowie errors.

Take the case of Scott Hatteberg. Hatteberg is presented as Exhibit C (right behind Jeremy Brown and the guy with titties) of Billy Beane's appreciation of players everyone else dismisses. Another non-athletic catcher, Hatteberg toiled for four seasons in Boston where, at least according to Michael Lewis, his subtle genius was overlooked by fans, coaches and front office alike. Hatteberg was a thinking man's player who did the sorts of things Beane worships — took pitches, worked counts, drew bases on balls. It's hard to believe that Red Sox Nation found nothing admirable in this, but that's Lewis's story; Hatteberg received no love in Boston, and in large part for that reason was set to retire at 32.

Good timing saved him. Just before Hatteberg traded in his bats for fly fishing rods, Oakland lost Jason Giambi to free agency. Beane saw in Hatteberg a poor man's Jason Giambi. Literally. Beane couldn't afford Giambi, but he could afford Hatteberg because no one else appreciated him. Hatteberg deferred retirement and, to hear Lewis tell it, he and the A's lived happily ever after. Lewis gushes about their symbiotic relationship. Hatteberg was "Billy Beane's creation" and he thrived in an environment where his unusual skills were appreciated, even encouraged.

Lewis neglects to mention that Hatteberg's actual performance did not improve. His on-base percentages at Boston and Oakland were nearly identical (.357 and .355) and his slugging percentage considerably higher with the Red Sox. The story got more intriguing after Hatteberg left Oakland four years later. He signed with Cincinnati as a free agent in 2006, and *that's* where he thrived. In his two full seasons with the Reds, the 36-year-old journeyman suddenly posted numbers worthy of a star, including an on-base percentage near .400.

A large part of Beane's genius, in Lewis's telling, concerns knowing when to obtain and release players; he buys low and sells high. But the opposite was the case with Hatteberg. Beane signed him for $900,000 but after three seasons had to pay him $2,450,000. Beane lost interest in him, and Cincinnati signed him to a one-year contract for the bargain basement price of $750,000. *Moneyball* claims Beane succeeded on a low budget because of mega-efficiency, but Hatteberg reflects Beane at his least efficient; at Cincinnati, Hatteberg's productivity-per-dollar was astronomically higher than at Oakland.

Hatteberg's success at Cincinnati took place after *Moneyball* was published, so one can't fault Lewis for ignoring it. But it is nevertheless revealing that when you map Hatteberg's career, you find something you couldn't possibly imagine based on *Moneyball*'s treatment of him. He got no better when he came to Oakland, and got much better when he left.

We haven't even gotten to the peak (or nadir) of Lewis's fairy tale treatment of Hatteberg. He credits the converted first baseman with the A's *pitching* success. A key for the A's was the revival of pitcher Chad Bradford. Lewis claims that "[Bradford's] confidence returned about the same time Scott Hatteberg started telling him what the hitters said on the rare occasions they got to first base against him." Since Bradford figures prominently in *Moneyball* as the kind of pitcher that Beane (virtually alone among general managers) appreciates, Lewis's "insight" here is a delicious example of the Buckner-Bowie tendency to tidy things up in dramatically satisfying fashion. The A's prospered because a quintessential Beane field player saved a quintessential Beane pitcher.

The emphasis on Bradford suggests *Moneyball*'s biggest flaw: it distorts the reason for Oakland's success. The team thrived primarily because of superb pitching. During its run of post-season appearances, the A's were second or third in the league in fewest runs allowed, whereas in some of those seasons, they finished in the bottom half in runs scored. At the heart of the pitching staff were three dominant starters: Mark Mulder, Tim Hudson, and Barry Zito. All three were early-round draft picks highly scouted and well-regarded — Mulder and Zito were selected in the top ten of their respective drafts. This was hardly a case of Beane spotting sleepers (like Jeremy Brown and Brant Colamarino) because of nuanced numbers. Indeed, Michael Lewis does not suggest that sabermetrics had anything to do with Beane drafting the three studs who led Oakland to greatness. Instead, he virtually ignores them. Lewis devotes a few paragraphs to the Big Three (making the strained claim that Beane appreciated them for quirky reasons), quickly dropping them and transitioning to an entire chapter on ... Chad Bradford.

If Oakland succeeded largely because of three touted pitchers, *Moneyball*'s juicy thesis begins to melt away. But Bradford is a guy who (at least according to Lewis), despite success in the minor leagues, scared off most general managers. No one trusted his success in the minor leagues because of his ungainly submarine throwing motion, but the Oakland front office, drawing on statistical insights, saw a diamond in the rough. Lewis tells us that "the Oakland A's pay Chad Bradford [just] 237,000 a year" and regard him as "one of the most effective relief pitchers in all of baseball." Ungainly, unappreciated, underpaid and underrated — a cross between Jeremy Brown and Scott Hatteberg. One can understand why Lewis, ever the gifted storyteller, devotes more than 40 pages to this relatively anonymous relief pitcher.

Which is fine, except that *Moneyball* implies that Bradford played a crucial role in Oakland's success. In a typical season, Zito, Mulder, and Hudson gave the team more than 650 quality innings and roughly 50 wins, whereas Chad Bradford never won more than seven games and topped out at 77 innings. What about saves? Bradford recorded hardly any because Oakland never trusted him to be their closer. In a book ostensibly written to explain a team's success, Michael Lewis treats three dominant pitchers as an afterthought and obsesses about a pretty good middle-reliever.

We saw how the ending of *Moneyball* (Jeremy Brown's home run, conjuring Babe Ruth) reflects Lewis's impulse to spin a tale that bears an awkward relationship with reality. As it happens, the very first sentence of *Moneyball* foreshadows the problem: "I wrote this book because I fell in love with a story." How true. As is the oldest cliché known to man: love is blind.

Lewis's blind love of his story produces any number of absurdities. Kevin Youkilis makes a brief appearance in *Moneyball* as another quintessential Beane-type player, referred to by the A's front office in literally worshipful terms: "the Greek God of walks." Youkilis isn't Greek, but that's the least of the inaccuracies. According to Lewis, Youkilis, then a minor leaguer whom Beane craved, "was a fat third baseman who couldn't run, throw or field" but walked a ton. Anyone who has seen Youkilis play with the Boston Red Sox will laugh at Lewis's assessment. Youkilis runs decently by major league standards, is a Gold Glove first baseman (who for awhile even held the record for consecutive games without an error), plays a solid third base, and throws fine. Unless Youkilis somehow dramatically improved his speed, fielding, and throwing after *Moneyball* was written, we have here another prime example of Buckner-Bowie. Kevin Youkilis as a talented if somewhat underrated player would not yield a satisfying story. To see him as another Jeremy Brown — a fat, non-athletic kid who walks a lot and therefore catches the eye of Billy Beane — is a temptation Lewis found irresistible.

If warped perceptions of various players led Beane and Lewis astray, that's not the biggest flaw in their thinking reflected in *Moneyball*. A more far-reaching flub concerns the revolutionary theory about pitching devised by a sabermetrician named Voros McCracken. McCracken hypothesized, then allegedly proved, something staggering. Simply put, the only items a pitcher controls, and thus the only statistics relevant to an assessment of his performance, are walks, strikeouts, and home runs. When a ball is put in play, and not over the fence, what happens is almost exclusively a matter of luck. No less an authority than Bill James stamped this finding "basically true" and "obviously very important." Billy Beane bought into it as well, which Michael Lewis holds up as part of the explanation for Beane's success.

If McCracken is right, balls put in play against the overpowering

Sandy Koufax or Roger Clemens were no less likely to be base hits (provided they didn't clear the fence) than balls put into play against baseball's weakest pitchers. McCracken's hypothesis seems even more staggering when we think about legendary "junk ball" pitchers over the decades, guys like Eddie Lopat and Mike Cuellar, who succeeded (according to everyone's eyes and the conventional wisdom) because they kept batters off-balance and induced weakly hit balls. And what about Mariano Rivera, who breaks bats on a regular basis? Is it possible that balls put in play against his cutter are no less likely to be base hits than balls put in play against some journeyman's fat fastballs? If McCracken is right, Koufax, Clemens, Lopat, Cuellar, Rivera and every other pitcher who enjoyed long-term success succeeded solely because of the combination of good control, keeping the ball from being hit at all (i.e., amassing strikeouts), and keeping it in the ballpark when it was hit. The notion that some pitchers induce weakly hit balls is urban legend. When balls are put into play, and not over the fence, all pitchers are equal.

McCracken's doctrine rocked cyberspace — after he published his findings on his website, he received 1,700 e-mails in two days. And for good reason. If true, his idea changes everything from the Cy Young Award voting to the player draft to the use of pitchers in a game and season — in other words, the evaluation of performance past, present, and future. Most pitchers' statistics become useless. The true evaluation of a pitcher should be gleaned solely from walks, strikeouts and home runs. The remaining category that measures the outcome of each at-bat, batting average on balls in play (BABIP), is a matter of luck that will even out over time. If a pitcher has an unsuccessful season despite good numbers with respect to strikeouts, walks, and home runs, that means balls hit against him happened to find holes. He had a bad BABIP, and BABIP is random. Next year, he figures to do much better. Conversely, the pitcher who does well despite faring not so great in terms of walks, strikeouts, and homers was the beneficiary of luck — a low BABIP that will presumably not carry over to next year.

Sabermetricians scrambled to test McCracken's hypothesis and confirmed its truth. That, at any rate, is Michael Lewis's fantastic version. In the real world, the best that can be said for McCracken's idea is that it would be true if it weren't false. Its falsity is easily demonstrated. Quite simply, if BABIP is a matter of luck, all pitchers' career BABIPs should be roughly the same. In a given season or two, a pitcher may be lucky or unlucky, but luck evens out over time. There remain pertinent variables, especially ballpark and defense. The pitcher who spends most of his career in a hitting-friendly park or on a poor defensive team will suffer when it comes to BABIP. That problem we can take care of by comparing pitchers who spend most of their careers with the same team. Of course, an inherent element of randomness cannot be escaped. If you flip a coin 100 times in 100 different trials you will not get the identical results each time. But the results figure to be close enough — reasonably close to 50-50 heads-tails in virtually all trials. Similarly, if McCracken were right, the variation among pitchers' career BABIPs should be minimal, at least among pitchers who played on the same team.

With all this in mind, a little poking around suffices to debunk McCracken. We will illustrate the point without making your eyes glaze over by looking at just four pitchers: Sandy Koufax, Johnny Podres, Jonathan Papelbon, and Manny Delcarmen. Koufax and Podres spent most of their careers together on the Dodgers in the 1950s and '60s, Papelbon and Delcarmen with the Red Sox in the 2000s, so we control to a large extent for variations among defense and ballpark. Koufax and Papelbon have the reputation of being extremely difficult to hit, and the other two do not. If conventional wisdom is correct, Koufax and Papelbon should have lowers BABIPs than Podres and Delcarmen. If McCracken is correct, there's no reason to expect Koufax and Papelbon to have any advantage. Here are the actual BABIPs — the batting average against from non-home run batted balls: Koufax, .259; Papelbon, .264; Podres, 282; Delcarmen, .292.*

In other words, the real world produces the results predicted by conventional wisdom and observation, not the results predicted by McCracken's hypothesis. For good measure look at Mike Cuellar, a quintessential junk ball pitcher famous for inducing weakly hit balls. Sure

---

*In the cases of Papelbon and Delcarmen, who are still active, the figures are through the half-way point of the 2010 season, before Delcarmen was traded.

enough, his BABIP (.267) was superb. Dave Stieb, who posted an even better BABIP (.263), managed to succeed over a long career despite a poor walk/strikeout ratio and yielding a fair number of home runs. A better example still is Catfish Hunter, a superstar despite giving up home runs by the bucket and not striking out all that many batters. His propensity to yield weakly hit balls produced the amazingly low BABIP of .246. Thus refutes McCracken.*

McCracken might respond that the variations we found were relatively small. Turning our findings on their head, he might say: "Koufax only .23 better than Podres proves I'm basically right." But it doesn't. Rather, it illustrates a key truth: baseball is a game of small advantages. Consider that a .300 batting average is considered an emblem of excellence, whereas .250 epitomizes mediocrity. The difference between .300 and .250 is one hit every 20 at-bats. Or take one of the categories McCracken considers crucial: strikeouts. Koufax averaged nine strikeouts per nine innings compared to Podres's seven — just two more per game. Koufax's edge over Podres in inducing weaker batted balls, and striking out more batters, are both statistically small. They, along with his other advantages (allowing fewer walks and home runs), add up to the difference between the game's greatest pitcher and a solid pitcher. Which is itself smaller than one might think — roughly one run every nine innings.

McCracken did contribute to a proper understanding of baseball by focusing attention on a major factor often underemphasized: luck. But he wildly exaggerated the role of luck when suggesting that pitchers have no control over batted balls that remain in the park. Apparently no bad deed goes unrewarded; McCracken's goof landed him a job as "pitching consultant" in the Red Sox front office. Not bad for a bored paralegal whose playing days ended in high school. Talk about luck!

The McCracken episode raises an important question. Among the many baseball luminaries taken in by the false theory were Bill James and

---

*The examples we have given are not exceptions. Rather, pitchers' career BABIPs show substantial variation across the board. For a thorough debunking of McCracken's theory, we refer readers to one of the few sabermetricians who wasn't bamboozled. See Tom Tippett, "Can Pitchers Prevent Hits on Balls in Play?" *Diamond Mind Baseball*, http://www.diamond-mind.com/articles/ipavg2.htm.

Paul DePodesta. How could these undeniably intelligent folks, who dedicate much of their lives to the study of baseball, get something so basic so wrong? The question looms large because the embrace of McCracken's folly was only an extreme instance of a more common phenomenon — sabermetricians missing something fairly obvious to anyone with a decent grasp of baseball. How can this happen?

We have glimpsed the explanation: the Buckner-Bowie phenomenon. The idea that the fate of a batted ball is pure luck has a seductive tidiness, calling to mind H.L. Mencken's quip: "For every complex problem, there is an answer that is clear, simple — and wrong." Stephen Jay Gould helped us understand why the "clear" and "simple" often trump the "wrong." The tendency to latch on to tidy, dramatic stories may be so strong that even the brainiest succumb to it.

If McCracken's idea fooled sabermetricians with nothing directly at stake, it's easy to understand how it fooled Billy Beane. Beane must, for a living, predict the performance of pitchers. McCracken's silver bullet made it easy to do so; just look at home runs, walks, and strikeouts. And it played to Beane's weakness, the idea that he can outsmart other general managers through awareness of numerical nuggets. His competitors would overrate pitchers who had done well only because they lucked out on batted balls, and underrate those who did poorly because of bad luck. Armed with McCracken's revolutionary insight, Beane would know better.

Moneyball*'s Central Fallacy*

A critical question remains. Beane's errors permeate *Moneyball* (usually presented as wisdom), but his success cannot be written off as a quirk. His teams accomplished too much, averaging 97 wins over a five-season stretch, and repeatedly making it to the post-season. How did his low-budget Oakland A's manage to do so well for so long?

The answer has three parts. The first we already noted: Beane's shrewdness or good fortune in landing three elite starting pitchers. Second, despite everything we've said, Beane did benefit from some saber-insights, such as closers being overrated and on-base percentage underrated. Third, and most important, *Moneyball* searched for the answer to a misleading question: how does Beane, with a shoestring budget, manage the miracle of competing with high-payroll teams? The answer is that there was no miracle to explain in the first place. A proper understanding of baseball reveals that a disadvantage in payroll is not as big a deal as is generally assumed.

By its very nature, major league baseball produces relatively balanced competition. The worst team in baseball history since 1900, the 1962 Mets, won a fourth of its games, and the very best teams (1927 Yankees, 1954 Indians, 2001 Mariners) lost almost a third. Such parity distinguishes baseball from other team sports. In football, the worst team, the 2008 Lions, was winless, and the best teams, the 1972 Dolphins and 2007 Patriots, unbeaten. Similarly, in basketball, dominant teams win over 80 percent of their games and the worst teams lose over 80 percent.

One reason for baseball's inherent parity is that individual superstars have a much more limited impact than in other sports. Take, for example, the player who commands the biggest bucks, Alex Rodriguez. A-Rod is an ordinary third baseman defensively, so any extraordinary contribution figures to come at the plate. A typical game features roughly 85 events (at-bats), and offensively A-Rod is involved in just four or five. More often than not, those few events are unremarkable. By contrast, LeBron James is the best player on the court virtually every game, and handles the ball on almost every offensive possession. Tom Brady rarely has an off-day, and is involved in roughly half the plays in a game. Baseball doesn't work that way. The game's best hitters fail substantially more than they succeed, and on the many days when he goes 0–4, A-Rod has hardly more impact on the game than the bat boy.

A-Rod is special because he can (or at least once could) hit 50 home runs — if 20 of his home runs were singles instead, the Yankees wouldn't have shelled out record sums to land him. Yet A-Rod's home runs have less of an impact than one might think. In a typical season, A-Rod bangs maybe six to eight home runs more than the average leading power hitter on other teams. Some of those surplus home runs come in defeats, and obviously his team would have won some of the other games without A-Rod's dinger. At the end of the day, A-Rod gives the Yankees just a few more wins than they'd manage if he were replaced by a lower-profile slugger whom other teams can afford to pay.

Moneyball makes a big deal about the A's maintaining their overall record while losing Jason Giambi and Johnny Damon to free agency, suggesting that they pulled off this feat because of Billy Beane's mastery at finding good low-cost replacements. But the book exaggerates the difficulty of the achievement. Just a few years earlier, the Seattle Mariners lost two of the greatest players of all-time, A-Rod and Ken Griffey, Jr., and improved tremendously. The last year they had both of these superstars was 1999, and the team won just 79 games. Griffey was traded for two journeymen and two minor leaguers. Critics charged that the Mariners had virtually given him away. Yet in 2000, Seattle won 91 games. Then they lost A-Rod to free agency, and now everyone *knew* they were doomed. Except in 2001 they won 116 games, nearly the best record in baseball history. That's right, they won 25 more games after losing A-Rod. From 1999 to 2001, the Mariners registered a staggering two-season improvement of 37 wins after losing two future Hall of Famers in their prime.

It wasn't magic. Before the 2001 season the Mariners acquired a pretty good rookie outfielder named Ichiro Suzuki and a second baseman, Bret Boone, who supplied far more power than anyone expected. In addition, the Mariners made small upgrades at several positions, especially on the mound. That they more than compensated for the loss of two immortals seems miraculous, but only until we realize that Griffey and Rodriguez, like Giambi and Damon, were overrated — all stars are. Again, the individual player simply doesn't have a decisive impact on most games.

Starting pitchers are the exception, the players who can provide a team with a major advantage. Unlike the field player, who participates in just a handful of plays, the starting pitcher may be involved in half. Yet the disproportionate role of the starting pitcher actually contributes to baseball's parity. Consider that in 1972, Steve Carlton won 27 games for a team that won 59 overall. With Carlton pitching, the Phils were championship quality; without him, a disaster. What separated the 1927 Yankees from routinely great teams was the historic combination of Babe Ruth and Lou Gehrig, but a dominant pitcher like Carlton could easily hold those two hitless. With the right person on the mound, one of the worst teams in baseball history would have an excellent chance of beating the game's greatest juggernaut.

Carlton presents an extreme case but illustrates a point that's true across the board; in any given game, one man can neutralize a superior opponent. Critically, that one man needn't be a star. An average pitcher on a very good day has the same disproportionate effect as a stud like Carlton, and all major league starters are capable of very good days. The 1927 Yankees, with a lineup dubbed Murderer's Row, had plenty of games where their bats were quiet — 40 times they scored three or fewer runs. A strong effort by the opposing pitcher single-handedly neutralized Murderer's Row.

If even mediocre pitchers can, on a good day, shut down top teams, the converse is equally true: the best pitchers have plenty of off-days. In that dominant 1972 season, Carlton gave up four or more runs ten times. Even the star pitcher on his good days guarantees nothing, because the other team's starter may shut down your offense. In 1968, Bob Gibson's ERA was a staggering 1.12. Almost every game he pitched was a gem. Even so, he lost nine times. A team that puts an outstanding pitcher on the mound every day, such as the 1969 Orioles, will still lose its share of games.

In addition, starting pitchers are a notoriously fickle lot. Over the last decade the big-budget Yankees have signed a long list of coveted free agent starting pitchers who turned out to be busts — Javier Vasquez, Kevin Brown, Kenny Rogers, Carl Pavano, Jared Wright, Randy Johnson, Jose Contreras, and Kei Igawa. Pitchers get injured more than field players, and they're less consistent even when healthy. It is not uncommon for a pitcher who wins 20 games to accomplish little or nothing the next season. Recent examples include Bartolo Colon (21–8 to 1–5), Roy Halladay (22–7 to 8–8), Curt Schilling (21–6 to 8–8), David Wells (20–8 to 5–7), Jon Lieber (20–6 to 6–8), Andy Pettitte (21–8 to 6–4), and Josh Beckett (20–7 to 12–10).

Another reason for baseball's inherent parity is the enormous role of luck. This tends to be the case in a low-scoring sport, where one bad break can determine the outcome. In soccer, the ball that hits the crossbar often decides a game, because a tie or one-goal margin is commonplace. For the same reason, luck permeates baseball. It often comes disguised. When a player mired in a slump hits a few ground balls through the infield, the crowd roars and the media speculate that he's coming alive. If the same ball is a few feet to either side, it's a routine out, maybe even a double play; the crowd boos and everyone laments the deepening of the player's slump. A few feet determine not only the fulminations of fans and media but also the outcome of ballgames. That ground ball that finds a hole scores two runs and wins the game; a little to either side yields a different result.

Baseball's "game of inches" quality is only one facet of the larger phenomenon of luck or happenstance. Close calls by umpires play a decisive role in many games, as does Mother Nature — the direction and strength of the wind determine whether a ball is a game-winning home run or a harmless fly. So too, the size and shape of the ballpark dictate the fate of many batted balls.

While baseball always featured a built-in parity, over time the changing nature of the sport has created even more parity. (It used to be that the best teams won two-thirds of their games. Now it's closer to three-fifths.) To a certain extent, this results from changes made by major league baseball. A player draft instituted in 1965, in which the order of selection varies inversely with a team's record, provided losing teams access to the top prospects. When the top free agents leave a team for greener pastures, the team is typically compensated with high draft picks. In addition, a "luxury tax" prevents teams from spending too much money without incurring a fee that funds cash-strapped teams.

But the principal reason for ever-increasing parity was captured by Stephen Jay Gould in an essay about the disappearance of .400 hitters. Gould debunked the suggestion that this development reflects anything disappointing about modern baseball. It's not that the great hitters are any less great, but that *everyone* is better. In a sport's infancy, superstars dominate; Wilt Chamberlain averages 50 points a game and Babe Ruth hits more home runs than any *team* in the American League. Feats like that become impossible as the level of competition improves. The 2009 version of Ted Williams cannot hit .400 because he faces better pitching and defense. A developing system features regression to the mean — no .400 hitters and no .200 hitters either.

Gould's analysis about individual players applies, by extension, to teams. A rising tide levels the current. With decreased dominance by superstars, the ability to buy marquee players produces diminishing returns. The extreme case drives home the point; If all players were interchangeable, a disadvantage in money would be irrelevant. Teams tend to bunch up towards the middle — none win or lose 120 games. This equalizing tendency occurs in part because of the advancement and dissemination of knowledge at every level from youth to the major leagues. Over time there is vast improvement in training and fundamentals, and expanded means of communicating these advances (through videotapes, the internet, and so forth), which raises the caliber of athletes across the board. But the biggest reason for the higher and more equalized level of competition is the expanded pool of available athletes. That, in turn, resulted primarily from three developments: advanced scouting, racial integration, and globalization.

Major league baseball has improved largely because of advances in identifying talent around the world. For baseball's first several decades, scouting was haphazard. Teams had a few scouts to cover the entire nation, and nothing but word of mouth to direct them to repositories of talent. We'll never know how many would-be major leaguers spent their baseball lives undiscovered while dominating sandlot or semi-pro ball in forsaken corners of the universe, but we have every reason to believe the number was high. In oral histories from the early twentieth century through the 1940s, one finds player after player discovered serendipitously. A few charming examples should suffice. Here's George Pipgras (in Donald Honig's book *Baseball When the Grass Was Real*) explaining how he came to the attention of a big-league team:

> When I came out of the army in 1918, I went up to Fulda, Minnesota, a little old country town, to pitch semipro ball. There was a train that ran right behind center field, and every so often when I was pitching, I'd notice the train would stop and just stand still out there in deep center field. I didn't know it at the time, but I was being scouted by the train conductor. He was a fellow that was interested in baseball, and he recommended me to the White Sox. Can you imagine that fellow stopping the train to watch a ballgame?

Were it not for this inquisitive conductor, Pipgras, who was 10–3 for the 1927 Yankees and won 24 games the following year, could easily have spent his life in little old country towns.

If the circumstances that led to Pipgras's discovery seem random, consider how 1930s pitcher Elbie Fletcher made the big leagues — through a contest run by a Boston newspaper "to recommend a high school player" who could eventually make the majors. Fletcher organized a campaign on his own behalf, enlisting friends and relatives to recommend him. He won the contest, and with it a free trip to the Braves training camp, where he pitched his way onto the team.

When players' fates are determined by the whims of train conductors and newspaper contests, you know that many quality players won't be discovered. Scouting was such that Paul Krichell and Tom Greenwade, the men who discovered Lou Gehrig and Mickey Mantle respectively, became part of baseball lore. In today's information age, someone like Gehrig or Mantle is likely to grace the pages of *Sports Illustrated* by the eighth grade, and would surely appear in some blog, "100 Best Young Players in America." The accompanying blog discussion would include the adolescent's performance in AAU competition, and if the trend continues, those games will soon be on ESPN. Who needs Tom Greenwade beating the bushes in Oklahoma mine country?

The introduction of African Americans and later players from all over the globe expanded the proliferation of talent astronomically.* One way to see the effect is to compare the shortstop position of the Yankees in the late 1960s to that of the Red Sox four decades later. The Yankees handed the position to Gene Michael, a decent fielder nicknamed "Stick" only because of his lean physique, not because he could hit — he couldn't. Michael held on to the position for five years in which he batted more than .235 only once and hit a *total* of 11 home runs. Michael could field okay, but was no Gold Glover. Yet for five seasons the Yankees could not find anyone better and didn't fret; Michael was considered adequate.

Fast-forward to 2004 and the Boston Red Sox. Their shortstop for several years, the formidable Nomar Garciaparra, had become disenchanted

---

*There are, of course, countervailing factors, such as an increase in the number of professional sports that siphon off athletic talent. On the other hand, the population has increased enormously over time, and that's in America alone. When globalization is factored in, the pool of potential athletes increases exponentially, and more than compensates for the loss of would-be professional baseball players to other sports.

and the Red Sox felt they had to trade him. They acquired Orlando Cabrera, a shortstop not considered in Garciaparra's league. In part because of the overrating of superstars like Garciaparra, it was universally believed that the trade damaged the Red Sox. But Cabrera, if no Nomar, was no Gene Michael either. He sports a lifetime batting average over .270 and his bat has some pop. He also fielded better than Garciaparra, and with him at short, the Red Sox won their first World Series in almost a century.

You'd think the front office would have been thrilled with Cabrera, but in this era of plentiful talent, you can afford to be picky. Cabrera lacked a good batting eye, so they let him go and signed Edgar Renteria, a somewhat stronger offensive player. After one year, Renteria gave way to a platoon of Alex Gonzalez and Alex Cora, followed by Julio Lugo, Jed Lowrie, Nick Green, Gonzalez again, and Marco Scutaro — nine shortstops in six years, and the Sox won with them all.

The musical chairs reflected the Sox's failure to find a guy who could give them what they wanted both at bat and in the field, and their vacillations over the proper balance between the two. But what's most revealing is the availability of all these shortstops of reasonable quality. The weakest of the nine would have delighted the Yankees in the days when Gene Michael held the job for five seasons. The main reason for the availability of so many quality shortstops is globalization. Renteria and Cabrera are from Colombia, Lugo from the Dominican Republic, Gonzalez and Scutaro from Venezuela, and Cora from Puerto Rico. Teams trying to upgrade now have a world to look at. (As of 2009, major leaguers hail from 22 nations and five continents. Twenty-nine percent of players come from abroad. The figure was 12 percent in 1980 and 8 percent in 1960.)

The Sox's experience with Garciaparra echoes what happened to the Mariners and A's a few years earlier; they lost their superstar and were none the worse for wear, because of the availability of solid replacements. Then, on account of the proliferation of quality shortstops, they traded theirs in for someone new year after year with no noticeable effect. With the extensive supply of good players, teams don't start the likes of Gene Michael for long.

Because of baseball's built-in parity, significantly enhanced by the game's improvement across the board, small-market teams don't face the enormous disadvantage people assume. It's better to be rich than poor, but the forces of parity blunt the effect of the dollar, helping low-payroll teams compete. That is why any number of small-market teams, most notably Atlanta and Minnesota, have been able to succeed for a period of years. Michael Lewis's premise, that only genius could account for Oakland's success, is flawed.

Postscript

A test of *Moneyball*'s thesis comes after the fact. If Billy Beane was indeed a step (or two or three) ahead of the pack, he figured to stay that way. So what happened to the Oakland A's following their successful run from 1998 to 2003? The short answer is that they plopped and then flopped. From 2004 to 2006 the A's averaged 91 wins per season, impressive though not the stuff that inspires books. From 2007 to 2009, they averaged just 75 wins. Only a handful of teams did worse. What went wrong?

The biggest problem was the loss of the Big Three pitchers (Zito, Mulder and Hudson) who, more than anyone or anything else, accounted for the team's success. When their contracts came up, the A's were not able to resign them; their accomplishments priced them out of Oakland's small market. The challenge, for Beane, was to find equal value in return. He lost Zito to free agency, and the player drafted with the pick given as compensation opted for the priesthood before ever making the majors. Beane traded Hudson and Mulder before their contracts expired, acquiring six prospects in return. But only one of them, pitcher Dan Haren, amounted to much. Haren pitched well for three seasons, then was traded for six more prospects, only two of whom, pitcher Brett Anderson and first baseman Daric Barton, have helped the A's (another player, Carlos González, was traded to Colorado and won the National League batting title in 2010) — and neither is, by any stretch, a star. All told, Beane replaced his Big Three pitchers with 13 players who collectively provided relatively little help.

As noted, *Moneyball* chronicled Beane's iconoclastic approach to the draft, marked by his preference for college players, particularly those with high on-base percentages, over the uber-athletic high school phenoms that other teams drooled over. We saw how the 2002 draft which the book centered around did not remotely live up to Michael Lewis's hype. In subsequent drafts, Beane fared no better. In the nine drafts from 1998 to 2006 (it's too early to evaluate the drafts after that), Beane followed his preference for college players, and with mediocre results. Only 25 of the nearly 400 players he drafted have made the majors for more than a cup of coffee. To be fair, the draft is largely a crap shoot and many other teams did no better. But the other teams' general managers do not purport to have novel theories for successful drafting, nor were they the subject of books celebrating their acumen.

To his credit, Beane seems to have recognized the error of his ways and adopted the more conventional approach to the draft. After an interview with him in January, 2010, ESPN.com's Howard Bryant reported that "the undervalued quality in the baseball marketplace is the high school player with little polish but high potential, which is exactly how Beane has drafted lately." In the 2010 draft, Beane reached a personal high of 16 high school draftees, including five of his first six picks. This from the guy who, according to *Moneyball*, hurled a chair through a wall when he learned that the A's had ignored his admonition and drafted a high school pitcher, Jeremy Bonderman, with their first pick in 2001. (Bonderman won 14 games for the 2006 World Series champion Tigers.)

Beane's reversal on drafting high school players was only one part of a broad reversal with respect to the ideas at the heart of *Moneyball*. Michael Lewis would not recognize the A's these days. Not only has the team been mired in mediocrity for several years, and resorted to drafting high school players, but in 2010 the A's were near the league lead in stolen bases and sacrifice bunts (the "small ball" Beane pointedly avoided in the *Moneyball* years) and only average in walks. Most of what *Moneyball* deemed central to Beane's success has been scrapped. Meanwhile, as we shall see in Chapter Three, other teams (including some which openly oppose sabermetrics) replaced Oakland as the success stories among small-market teams.

It may be thought that the errors we have identified by Michael Lewis, Billy Beane and Voros McCracken are their own, and it's unfair to judge sabermetrics by a few blind spots or goofs or by one general manager failing to sustain an admittedly impressive run of success. Fair point — in theory. In reality, as we shall now see, sabermetrics is at heart a deeply flawed enterprise.

CHAPTER 2

Where Sabermetrics Goes Wrong

The tale of the revolution Bill James wrought shouldn't be taken to imply that baseball was traditionally marked by indifference towards statistics. Even in the nineteenth century, some baseball fans and scribes were obsessed with numbers. Box scores published in newspapers nationwide fed the obsession, and underwent an ongoing tweaking because they failed to satisfy the thirst for numbers. Long before James's first *Baseball Abstract* reached a few dozen readers in 1977, entire books were devoted to baseball statistics. While crusty managers insisted they needed nothing but their own eyes to understand the game, many fans relished data.

However, pre–James, the data made little sense. Even major league baseball's official statistical categories were highly flawed. The weaknesses of some statistics, like batting average and saves, are by now old hat. Batting average treats singles no differently from home runs, and ignores walks. Saves reward the relief pitcher who succeeds where almost no one fails (pitching one inning to protect a three-run lead), while ignoring major contributions (keeping a game close or tied). Today, every thinking fan knows that these statistics are overrated. That wasn't the case when James came along.

Many other mainline statistics are equally flawed. Take Earned Run Average (ERA), long considered the most reliable indication of pitching success, and to this day a major determinant of voting for the Cy Young Award and Hall of Fame. ERA is problematic on numerous levels but we'll highlight just one. A pitcher who leaves the game with men on base gets charged with runs if the relief pitcher allows these runners to score — hence the spectacle of a pitcher watching from the dugout while his ERA is determined by the effectiveness of his replacement.

The problem of inherited runners is an extreme example of a flaw that ERA shares with many statistics: it is teammate-dependent. A batter will drive in more runs when his team puts men on base in front of him, and will score more with strong hitters behind him. A catcher will throw out more or fewer runners depending on whether the pitchers keep them close. Many individual statistics are significantly influenced by one's teammates.

Numerous other statistics suffer from a different flaw: lack of sample size. The world would instantly become a better place, or at least baseball telecasts would become more enjoyable, if we were spared all stats which lack an ample sample size. We're treated to each hitter's lifetime batting average against the pitcher, which usually spans fewer than 20 at-bats. We learn a hitter's batting average that year with runners in various situations, involving at most a dozen at-bats. Statistics based on such small sample size often describe random relationships. It takes time for the world of cause and effect to reveal itself.

"Clutch hitting" gives rise to the greatest folly in this regard. In any given year, certain players are hailed for their success when batting in one-run games from the seventh inning on, or whatever other concoction is offered as the measurement of clutch hitting. Other players are vilified for their failure in such situations. Yet these calculations are based on far too few plate appearances to be meaningful. For years Alex Rodriguez received flack in New York because of his alleged inability to deliver when it matters most. In 2007, Rodriguez was spectacular when it came to at-bats in the late innings of close games. Does anyone believe that Rodriguez suddenly developed the knack or character for clutch performance?

Reggie Jackson had the ballyhooed title "Mr. October" bestowed on him because he shined in several post-seasons, particularly his legendary three home runs in Game 6 of the 1977 World Series. What's less well-known is that Jackson had several poor post-season series. (In five different series, he batted under .200.) Was he mega-clutch sometimes and a choker the other times? Much more likely, he performed in the post-season exactly the way he did in the regular season. Indeed, his overall post-season numbers are similar to his regular season numbers. He had his great moments because he was a great player — clutch hitting had little to do with it. Similarly, David Ortiz was hailed as Mr. Clutch for his fabulous performances in the 2004 and 2007 post-seasons (.400 with five home runs, .370 with three home runs), but in 2008 was pathetic (.186 with one home run in 43 at-bats). Did Ortiz lose the clutch touch? Far more likely, he experienced nothing but a player's normal variation. Any notion to the contrary reflects a misunderstanding of the limited sample size that renders most such statistics meaningless.

Another problem with baseball statistics is the ever-proliferating category that we call the "Munson Statistic" in honor of one of its earlier manifestations. The Munson Statistic throws together two or more numbers to create a worthless blend. In 1977, much was made of Thurman Munson's successful quest to become the first American League player in a quarter-century to bat .300 with 100 RBI in three consecutive seasons. We loved Munson, but not this gimmicky statistic.

The problem starts with the arbitrariness of the particular numbers. What if players hit .295 with 100 RBIs for three consecutive years? Or hit .300 with 98 RBIs? In addition, what's so special about the *consecutive* part of the equation? Was Munson necessarily any better from 1975 to 1977 than someone who *averaged* .300 and 100 for those three seasons but dipped below the magic mark in one of those categories for one of the years? Munson's RBI totals were 100, 102, and 105. Is that more impressive than the player who drove in 125, 130, and 98?

The media bombard us with variations of the Munson Statistic, often in support of a player's election to the Hall of Fame. *Boston Globe* sportswriter Dan Shaughnessy pushed Jim Rice for the Hall by virtue of this accomplishment: "When Rice retired in 1989, he was one of only 13 players with eight or more seasons of 20 homers and 100 RBIs." One baseball blogger, in a post making the case for Rice, pointed out all of the following: Rice is one of 17 players with a career average of .290 and 350 home runs; the only player since Babe Ruth and Jimmie Foxx to have three straight 39-homer seasons while batting .315; and, our favorite, "one of only 13 major leaguers to have hit .300 with 375 HR and 1,400 RBI in a 14-season stretch." Such statistics represent what some social scientists call "post-hokey" analysis, hunting for data to support a pre-ordained conclusion and finding significance in categories that never would have been considered meaningful in advance. If you consider this sort of statistic legitimate, the silliness that follows will last a lifetime. Roy White is one of a handful of players who managed 10 home runs, 14 stolen bases, and 75 walks in four consecutive seasons. Julio Franco is one of a few who batted .300 in two different seasons after the age of 40. All the others are in the Hall of Fame. Franco must belong in the Hall. Put his plaque next to Roy White's.

One last species of ridiculous statistic is the pervasive "Whenever." The Red Sox are 16–3 whenever David Ortiz hits a home run or 3–18 whenever their starting pitcher doesn't last five innings. The Cubs are 4–9 whenever manager Lou Piniella is ejected and 8–11 whenever they turn no double plays. Such statistics are typically inane, for any of several reasons. Yes, the Red Sox tend to win when Ortiz hits home runs. Some announcer with too much time to kill during too many pitching changes, and only a limited grasp of statistics, will suggest that this item demonstrates Ortiz's value. But, of course, in a low-scoring game like baseball, a home run by *any* player will correlate with the team's success. There's no particular reason to think that Ortiz's home runs correlate with Red Sox wins any more than home runs by any other player. If they did, it would probably be mere coincidence, but at least it would be something worth considering. Usually, the Whenever statistic is not accompanied by any basis of comparison.

Even so, some heavy thinkers traffic in Whenever statistics. In his best-selling book *Men at Work: The Craft of Baseball*, political pundit and baseball enthusiast George Will eagerly trotted out variations on the theme, such as the fact that in 1988, 31 of Jose Canseco's 46 home runs tied the game or gave Oakland the lead. The implication is that Canseco bears down in key situations, but that can't possibly be established unless we know how these numbers compare with those of other players and, if favorably, whether they hold true across Canseco's career. More likely, it is a statistical quirk, which is a polite way of calling it meaningless. Just like the following item, dutifully passed along by Will: "The 1986 *Elias Analyst* reported that scoring the first run gave the typical American League team a 2–1 edge on its opponents.... National League teams scoring first [also] won 67 percent of the time." If it's surprising that someone as smart as Will attaches significance to these data, consider that Tony La Russa, one of the most cerebral managers ever, does as well. Will quotes La Russa at length on the importance of the first inning, with La Russa basing his claim on these same data.

They are missing the obvious. Consider that in soccer the team scoring first wins close to 90 percent the time, whereas in basketball the team scoring first wins just over 50 percent of the time. In other words, the correlation between scoring first and victory varies inversely with the amount of scoring in the sport. *Of course* the team scoring first in baseball usually wins — the margin of victory in baseball is often two runs or less. Until someone supplies data suggesting otherwise, there's no reason to assume the result any different for the team which scores second or third or fourth. Scoring *at any point* will correlate with victory. If the *Elias Analyst* reported that teams outscoring their opponent in the third inning win most of the time (as they surely do), would La Russa adjust his lineup to have his team's best hitters come up in the third inning?

The "first team to score" statistic can be even more misleading than we've suggested. This statistic resonates with us because we wrestled in high school and were frequently admonished to get the initial takedown because the wrestler who scores first wins 80 percent of the time. Of course, as in baseball and soccer or any low-scoring sport, two points (whether the first two, or next two, or last two) in wrestling will always correlate with victory. But the invocation of the 80 percent statistic also reflected a more profound misunderstanding. The better wrestler generally gets the first takedown — and the second and third, for that matter. He does not win the match because he gets the first takedown; he gets the first takedown because he's the better wrestler (which is also why he wins the match). Such misattributions of cause and effect plague the interpretation of statistics. If the Red Sox win 95 percent of the games in which Jonathan Papelbon appears, that's because they put him in when they are ahead rather than because putting him in creates victory.

We rehearse the vast universe of meaningless statistics to convey the world Bill James sought to revolutionize. James's odyssey amounted to a quest for meaningful data. His task tended to be twofold: (1) identify the flaw in prevailing measurements, and (2) substitute a new measurement that solves the problem. Not surprisingly, the second part proved a lot more difficult than the first.

For example, pre–James the prevailing measurement of defensive excellence was fielding percentage. James recognized that this statistic grossly exaggerates the significance of errors and undervalues a player's ability to get to balls. A player with limited range but good hands might earn a high fielding percentage while actually hurting his team. Conversely, the speedy shortstop who ranges far to get to a ball no one else could, but bobbles it for the error, would receive a statistical debit, punished for his unique skill. So James invented "Range Factor" and other defensive statistics which took greater account of a player's ability to reach balls. The problem is that his new statistics were deeply team-dependent. The infielder who plays on a team with sinker-ball pitchers will "reach" numerous balls, even if his range isn't all that good.

James's solution is always more data. The logical extension of his program is the precise calculation of each player's total value, and James's "Win Shares" allegedly approaches that goal. James doesn't settle for quantifying the past. The annual *Bill James Handbook* offers detailed "projections" for every batter and pitcher for the next season. For example, the 2008 handbook projected that in 2009 Dustin Pedroia would bat 642 times, hit 130 singles, 52 doubles, 5 triples, 15 home runs, and draw 58 walks. (That actually just scrapes the surface.) James's discussions of these projections shows that he leaves no stones unturned — he even projects whether and how badly players will get injured. Of course, James does not expect that he will accurately predict each player's performance. But the very effort betrays the mindset we saw in *Moneyball*, where Billy Beane claimed baseball is reducible to a social science.

Sabermetricians of all stripes took the lead from James in undertaking hyper-ambitious efforts to quantify every aspect of player performance. For example, a Maryland meteorologist named Clay Davenport devised "Equivalent Average" (EqA) which takes into account everything a player does at bat and on the bases, while factoring in his team, league, position, and ballpark, to arrive at a single number allegedly capturing his offensive value. John Thorn and Pete Palmer offered something similar that they call "Linear Weights."

The mission is doomed. We glimpsed why last chapter, in connection with Oakland's effort to calculate the runs saved by Johnny Damon's defense. The number of runners who gambled on an extra base because of Damon's weak arm (to pick just the one variable we emphasized for convenience) simply cannot be measured. The problem is no different with respect to offense. Certain offensive contributions, such as breaking up double plays or advancing runners with ground balls to the right side, are almost impossible to quantify, and contributions less subtle will also fail to register.

Take Mickey Mantle and Roger Maris, who in the dream 1961 season jointly chased Babe Ruth's home run record. Who was the more valuable player, Mantle or Maris? If they haven't done it already, sabermetricians could make that calculation in about as long as it took Mantle to get down the line to first. (Because Mantle and Maris were teammates, they don't even have to adjust for ballpark.) Of course, if anyone does the calculation, a few years later someone else will come along and, based on a refined notion of the proper relationship between on-base percentage and slugging percentage, reassess Mantle and Maris. A few years after that, someone may establish that hitting in the eighth and ninth innings is especially important, which will require further refinement.

In reality, all the sabermetrical analysis in the world, the AVM system, Win Shares, EqA, various statistical formulae emphasizing .OPS or .OBP in whatever permutations, adjusting for God-knows-what, all of the above will almost surely omit a number critical to the assessment of Maris and Mantle: zero. That happens to be the number of intentional walks received by Roger Maris in 1961.

That's right, in a season in which he hit more home runs than any player in the pre-steroids history of baseball, Maris did not receive *a single intentional walk*. Amazingly, he was the only Yankees regular who never received a free pass. (Even singles hitters Tony Kubek and Bobby Richardson received one!) To put this in perspective, players who hit 50 or more home runs typically receive 15 to 20 intentional walks in that season. Maris received not a one. Surely, there were plenty of times where he came up with first base open, a right-handed pitcher, and circumstances dictating that it made sense to give him the base rather than risk the long ball. Why was he never walked intentionally? The two-word explanation is: Mickey Mantle. Mantle, who batted behind Maris, was not only as potent a home run threat, but a more feared hitter overall. To put Maris on base to face

Mantle made no sense. Pitchers' unwillingness to walk Maris intentionally meant more opportunities for him to hit with runners in scoring position. Equally important, concern about Mantle on deck surely translated into pitchers avoiding walking Maris semi-intentionally as well. In short, he got better pitches to hit because Mantle was behind him. Whereas Mantle received no similar protection.

How much of Maris's performance could be attributed to Mantle? We can't know for sure, but this much we do know: during the 13 games Mantle didn't start, Maris was pathetic, managing just eight hits in 49 at-bats. That's a limited sample size, but in 1962, when an injury limited Mantle to three pinch-hitting appearances over a 30-game span, Maris again performed poorly, hitting just .191 and with reduced power. In total, for 1961 and 1962, with Mantle behind him in the lineup Maris hit 70 points higher than without Mantle behind him. (The sample size is non-trivial: more than 800 at-bats with Mantle behind him and 350 without.) More importantly, with Mantle behind him, he hit a home run every 11 at-bats and without him one every 20 at-bats — the difference between a solid player and an MVP.*

That's not to say Maris did nothing for Mantle. Fifty-three times Mantle came to bat after a Maris home run, perhaps facing a shell-shocked pitcher. But wait; do pitchers fare badly immediately after giving up a home run? Maybe they bear down and do better. Maybe some pitchers do better and some do worse. These questions have to be part of the calculation if anyone wants to determine the relative value of Maris and Mantle. Such factors and a dozen other variables that we'd have trouble even conjuring, much less calculating. Quite simply, no one can *ever* quantify a player's value with precision.

---

*In his book *The Bill James Gold Mine 2009*, Bill James categorically rejected the notion that batters are affected by who hits behind them, noting that "it's been looked at many times." Apparently whoever did the looking ignored Mantle and Maris. James's comment reflects a regrettable tendency among sabermetricians: worshipping the rule and ignoring exceptions. Which is a shame, because exceptions are, well, exceptional. And even if one dismisses Maris's vastly superior performance when Mantle batted behind him as a fluky outlier, one simply cannot dismiss the brute fact that Maris was never intentionally walked with Mantle on deck. If nothing else, in 1961 he received an extra 15 at-bats with runners in scoring position.

It doesn't follow that we shouldn't figure out what we can. Knowledge is a good thing — usually. Sometimes we're better off ignorant. Consider what the sabermetricians have to say about base-stealing. Their work in this area is often cited, with some justification, as among their clearest contributions to baseball understanding. The records of players before the 1980s show that would-be base-stealers were thrown out quite a bit. For example, Pete Rose, known as a heady ballplayer, was out stealing 43 percent of the time. That's just a little worse than Bob Meusel, the most proficient base-stealer on the 1927 Yankees. And Duke Snider. (We will leave it to sabermetricians to figure out why so many base-stealers were safe 57–58 percent of the time.) Today, anyone who is thrown out more than 40 percent of the time isn't allowed to keep trying. Sabermetricians won this battle. They demonstrated that unless you are safe roughly 70–75 percent of the time (the precise figure depends on the era, specifically the amount of scoring), attempting a stolen base actually detracts from a team's run-scoring.

This seems like an important discovery, yet it illustrates the pitfalls of sabermetrics. Consider that leading sabermetrician James Click wrote an eye-popping essay for *Baseball Prospectus* arguing that Rickey Henderson's baserunning was a virtual wash. (Henderson stole successfully 81 percent of the time, which doesn't beat the break-even point by much.) The precise conclusion was that if Henderson had been like the slow-footed Pete Incaviglia on the bases, his teams would have won just five fewer games in 25 seasons. Rickey Henderson? By far the greatest base-stealer of all-time — the guy who stole 130 bases in a single season? It's not just Click. Using a similar analysis, Bill James concluded that Henderson's base-stealing during his record-shattering season in 1982 produced a net gain of just 4.5 runs for Oakland. What next — Barry Bonds's home runs barely helped the Giants?

Here is where a little knowledge is indeed a dangerous thing, and blissful ignorance helps wins ballgames. In a board game like Strat-O-Matic, the 70–75 percent yardstick might be a good guideline for whether to run. In real life, the figure tells us precious little. An easy way to see the point is to compare Henderson to another historic player who succeeded in stealing at close to his percentage: David Ortiz. Yes, through the 2008 season Big Papi was safe on 77 percent of his stolen base attempts.

Now consider the obvious difference between the two. The lumbering Ortiz succeeds at stealing only because he rarely tries (ten steals in 13 attempts). An element of surprise — or indifference — works to his advantage. When Ortiz is on first, the pitcher gives no thought to a steal. The tiny risk of an Ortiz steal is not worth multiple throws to first base, or pitch-outs, or the other adjustments (such as pitch selection) that reduce the likelihood of a successful stolen base. Of course, the opposite was the case with Henderson. It took a total focus by the defense, especially the pitcher, to keep his stolen base rate at 81 percent. Absent such effort, Henderson was likely to stand on third base after two pitches. Accordingly, the pitcher looked over to first incessantly and often threw over there several times, and had to be judicious about using off-speed pitches, which are easier to steal on. Did all of the distraction, and the predictable fastballs, help the batters behind Henderson? Well, this much we know: quite a few players (Dwayne Murphy with the A's, Don Mattingly with the Yankees, Edgardo Alfonzo with the Mets) had their best seasons with Henderson batting in front of them.

Unlike previous sabermetricians who disparaged base-stealing, in his essay on Henderson's baserunning James Click at least addressed this issue — but barely. He devoted a few perfunctory paragraphs to the idea that base-stealers help the batters behind them. Based on five years of data, he claimed that while batters do improve when the top 20 percent of base-stealers are on base, the effect is minor. Click concluded that the threat of the stolen base, even by the likes of Rickey Henderson, does not substantially assist an offense. This analysis is, to say the least, inadequate. Lumping together the top fifth of base stealers dilutes the effect of the guys at the top. Indeed, Click supplies no data on the batters behind Henderson. (It wouldn't have helped if he did, because his data come from the early 2000s, when Henderson was long past his prime.) His stunning conclusion that Henderson's baserunning added virtually no runs to his teams misses what may have been Henderson's major contribution — transforming the game by driving pitchers crazy.

Click never addressed the possibility that a guy like Henderson does more than help the batters immediately behind him — there's a potentially significant delayed effect when pitchers focus their attention on keeping

Henderson from stealing. With an on-base percentage of roughly .400, Henderson reached base his first two plate appearances at least 25 games a year. On those occasions, by the third or fourth inning the pitcher had likely made a dozen throws over to first, stood out on the mound (sometimes in summer heat) for several more minutes, and exerted significant mental energy. On account of all that, the odds of the starting pitcher tiring and coming out of the game earlier increased, which is no small deal. (Or, at a minimum, the fatigue might reduce his effectiveness in his last inning.) If the starter goes five innings instead of six or seven, he is usually replaced by one of the weaker pitchers on the staff. How many games per year did Henderson make that happen?

The answer, of course, is that we can't know. While Click apparently did not consider the possibility of this delayed effect from Henderson's baserunning, there would have been no way to test such a possibility in any case, for the same reason we cannot assess how much Mickey Mantle and Roger Maris helped one another — too many variables. You can look at how long pitchers last in games when Henderson reaches base compared to games when he doesn't, but maybe he gets on base more when the pitcher doesn't have it. (In other words, in games where Henderson does reach and the starter does depart early, it could be because *everyone* was getting on base.) Conversely, the pitcher who keeps Henderson off base is on his game. It's not that he succeeds because he keeps Henderson off base. Rather, he keeps Henderson off base because he's succeeding. Thus, the data tell us nothing about Henderson's effect on a pitcher.

Put aside the delayed effect. We cannot even quantify the effect of Henderson on the batters directly behind him. Yes, Dwayne Murphy and Edgardo Alfonzo (to pick the seemingly most obvious beneficiaries of Henderson on the bases) had their best seasons with Henderson in front of them, but they happened to be around the age where players most often thrive. Besides, when Henderson left or joined a team, other changes took place as well. Perhaps the loss of his manager or batting coach or personal trainer affected Murphy as much as the loss of his leadoff man. To get meaningful data you'd need to see how Murphy did, with and without Henderson on base, in the same situations — same pitcher, outs, ballpark, weather, and same Murphy. Obviously, this is impossible.

Sabermetricians are wary of stolen base attempts and sacrifice bunts because these tactics violate their first commandment: thou shall not give away outs. By their lights, Rickey Henderson, thrown out stealing 335 times, was a gift that kept on giving — to opponents. But their focus is too narrow. What matters is avoiding making outs, whether you "give them away" or not, and players like Henderson help their teammates avoid making outs, albeit in ways that can't be measured.

The examples of Mantle/Maris and Henderson only scrape the surface of why the sabermetrical mission of total quantification is a fool's errand. Typically, the sabermetrician supplies only base rate data (meaning the relative frequency of something in general, in the absence of information specific to a particular event). In the case of the utility of stolen bases, the base rate is 70–75 percent — overall, a success rate in that range will neither gain nor cost a team runs. Quite apart from the value of the threat to steal, the base rate information fails to speak meaningfully to each particular situation. The value of a steal at a given moment depends on the inning, the batter up, the pitcher, the score of the game, and much more, and there will never be enough data relevant to the particular situation to provide more than an educated guess about that decision. We now turn to an example of historic proportions which exposes the shallowness of sabermetrics.

Babe's Baserunning Blunder — A Case Study

To some sabermetricians, Babe Ruth getting caught attempting to steal to end Game 7 of the 1926 World Series was a blunder perfectly illustrating what happens when players or managers misunderstand the things sabermetrics illuminates. Indeed, Babe's alleged goof merited several pages in *Rob Neyer's Big Book of Baseball Blunders: A Complete Guide to the Worst Decisions and Stupidest Moments in Baseball History*, a book by a noted sabermetrician. At the time, the Yankees trailed by a run with the formidable Bob Meusel at bat, followed by Lou Gehrig. For Ruth, who stole successfully at just a 55 percent clip that year (roughly his career rate), to attempt a theft in that situation seems crazy. Indeed, long before the advent of sabermetrics, Ruth's attempted steal was considered folly. Rogers

Hornsby, who made the tag on Ruth, called the attempted steal "the biggest break any of my teams ever got. It also goes to prove that the World Series isn't won — it's lost." The pitcher, Grover Cleveland Alexander, chimed in, "I'll never know why the guy did it," and Yankees General Manager Ed Barrow called it "the only dumb play I ever saw Ruth make." Decades later, in his book *Yankees Century*, Glenn Stout wrote that Ruth "had made a career of careening between the incredible and the incorrigible. Now he added the inexplicable to his resume."

To this conventional wisdom, sabermetricians add the numbers. While, as noted, the success rate of stolen bases needed to justify an attempted theft differs in different eras, it is typically calculated to be 70–75 percent and is never as low as Ruth's 55 percent. The idea of seeking an extra base with a predicted success rate well below the proper standard constituted the ultimate violation of the sabermetricians' first commandment: Thou shall not give away outs. Ruth gave away the World Series!

This analysis demonstrates one of sabermetrics' critical limitations; no two situations are identical, undermining the value of the "relevant" data. The notion that a player should not steal absent a 70–75 percent likelihood of success is a generalization based on analysis of all situations. The figure is so high largely because a failed attempt not only costs you one runner but also reduces (or, in the case of a third out, eliminates) the possibility of a multi-run inning. However, where one run is desperately needed, the 70–75 percent standard must be adjusted downwards. Ruth faced such a situation. Down a run in the bottom of the ninth, with future Hall of Famer Alexander mowing down the Yankees, multiple runs seemed far-fetched. Scoring one run was paramount; tie the game and get into extra innings, where Alexander would eventually tire. Under the circumstances, the math probably favored Ruth's stolen base attempt.*

---

*For Ruth to score from first with two outs required base hits from Meusel and Gehrig. (A Meusel extra-base hit might have scored Ruth from first, but Meusel had just 37 extra-base hits all season, so that possibility doesn't much alter the math.) If Ruth stole successfully, he needed *only* Meusel to get a hit. Whether Ruth stole or not, Meusel had to get a hit for him to score, so the calculations came down to Ruth's chances at stealing successfully versus Gehrig's chance of a hit. Gehrig batted .313 that season, so his chance of a hit, especially against the great Alexander, seems well below Ruth's chances of a successful steal. To be sure, as discussed in the text, both those odds are impossible to quantify.

But, sabermetricians will reply, all we've demonstrated is that the 70–75 percent figure did not govern — we simply need to find the appropriate numerical standard for those situations in which a team is playing for just one run. But this calculation, too, depends on case-specific variables that defy generalization, particularly the likelihood that subsequent batters will get base hits. These figures can only be estimated within a very wide range. When Ruth stole, Lou Gehrig was on-deck. Gehrig hit .313 that year, but what were his chances against this particular pitcher on this particular day? Was the 23-year-old intimidated by a World Series Game 7? Simply not swinging the bat well? Was Alexander nearly unhittable on this day? Or perhaps he was beginning to tire and the future Hall of Famer Gehrig was focused and strong? Depending on these and assorted other non-quantifiable factors, Gehrig's chance for a base hit would vary considerably. The range? Probably somewhere between .200 and .400. Any precision is illusory.

The same problems apply to the other allegedly crucial figure: Ruth's 55 percent success rate. The situation Ruth faced in Game 7 differed significantly from the varied circumstances of his 20 regular-season attempts. Those attempts were against different pitchers and catchers. Ruth might reasonably have thought that the best predictor of success in Game 7 was not his regular-season attempts against other batterymates, but his successful steal in Game 6 against Alexander and catcher Bob O'Farrell. Perhaps he had Alexander's move figured out, or noticed that O'Farrell wasn't throwing well. But even the Game 6 steal might not bear directly on Game 7. Ruth had to consider whether Alexander was holding him on more closely, shortening his stride, throwing fastballs or breaking balls, whether the infield was fast or muddy, whether an element of surprise worked in his favor, and more. Depending on those many issues, Ruth's season-long 55 percent success rate might be adjusted to a likelihood of success between, say, 20 percent and 80 percent. Thus, the saber-inspired notion that Ruth screwed up by attempting to steal amounts to guesswork. Sabermetricians' base rate data, culled from computers, was trumped by variables that could be assessed in real time only through intuition and informed judgment.

What is true of stolen bases applies to most in-game decisions. In his book *The Sinister First Baseman*, well-regarded sabermetrician Eric Walker attacked baseball insiders who ignore his data. At one point Walker remarked, "What are the cumulative odds of a runner on second with one out eventually scoring? What are those for a runner on first with none out? If you don't know those things to a nicety, you're not making decisions, you're making guesses." His immediate point, of course, concerns the sacrifice bunt. Why give away the out to get a runner into scoring position unless you are more likely to score in that situation? Yet for decades managers frequently resorted to the sacrifice bunt with no awareness that teams score more with a runner on first and no outs than with a runner on second and one out. While this base rate information should give the manager pause, Walker misses the fact that even if you *do* know the base rate data to a nicety, you're making guesses. The "cumulative odds" of scoring with a runner on first and no outs versus a runner on second and one out is of limited usefulness, because you never face a "cumulative" situation.

Take the climactic point in Game 4 of the Red Sox–Yankees 2004 ALCS — ninth inning, Yankees lead by a run, Dave Roberts on first with no outs and Bill Mueller at bat. The Red Sox chose to steal, but could just as easily have bunted. Terry Francona doesn't much like the bunt, but this was Mariano Rivera on the mound, who rarely gives up more than one hit in an inning. To make a numbers-based assessment of whether to bunt, Francona would have needed to know the odds of scoring with a runner on second and one out (versus runner on first, no outs) with these particular batters against Rivera, but such data derive from a tiny sample size. He'd need to know how often the sacrifice fails — with Mueller at bat and Rivera on the mound — and leads to a force-out at second or even a double play. Quite simply, the base rate data that Eric Walker thinks so critical does next to nothing for the manager in a specific situation. Nor can he await a fax from the team statistics guru telling him the computer's recommendation, because one cannot possibly feed the computer all the relevant data before the next pitch. Indeed, one can't feed it all the relevant data period, because of potentially crucial and non-quantifiable factors peculiar to the situation at hand, such as how well Rivera is throwing.

Even if you could feed the computer the relevant data, it would be all too little, for an additional reason. Baseball statistics are observational only, and the hypotheses they give rise to do not allow for prospective study. Take the suggestion, discussed above, that Roger Maris hit better with Mickey Mantle batting behind him. We supplied data to support that conclusion, but the data hardly prove that manager Ralph Houk was right to bat Mantle behind Maris. The first question he'd need to ask is whether Maris's success with Mantle behind him amounts to a real finding or a random phenomenon rooted in a small sample size. Assuming he determined that it was real, he'd need to consider the converse: might not Maris protect Mantle equally well? How could he establish which way they were better off?

The obvious answer is to switch the order for awhile, and see how Maris, Mantle and the Yanks fare with Maris behind Mantle as compared to how they'd done previously. In fact, this experiment would not yield reliable information. Experiments provide the most useful information when the scientific method is used — all relevant factors kept constant except one (in this case, where Maris and Mantle bat). If you vary only the factor in question, the results can confidently be attributed to the change in the single variable. Baseball does not permit such a controlled experiment. The flipping of Maris and Mantle in the lineup will necessarily be accompanied by numerous other changes as well — the teams the Yankees play, the pitchers they face, the weather, the performance of the batters before and after Maris and Mantle and, most importantly, the players themselves. Mantle and Maris will slump or streak on their own accords, because of the normal flow of player performance or abnormal developments such as injury. By the time the experiment has obtained a substantial sampling of data, they will no longer be the players they were at the start of the experiment. In short, any hypothesis about which batting order best serves the Yankees can never reliably be tested.

This example demonstrates a major limitation of sabermetrics that often seems to escape its practitioners. Sabermetricians produce data about the past, but the data do not prove cause and effect. They can only generate hypotheses, and until these hypotheses are tested, the predictive value of the data remains unknown. In order to evaluate a hypothesis, one must do a forward-looking study, and baseball can never provide laboratory conditions for such study — too many variables cannot be controlled, and many things change over time.*

It does not follow that sabermetrics is useless. If observational evidence is all you have, run with it. If Mantle, Maris, and the Yankees did great for the 50 games where Mantle batted behind Maris, and poorly when they were flipped, you might as well put Mantle behind Maris. But the recognition that you base your move on a hypothesis only, not a proven fact, has important ramifications. We should never be slaves to the numbers, for a proper understanding of baseball requires recognition that a great deal cannot be quantified. Don't lose sight of Rickey Henderson's value on first or Mantle's value in the on-deck circle, just because these things don't show up on an AVM grid and can't be proven.

In fairness to Bill James, he acknowledges that his Win Shares does not capture everything. In *The New Bill James Historical Abstract*, he explained that he adjusts a player's ranking for things like World Series performance, disruptive or leadership behavior, and "special contributions of the player utterly beyond the reach of the statistics." It might seem that the latter provision accommodates the kinds of non-quantifiable contributions we've talked about throughout this chapter, but James has something different in mind. His discussion of the "beyond statistics" exception consists of three names and a sentence: "Jackie Robinson, Hal Chase, Eddie Grant. You see where I'm going with this." Robinson integrated baseball, Chase reputedly threw games, and Grant was killed in combat during World War I. In other words, James's notion of special contributions beyond statistics involves a handful of unique circumstances. We have in mind something else. While the non-quantifiable contributions of Mickey Mantle and Rickey Henderson are particularly large, they stem from nothing exotic — they are engrained in the marrow of the game. So, for that matter, are breaking up double plays and forcing defensive mistakes

---

*Medical research exemplifies the point. Based on observational evidence, a large number of vitamins and micronutrients have been suggested (and, sadly, often accepted) as effective for reducing incidence of heart disease and cancer. Unfortunately, prospective studies disproved these observation-based hypotheses, establishing no beneficial effect. So, too, most of the hypotheses of sabermetricians could well be false. We will never know, because controlled experiments are impossible in baseball.

through aggressive baserunning, keeping runners from advancing by getting quickly to balls in the alley (and having a reputation for a strong arm), hitting the cutoff man, and backing up errant throws. No statistics measure these things, but they are surely relevant to player evaluation.

Consider the case of Pete Rose. Usually, discussion of Rose and the Hall of Fame centers around gambling. But let's come at this from a different angle and ask a surprising question: is it so clear that Rose belongs on the merits? Sure, he managed 4,256 career hits, an astonishing 1,256 above the 3,000 mark which usually guarantees induction. Base hits are the name of the game. How can anyone even begin to suggest that the hit king does not have Hall of Fame credentials? Well, for starters, as sabermetricians have preached for decades, base hits are *not* the name of the game. On-base percentage (OBP) and slugging percentage (SP) are more important, and Rose was not great in either department.

Rose lacked power and speed — historically a near-fatal combination for Cooperstown wannabes. He never hit more than 16 home runs and as often as not managed only single digits in that department. If that's an unfair metric for a leadoff hitter, look at stolen bases; his season high was 20, and he was caught stealing an alarmingly high 43 percent of the time. And, most importantly, look at OBP. Rose's career OBP of .375 is virtually identical to that of Lenny Dykstra, Willie Randolph, and Brett Butler, top-of-the-lineup guys who aren't getting to Cooperstown unless they pay admission.

Of course, OBP isn't everything. To many sabermetricians, OPS (the sum of OBP and SP) is the best gauge of offensive production.* For both career and five best years, Rose's OPS is equaled or surpassed by a long list

---

*Sabermetricians have labored to find the proper relationship between OBP and SP. Many settled on the product of OBP and SP, which slightly enhanced the importance of OBP over SP. However, OPS, the simple sum of OBP and SP, is what entered the baseball lingo. The reason was simplicity: Fans and media could understand the rationale behind adding the two figures and could easily do the calculation, whereas the reason for multiplying was not intuitive and only a mathematical savant could multiply two fractions in his head. But, in any event, the quest for the exact relationship between OBP and SP is misguided. The relative value of a walk versus a single or an extra-base hit depends on the situation, including whether and where there are baserunners, the score, the inning, and the number of outs. When you also factor in the speed of the baserunners (an important variable), the range of permutations approaches infinity.

of players who never received serious Hall of Fame consideration, including: Dwight Evans, Fred Lynn, Bobby Murcer, Dave Parker, Reggie Smith, Charlie Keller, Boog Powell, George Foster, John Olerud, Darryl Strawberry, Jimmy Wynn, Eric Davis, and Ken Singleton.

So why is Rose universally considered a shoe-in Hall of Famer (apart from gambling)? One reason is that he played 23 years, thereby amassing career statistics off the charts. But extraordinary longevity should not a Hall of Famer make. Bill James once remarked that Rose had a "Hall of Fame career or two." James is half right; Rose had two careers all right, but *neither* is Hall of Fame caliber. Putting them together doesn't establish greatness, any more than a writer's two solid 300-page novels can be thrown together to produce a brilliant 600-page epic. If Rose had retired after 15 seasons (before he became "hit king"), his statistics would not have been Hall of Fame caliber. In his second career Rose was a below-average player — very limited power, no speed, and the failure to shine even in those categories where he previously excelled. Should eight years of mediocre performance elevate someone to the Hall of Fame by padding career statistics?

But here's where we see the limitations of OBP and OPS and all the other saber-measurements. Numbers alone should not determine Hall of Fame qualifications. Rose was a great leader on one of baseball's great teams, and displayed boundless hustle. It is almost inconceivable that he ever failed to advance a base or make a play in the field for lack of effort or alertness, and he certainly took many extra bases. In short, he belongs in the Hall because be brought to the table greater intangibles than any player — something entirely missed if one relies exclusively on numbers as the measurement of a player's contribution.*

Because statistics leave much untold, to appreciate a player's strengths and weaknesses you need to see him play a lot. Bill James grew up in Kansas, following the A's (before they moved to Oakland) and later the Royals. It therefore comes as little surprise that he supplies endless nuggets

---

*To be fair to Bill James, he not only considers Rose an easy Hall of Famer, but ranks him quite high (33) among players all-time. In our view, James arrives at a reasonable assessment of Rose because he makes two errors that cancel out — he underrates intangibles but overrates what he calls "career value," giving Rose too much credit for an extremely long career.

of insight into players on those teams. For example, Amos Otis was so good at reading pitchers that he would steal bases standing up. Diminutive Freddie Patek frequently flied out to deep left and center — not quite strong enough to hoist the ball over the wall. Hal McRae, for better and worse the most aggressive baserunner in the game, was constantly thrown out on the bases. On and on with such items that only a serious follower of those players could possibly know.

It's a different story when James talks about players on other teams. Here, he often whiffs. He writes that Roy White "did everything well" and discusses White at some length without mentioning his throwing arm. In New York during the 1960s and '70s, no conversation about Roy White would last 15 seconds without mention of his paper arm. He sometimes took a half-dozen steps before making a throw, perhaps because he ran faster than he threw. You wouldn't know about White's arm from any data — his total of outfield assists was adequate. In fact, in 1968 he had 14 assists, five more than Roberto Clemente, whose arm was legendary. This tells us nothing about White or Clemente, and everything about the limitations of statistics. Like RBI and many other stats, assists reflect opportunities. The weaker your arm, the greater number of opportunities. (That's why one year raggedy-armed Mickey Rivers actually led the American League in assists.) People tested White every chance they got, but feared Clemente.

White isn't the only Yankee from that era whose foibles elude James. He ranks Horace Clarke in the all-time top 100 second baseman, and his accompanying comments omit mention of what Yankees followers universally regarded as a big weakness: Clarke's tendency to bail out on the double play. This weakness, like White's weak throwing, does not show up in the box score. James claims that White and Clarke were underrated because they were scapegoats on poor teams. But non-quantifiable weaknesses help explain why those Yankees teams were poor despite having a number of players James ranks highly.

James's Win Shares calculus does include a defensive component, but its value is unclear. He acknowledges that Win Shares is "almost incomprehensibly complicated," and we'd quibble with the "almost." The defense component is actually the relatively easy part to understand, though hardly convincing. To give you an idea, a second baseman's defensive ranking is based 40 percent on Double plays vs. Expected Double plays, 30 percent on Assists as a Percentage of Team Total, 20 percent on Error Percentage and 10 percent on Putouts as a Percentage of the Team. Presumably James would say that Horace Clarke's tendency to bail out on the double play is captured by comparing his Double plays to Expected Double plays. If you're skeptical about the ability to quantify such things, and unconvinced that Double plays vs. Expected Double plays captures 40 percent of a second baseman's defensive merit, join the club.

We don't mean to come down too hard on James, whose ranking of the top 100 players at every position, driven by Win Shares, is harmless fun. Indeed, given that these rankings provide the format for his priceless reflections about every subject under the sun, they serve a most valuable purpose. But these rankings reflect the over-valuing of data at the expense of what can't be quantified. We know that James misses important aspects of the play of Roy White and Horace Clarke because they happen to be players we saw regularly. It's safe to assume that he misses aspects of numerous players that he didn't get to see much. Of course, one shouldn't expect omniscience from James or anyone else. It's just that his Win Shares conceit fosters a misleading sense that most everything in baseball can be quantified.

The world at large was introduced to James in 1981 by a laudatory article in *Sports Illustrated*. The author, Dan Okrent, ended his essay with a fitting epigram for sabermetrics: "It's all there in the numbers." In the real world, observation, intuition, and common sense are parts of the package needed to make sensible player evaluations and game decisions. When data trump all else, you end up drafting Jeremy Brown and underrating Rickey Henderson and Mickey Mantle, among numerous other errors.

Those who make such errors because they are overly attached to numbers over-corrected for generations of insiders who under-utilized numbers. These two paradigms present mirror images of one another. *Moneyball* describes baseball's titanic struggle between old school and new school, but each is terribly flawed.

Our serious misgivings about the new school should not be construed as suggesting that managers should throw their hands up and blindly follow hunches or intuition. That would amount to a return to the failed old school approach. What is needed is a third way, neither indifferent to sophisticated statistics nor over-valuing them. To illustrate what such an alternative might look like, let's look at an example of a real-life conundrum that confronted a manager and how it would be handled by the pre–*Moneyball* or old school model (baseball before the invasion of sabermetrics), the *Moneyball* or new school model (baseball under the increasingly popular sabermetric approach), and a proposed post–*Moneyball* model.

Before Game 3 of the 2003 American League Championship Series between the Yankees and Red Sox, Yankees manager Joe Torre faced an intriguing decision: whom to play at third base — the regular, Aaron Boone, or his back-up, Enrique Wilson. During the regular season, Boone hit .267 with 24 homers whereas Wilson hit .230 with just three. These numbers accorded with their careers — Boone reasonably solid, Wilson weak. But the Red Sox pitcher was the dominant Pedro Martinez, and Wilson happened to have a history of success against Martinez — a staggering 7-for-8 during the 2003 season and 10-for-20 during his career.

Under the traditional approach, this was a no-brainer. Although the old school didn't much value numbers, this sort of elementary statistic they could handle and wouldn't dare dismiss — Wilson hit at a .500 clip against Martinez, with an off-the-charts .875 for the current season! How could you not play him? Joe Torre, an unapologetic old school guy, did the old school thing and played Wilson. Boone and his teammates understood. As Derek Jeter explained, "There's always situations like that in baseball, where guys own certain pitchers. That's just how this game goes."

Sabermetricians scoff at such thinking. The issue, once again, is sample size. If you flip a coin eight times over enough trials, you will get some streaks of seven heads or seven tails. Twenty at-bats is more meaningful, but still far too few. The better predictor of success was Wilson's and Boone's overall numbers, not their respective numbers in a few dozen at-bats against Martinez. But be careful. Dismissing Wilson's 20 at-bats as too few to take seriously is not necessarily statistically savvy. Given that batters overall hit roughly .200 against Martinez, and Wilson hit .230 against the league, the probability of Wilson doing so well against Martinez in even a limited number of at-bats is very slim — so much so that it may reflect something real rather than random.

As every good geek could tell you, the solution is to crunch the numbers. You can determine with numerical precision the odds of someone with Wilson's overall numbers going 10-for-20 against someone with Martinez's overall numbers, which in turn will determine the likelihood that it was a mere random occurrence. Through a maze of formulae, factoring in Wilson's and Boone's overall batting as well as their respective performances against Martinez, the computer will tell you who should play.

We don't have to guess what conclusion the computer would reach because a leading sabermetrician happens to have written about something almost identical to the Wilson/Martinez conundrum. James Click devoted an essay to the significance of Mike Redmond's surprising success at the plate against Tom Glavine. Redmond, a career .285 hitter, hit .438 against Glavine. Wilson vs Martinez, Redmond vs Glavine — same idea. In each case, a journeyman batter seemingly owned a Hall of Fame–caliber pitcher. However, Redmond's dominance over Glavine spanned 48 at-bats, more than twice as many as Wilson's against Martinez. Even so, after a complex series of calculations replete with terms like "binomial distribution," Click reached the following conclusion: "Almost certainly, Mike Redmond doesn't own Tom Glavine. He was just lucky.... Going forward, there is no statistical reason to expect Redmond to hit any better against Glavine" than anyone else. Extrapolating from that situation to the similar situation facing the Yankees in 2003, it seems that the Yanks should have played Aaron Boone — the opposite decision reached by Joe Torre using the old school approach.

In our view, both approaches are flawed. For Torre to take a knee-jerk "Wilson 'owns' Pedro" attitude is to choose the dark ages over the information age. The Boone/Wilson decision must be informed by the kind of analysis done by Click gauging the likelihood that Wilson's success was a matter of chance. Don't play weaker players based on what may amount to a series of coin flips. At a minimum, you need to probe the possibility that Wilson's success reflects chance more than anything else.

But this example also shows the limitations of sabermetrics. Click's sophisticated numerical calculations cannot resolve Torre's conundrum.

The number-crunching leaves out too much, starting with a calculation that only the baseball insider can attempt. Is there some logical explanation for Wilson's surprising success against Martinez, some odd alchemy between the two players? Could it be, for example, that Wilson handles a certain pitch that happens to be Martinez's baby? To the extent that Torre can reasonably explain Wilson's success, the likelihood that it is real, and not random, goes up. In other words, a limited sample size becomes more meaningful if accompanied by understanding. And observation. Wilson's 20 at-bats supply useful information to the trained eye. Were the hits mostly bloops or line drives?

Sabermetricians correctly note that Wilson's success was fully explainable by laws of probability and does not justify the conclusion that he owned Pedro. However, it is also possible that Wilson *did* own Pedro — some hitters own some pitchers, after all. Sabermetrics cannot sort out the few hitters who actually own pitchers from the majority of cases which amount to random deviations. The batter who really does own a pitcher, who would end up 100-for-250 against him, begins at the same 10-for-20 as the lucky hitter who would end up 50-for-250. The new school manager who plays Boone over Wilson will feel satisfied that by playing the better player he was not seduced by a random hot streak, but he may unknowingly bench a player who would have bashed his personal patsy.

In addition, even success that's essentially random may nevertheless be predictive of (over)performance, when we factor in player psychology. Enrique Wilson is a professional athlete, not a student of probability, and he lives in a culture where the thinking about these matters remains primitive. The media and his teammates have been saying he owns Pedro Martinez; he likely believes it. Indeed, prior to Game 3 of the series Wilson told MLB.com that he feels more comfortable batting against Martinez than any other pitcher. Surely, confidence matters. Wilson's belief that he owns Martinez, in other words, can create a self-fulfilling prophecy. To what extent? We cannot put a number on it (a recurring theme), but if Wilson feels especially comfortable against Martinez, that has to be worth *something*.

The ultimately decisive question is: what do you stand to lose by playing Wilson? The seventeenth century French philosopher Blaise Pascal argued that we should believe in God just as a matter of sensible wagering. If you put your chips on non-belief, and you're right, what have you gained? But if you're wrong, you may lose eternal bliss. Conversely, if you choose to believe and you're right, you're golden. And if you're wrong, no harm no foul. There are serious problems with Pascal's reasoning as a justification for belief in God, but when it comes to choosing between Aaron Boone and Enrique Wilson, his wager provides the firmest foundation for decision.

Let's hypothesize that Wilson's success against Martinez is a function of something real, that Wilson really does own Martinez for some reason having to do with the mesh of their pitching/batting styles. Maybe he won't maintain the sizzling .875 average he amassed during the regular season in just eight at-bats, but he still figures to be the best player in your lineup against Martinez. Based on overall ability, Boone will likely be the worst. (He was the weak offensive link on the power-studded Yankees of 2003.) Playing the best hitter in your lineup as opposed to the worst is about as good as you can do when it comes to managerial decisions. Now imagine the reverse: Wilson's success has been a fluke, and starting the next at-bat he will revert to the kind of weak performance we'd expect from a .230 hitter against a lights-out pitcher. But how much better would Aaron Boone do? Presumably, hardly at all. Either infielder figures to be the weakest hitter in your lineup. The .200 Boone might manage against Pedro beats Wilson's .180, but that difference amounts to just one hit every 50 at-bats. We'd play Wilson because, even if his success against Martinez has been random and will not carry over, the down side is negligible.*

Of course, this calculation could theoretically be quantified, as we started to do when we pointed out that the advantage of playing Boone might amount to one hit every 50 at-bats. Accordingly, one might argue that we are following rather than resisting sabermetrics. But *every* decision in baseball ultimately comes down to a probabalistic assessment of out-

---

*As it happens, Wilson went just 1–7 against Martinez in the series, but playing him nevertheless worked out for the Yankees. Although he went 0–4 in game 3, Torre started him in Game 7. Wilson singled in three at-bats, but was replaced by Boone after Martinez was removed in the late innings. Boone subsequently hit the dramatic series-ending home run in the eleventh inning.

comes, even if subconscious. The question is what goes into such a determination. Back in the 1860s, when Harry Wright decided whom to start at second base for his Cincinnati Red Stockings, he implicitly determined who would "create more runs" (to use a saber-term) for his team or prevent runs against, but he did so solely on the basis of hunch and observation. A century later, Tony La Russa rifled through index cards, though the data remained unsophisticated. Today's sabermetrician introduces reams of complex data and a mathematician's ability to interpret them. And those of us who respect such numbers but consider them inadequate, supplement the data with concepts rooted in psychology (self-fulfilling prophecy) and philosophy (Pascal's Wager) and whatever else might be at hand.

Useful knowledge outside the numbers may involve baseball savvy, such as recognizing what Mickey Mantle did for Roger Maris and Rickey Henderson for Dwayne Murphy, even if these phenomena can't be quantified. But one also benefits from awareness of concepts farther afield. James Click's essay about Mike Redmond and Tom Glavine never raised the possibility of a self-fulfilling prophecy or asked what the manager had to lose by playing Redmond even if he recognized that Redmond's success against Glavine might well be random. This reflects a common failing of sabermetrics, akin to Billy Beane's infatuation with Jeremy Brown and disregard for the judgment of scouts that Brown could not play; over-reliance on numbers tends to crowd out extra-numerical insight.

The Revolution Arrived—The Case of Grady Little

A critical event in sabermetrics' takeover of baseball was Game 7 of the 2003 ALCS, the same series that featured Joe Torre's dilemma of whom to play at third base against Pedro Martinez. Pedro gave his own manager, Grady Little, a dilemma, too — when to take him out as he nursed a three-run lead but seemed to be faltering. In the eyes of the saber-minded Red Sox front office, as well as most of Red Sox Nation, Little flunked the test.

The Red Sox had amassed data showing that Martinez's performance suffered substantially from the seventh inning on and was particularly shaky after he'd thrown 105 pitches. Before Game 7, general manager Theo

Epstein reminded Little of Martinez's late-inning struggles. Nevertheless, Little allowed Martinez to throw 123 pitches, which included facing five batters in the eighth inning. Four of them reached base and the Red Sox's lead disappeared before Little mercifully removed his gassed ace. The Yankees won in 12 innings and Little was history.

One can view this episode as proof of the merits of sabermetrics. Old School Grady Little essentially based his decision about whether to remove Martinez on a cliché ("Go with the girl who brung you to the dance") rather than on data, and this folly extended the Red Sox curse. Case closed? No. For one thing, the data on Martinez's late-inning struggles were quite limited — just 53 batters. In addition, a strikingly similar circumstance presented itself almost 40 years to the day earlier. On October 15, 1964, also in a Game 7 against the Yankees (this time the World Series), another manager had to decide how long to stick with his fading superstar. Cardinals manager Johnny Keane decided to sink or swim with Bob Gibson, who was pitching his third game of the series and on just two days' rest. Gibson took a four-run lead into the ninth, where he staggered, giving up two home runs, one to the light-hitting Phil Linz. With the lead down to two and a dead man walking on the mound, Keane elected not to go to the bullpen, even though the formidable Ray Sadecki (who won 20 games that season) was ready to come in. Gibson retired the last batter on a pop-up, and Keane explained that he never contemplated removing his ace, because "I had a commitment to his heart."

With everything on the line Keane preferred attaching his fortunes to Bob Gibson's indomitable heart, even if Gibson's *arm* seemed to be falling off. Basically he made the same decision as Grady Little, only it turned out better. Of course, Keane did not have at his disposal the detailed information available to Little. If he had, it's possible he'd have decided differently, but it's at least equally plausible that Keane's sense of Gibson's character would have trumped any data. Statistics are not the only path to insight. Data about performance after certain pitch counts simply do not tell us whether a great athlete may be able to summon something extra on a particular occasion. As a general proposition, managers should be wary of making decisions based on subjective notions of this sort. But Keane and Grady Little faced a very specific situation, not a general one.

Sometimes, in the specific situation, trusting in character pays off. Remember Kirk Gibson's famous pinch-hit home run against Dennis Eckersley in the 1988 World Series? If Tommy Lasorda followed logic, he might have concluded that the crippled Gibson was not the man to send to the plate. But his Gibson, like Bob, was a warrior, which Lasorda rightly took into account.

Every decision involves a case of "compared to what"? Grady Little did not have a stud closer in his bullpen. If he had yanked Martinez, he would have depended on journeymen Mike Timlin, Alan Embree and Scott Williamson for the toughest five or six outs. They had pitched superbly in the series, but Little had seen them all season, when they were mediocre, and had reason not to be optimistic about their prospects against the potent Yankees lineup with the season on the line. The best move under those circumstances is impossible to gauge, but one thing is certain: If he had pulled Martinez, and the bullpen had relinquished the lead, Little would have been pilloried far and wide — including by many of the fans and media who pilloried him for leaving Martinez in.

Finally, what transpired in the eighth inning of that game has suffered the usual distortion of memory. Martinez had thrown just 100 pitches through seven innings and had a three-run lead to work with. He started the eighth by inducing a pop-up for the first out. Then things started to go south. Derek Jeter doubled and Bernie Williams singled him in. The score was now 5–3 and Martinez had thrown 115 pitches. The next batter, Hideki Matsui, doubled. At that point, the tying runs were in scoring position, and Little's idea that Martinez could will his way to victory looked shaky at best. Little probably should have yanked Martinez then, but we need to recall exactly what transpired next — Jorge Posada hit a weak pop-up that happened to fall safely in shallow center field. That's right, the game-tying hit that erased the Sox lead and sealed Grady Little's fate was a seeing-eye bloop. The ball floated so high that Posada, no speed demon, coasted into second base. Through the ages Little's critics will note that Posada doubled off the moribund Martinez, and few will remember that this "double" was pure luck.

Sabermetricians say that taking Martinez out after seven innings (or after Jeter's double in the eighth at the latest) was demonstrably the right thing to do. We say there was no demonstrably right thing to do. Little had to weigh different species of knowledge that don't lend themselves to comparison. How do you balance Martinez's poor performance after 105 pitches during 2003 against his competitive spirit and the fact that he is one of the greatest pitchers of all time? Was it really unthinkable that he could withstand arm fatigue on a single historic occasion, as Bob Gibson did in similar circumstances in 1964?

You follow your gut, or your best guess, and then you watch the game unfold in its unpredictable glory. Unless you're a devout sabermetrician, in which case you think the decision is made for you by the numbers. If you take the latter approach, you may sleep easier (win or lose), but you misunderstand messy reality and shortchange the beauty of the game.

The problem that animated Bill James's revolution was colossal ignorance pervading the baseball world. He helped cure it. The problem he inadvertently ushered in was excessive faith in a particular path to knowledge and insufficient appreciation of how much can never be quantified. James has acknowledged a problematic aspect of the revolution he wrought. Before resurfacing in the Red Sox front office, he spent years in relative seclusion, disheartened by the direction things had taken. He stopped producing his annual *Baseball Abstract* after 1988, and explained why with a curious mea culpa. While crediting himself with "growth in the access to and understanding of meaningful baseball statistics," James acknowledged "an unchecked explosion in meaningless ones" and lamented that he bore some of the responsibility. "I didn't create this mess, but I helped."

In fact, to be fair to James, the baseball world was awash in meaningless statistics before he arrived on the scene. Still, he is right to see that while he began as the solution, he ended up as part of the problem. But the principle problem with sabermetrics is not that it adds considerably to the vast sea of useless or misleading data, though it does. The bigger problem is that it promotes a mindset which gives data a centrality that distorts baseball decision-making and, more importantly, hinders baseball appreciation.

While at times James embodies the flaws of the movement he created, he is a gifted historian with a passion for the game and a deep appreciation of its quirky quality. The problem lies not with James himself but with the sabermetric monster he unleashed. Looking at the ideas that became associated with his name, Karl Marx quipped that he was not a Marxist. Bill James is no Jamesian. Throughout his voluminous works, he sprinkles recognition that much in baseball can't be quantified, that his formulae should be seen only as imperfect tools to guide understanding, that the game cannot be reduced to a social science, and that its greatness lies beyond the numbers. But many of James's acolytes are less discerning. Endless harm is done by those who misunderstand and misappropriate the spirit of a revolution.

The following passage from Alan Schwarz's *The Numbers Game* illuminates the problem:

> Two members of the Stanford University statistics department, working under a National Science Foundation grant, used sophisticated Marko analysis to devise a new batting statistic called Offensive Earned Run Average.... Scientists see things in baseball statistics the way astronomers do in the deep, night sky: connections, evolution, meaning. They use their telescopes or equations and theories to explore which statistic — home runs, on-base percentage, or some gadget of their own devising — might share an orbit with runs and wins.

Bill James sees numbers as a tool to enhance understanding of baseball. Others see baseball as a tool to enhance understanding of numbers. These include sabermetricians, leading some of their brethren to disillusionment. John Thorn, a prominent sabermetrician, explained, "While I still believed that numbers could reveal things about the game that were invisible to the naked eye, my own eyes had glazed over as the combination of fantasy baseball and mathematical arcana conspired to squeeze the life from the game I loved."

Thorn bears some of the blame. In the introduction to *The Hidden Game of Baseball*, he and coauthor Pete Palmer announced their aim to enhance baseball appreciation: "The complex texture of the game, which for many is its real delight — the thing that pleases the mind as well as the eye — cannot be grasped while the game is in progress. And that's what statistical analysis allows us to do." Then Thorn and Palmer got down to helping us grasp baseball's delight with things like "Linear Weights," a formula for capturing a player's offensive value: Runs = (.46)1B + (.80)2B + (1.02)3B + (1.40)HR + (.33)(BB + HB) + (.30)SB − (.60)CS − (.25)

(AB – H) – .50(OOB). Does anyone believe that such a formula enhances baseball appreciation? Can it really capture the value of a player's contribution?

Bill James has punched enough holes in Linear Weights to fill a donut factory. Unfortunately, James's solution was a far *more* complex formula impossible for anyone but a mathematician to follow. As baseball writer Tom Boswell says, "The more ambitious the stat, the more complex and arbitrary it almost always becomes. What it gains in sophistication and the intuitive wisdom of its creator, it loses in simplicity and objectivity. How can you love a stat, or use it in arguments, if you can't really explain it?"

The early days of sabermetrics replaced batting average with on-base percentage plus slugging percentage as the key metric for evaluating hitters. It also documented that bunting, stolen bases, and intentional walks were unthinkingly overused. These were tangible contributions, easily grasped by fans and applied by teams. Later phases of sabermetrics were increasingly esoteric and of little practical value — mathematicians talking to one another in code.

The vastly diminishing returns from sabermetrics might seem harmless, except the obsession with numbers trickled down and, as Thorn aptly put it, squeezed the life from the game. In his song "Talking Baseball," Terry Cashman chose as his refrain "Willie, Mickey, and the Duke." The song, focused on baseball in the 1950s, didn't have to single out these three. The decade (and the song) included Henry Aaron, Ralph Kiner, Roy Campanella, Bob Feller, and Warren Spahn, among others who were at least Duke Snider's equal. Why Willie, Mickey and the Duke? Because Willie Mays, Mickey Mantle, and Duke Snider played center field in New York at the same time, each starring for one of the three New York teams, and there wasn't a baseball fan in New York who didn't argue about which of the three was top dog. As that argument was woven into the fabric of the game, it makes perfect sense that a song called "*Talking* Baseball" would celebrate it. Baseball without the fans is like the tree falling in the forest unseen and unheard. Fans give the game reality and meaning, particularly when they argue about it passionately. The argument was never more passionate, nor the game more meaningful, than when the Giants, Yankees, and Dodgers competed to be King of the Hill in New York, then the sport's indisputable Mecca.

Fast-forward half a century and imagine a barroom debate between partisans of Mantle and Mays. Mays was more durable and overcame playing in a pitcher's park but Mantle, a switch-hitter and superb bunter, had more tools. And so forth. A great debate, free of the illusion (except for those who partake of too much beer or partisanship) that there is a right answer. But now some guy comes in waving Bill James's *Win Shares* and claims to resolve the debate in favor of Mays. "You can't argue with Bill James, who came up with this advanced formula precisely to rank players. It's all there in the numbers," he says, patting the fat book. An argument killer, but only until someone else comes in waving *The Hidden Game of Baseball* and insists that the Linear Weights formula yields a different and more reliable conclusion. Only someone with an extreme aptitude for mathematics will stick around to hear these two duke it out. Others will leave. They don't care a fig for these arcane formulae, and they sense that the game is now seen differently. Their own views of Mays and Mantle, based on impressions, observations, and comprehensible data, have been overtaken. They feel silly arguing about a question that could be fed to a computer.

Again, up to a certain point sabermetrics enriched the arguments. For example, until the 1980s, Mantle's partisans would not have thought to emphasize his superior on-base percentage. Such knowledge they could understand and use. The same cannot be said for Win Shares and Linear Weights and the like. They kill arguments not in service of truth, but only in service of the mistaken notion that one can grasp the essence of a sport through esoteric formulae.

In a *New York Times Magazine* article about the spread of sabermetrics to basketball, Michael Lewis (the author of *Moneyball* branching out to basketball) quotes Sam Hinkie, "the head of basketball analytics" for the NBA's Houston Rockets: "I care a lot more about what ought to have happened than what actually happens." This staggering statement captures the impoverished perspective of sabermetrics, sports as a plaything for social scientists, a laboratory to manipulate probabilities and chart results in order to assist the next simulation. The game itself conveys no beauty or meaning.

We don't begrudge the Rockets charting the fact that since 2003 Kobe Bryant has missed 86.3 percent of his three-point shots from farther than 26.75 feet at the end of close games. (We're not making this up.) If that knowledge truly assists the Rockets in defending the Lakers down the stretch, good for them. But we do begrudge them their attitude which reduces Kobe Bryant, indeed the entire game of basketball, to sets of numbers. Lewis concludes his article by describing Bryant's long-range buzzer-beater that defeated the Rockets. According to Lewis, Shane Battier, the Rocket defending Bryant, who forced him to take a low-percentage shot, just laughed. "The process had gone just as he hoped. The outcome he never could control."

What is missing from Lewis's account is any sense of appreciation of Kobe Bryant's dramatic heroics. To him and the Rockets front office, Bryant had merely rolled the dice. Indeed the Rockets, drawing on their mathematical mastery, forced him into an unfavorable roll where there was just a 13.7 percent chance of success. The Rockets deserved all the praise. Bryant was irrelevant, his shot (whether successful or not) an uncontrollable event. Ponder again the terribly revealing words of Lewis's protagonist: "I care a lot more about what ought to have happened than what actually happens."

Basketball is about Kobe Bryant, not Sam Hinkie. Sports is about what *actually* happens thanks to the unpredictable performances of those in uniform, not what *ought* to happen thanks to the maneuvers of "basketball analytics" in suit and tie. Indeed, much of the power and beauty of sports lies in the gap between what ought to happen and what actually happens, in the probability-defying performance of stars like Bryant, in the rich and unpredictable events that unfold when talented athletes bring to the playing field not data points but a thirst to compete. May the best team win — the one that performs best on that day in that place, not the one with the shrewdest statistical gurus in the front office.

Lewis described how his man Hinkie flipped out when a Lakers player hit an off-balance three-point shot. "That Ariza shot, that is really painful," Hinkie said. "Because it's a near-random event." Of course, every basketball fan understands the frustration when good defense is thwarted by bad luck. But Hinkie's pain is different. He takes this personally; the improbable undoes his painstaking work. When Kobe Bryant drives instead of taking a jump shot, Hinkie's reaction reveals the mind of a sabermetrician at work. "That's three-eighths of a point. These things accumulate." Whether Bryant drives depends on how the Rockets defend him, and that in turn depends on Hinkie's crew charting his every move and crunching every number. That's something Hinkie can control. That, for him, is what it's all about. Trevor Ariza's unlikely shot? That's just what *actually* happens, a regrettable deviation from what *ought* to happen.

We look at it very differently. You can dismiss Ariza's three-point shot, or Bryant's long-range game-winner, as "near-random events" that are unfair and somehow beside the point. Or you can celebrate them as wondrous events lying at the heart of sports.

CHAPTER 3

The Third Wave

Although the Society of American Baseball Research formed in 1971, the first wave of sabermetrics as we know it consisted primarily of the ruminations of Bill James in his annual *Baseball Abstract* starting in 1977. In highly entertaining fashion he raised numerous issues, and ranked and discussed virtually every ballplayer who ever lived (or so it seemed). As discussed in the previous chapters, James established that baseball had long languished in ignorance that could be reduced by statistical and mathematical analysis.

The second wave of sabermetrics can be traced to 1984 and publication of the first significant book by self-proclaimed sabermetricians not named Bill James — *The Hidden Game of Baseball*, by John Thorn and Pete Palmer. The second wave, which spans roughly two decades and produced an enormous volume of work by James and a coterie of his followers, fulfilled the promise of the first wave. Some of sabermetrics' central tenets became widely accepted, such as the importance of on-base percentage and the imprudence of "small ball" (risking or accepting extra outs to gain a base, particularly through bunting or stealing).

Allowing for a degree of arbitrariness that always accompanies a taxonomy of this sort, *Moneyball* can be considered the culmination of the second wave. By probing the success of Billy Beane's Oakland A's, it purported to establish that a team can gain a substantial advantage by putting into practice the insights gleaned from sabermetrics. *Moneyball* not only documented the second wave, but triggered the third: the infiltration of sabermetrics into baseball's front offices. A half-dozen teams essentially declared themselves saber-teams: Toronto, Seattle, Boston, Tampa Bay, Cleveland, and the Los Angeles Dodgers all hired Billy Beane acolytes to important front office positions, thereby providing a laboratory for assessing sabermetrics in action.

The record has been unimpressive. The Red Sox, with Beane-worshipper Theo Epstein as general manager assisted by Bill James himself, have thrived, winning the World Series in 2004 and 2007 and qualifying for the post-season virtually every year. It's unclear, however, what lessons can be derived from the Sox's success, because during most of the James/Epstein era they enjoyed baseball's second-largest payroll. The team won two World Series thanks, in large part, to players (Curt Schilling, Josh Beckett, Manny Ramirez) whom every team craved but few could afford and whose greatness was recognized even by those who don't know a slide rule from a slide step. The same, however, could not be said of another team that openly embraced sabermetrics, the Tampa Bay Rays. The Rays reached the World Series in 2008, and put together a formidable team poised to succeed for years to come, on a shoestring budget.

The Seattle Mariners, too, enjoyed some success, but it was short-lived. When old-time scout Jack Zduriencik was hired as the Mariners' general manager before the 2009 season, he made a point of surrounding himself with sabermetric faithful. He inherited a cellar dweller that had won just 61 games, and in his first year the team soared to 85, allegedly one of the great sabermetric success stories. However, the Mariners collapsed in 2010. Another former Beane assistant, Paul DePodesta, became the Dodgers' general manager in 2004, and endured a similar topsy-turvy experience: The Dodgers went 93–69 in '04, then 71–91 in '05, before DePodesta was fired.

Other saber-friendly teams fared no better. Toronto hired Beane's right-hand man, J. P. Ricciardi, as general manager in 2001 and played .500 ball throughout the decade (642–653) before Ricciardi was let go after the 2009 season. In 2002, a Cleveland Indians team that already employed prominent sabermetrician Keith Woolner in the front office hired as general manager the saber-sympathetic Mark Shapiro. The Indians, who averaged 93 wins the previous seven seasons, were sub–.500 (635–661) during Shapiro's first eight seasons. Thus, looking at the various saber-run teams without a treasure chest of money, we find more failure than success.*

---

*There's an irony in the failure of Ricciardi especially. In a *Sports Illustrated* article defending himself against *Moneyball*'s critics, Michael Lewis made a huge deal of Ricciardi's success in his second year at Toronto. The team's win total rose from 78 to 86. The next year, following publication of Lewis's article, it fell to 67.

But perhaps the most revealing team in the post–*Moneyball* era was one that did not hire sabermetricians nor in any way embrace the saber-revolution, yet succeeded Oakland as the leading small-market, low-budget success story: the Minnesota Twins. Indeed, the Twins outperformed Billy Beane's A's in terms of win per dollar throughout the 2000s, suffering only one losing season and winning their division five times.

The Anti-Saber Twins

Moneyball implies that the way for a team to outperform its payroll lies in adherence to sabermetrical insight. The Twins present a different model. They not only explicitly disavow sabermetrics, but have succeeded in large part by ignoring one of Billy Beane's alleged insights: the folly of drafting high school players. Minnesota's starting lineup in 2010 featured five players drafted out of high school, most notably superstars Joe Mauer and Justin Morneau.

Rob Gardenhire, the Twins manager throughout the long successful run, told an interviewer in April 2010 what he thought of sabermetrics: "I like the human element and I like the heart way better than I like their numbers. And that's what I'll always stay with." Assistant General Manager Rob Antony confessed (actually boasted) to an interviewer that he was unaware that BABIP stood for "batting average on balls in play." Antony acknowledged that the Twins concern themselves with no statistics more complicated than OPS and WHIP, prompting espn.com's Rob Neyer to remark on the team's "utter lack of sophistication regarding statistical analysis."

There appears to be no unifying motif when it comes to Minnesota's approach to the game. Instead, throughout the decade the Twins jumped around in every major statistical category. They ranked as high as third in the league in runs scored and as low as last. Their stolen base totals ranged from third to tenth and walks from fourth to tenth. In 2004, they won 92 games while finishing tenth in batting average and third in stolen bases. Two years later they won 96 games while leading the league in batting average and falling to sixth in steals. They led the league in ERA in 2004 but were just seventh the year before and 11th in 2009.

There was a single statistical constant: walks allowed. The Twins staff was first or second in fewest walks allowed in almost every season. It's hard to know exactly why Twins pitchers walked so few batters (a phenomenon dating all the way back to 1984), but this curious achievement hardly explains the team's success. Minnesota's brilliant run this decade was preceded by eight consecutive losing seasons from 1993 to 2000, though the walks allowed were low in those years as well.

So what explains the Twins' success? The two primary ingredients are a shrewd general manager (who made good draft picks, good trades, and hired a good manager) and luck. The role of luck in baseball, discussed in Chapter One in connection with actual games, carries over to the process of assembling a team. The Twins' most important acquisition, Joe Mauer, actually resulted from the team's cash-strapped status. The Twins had the first overall pick in the 2001 draft, which featured pitcher Mark Prior as the consensus top prize. But Prior was so highly regarded that the Twins knew they would never be able to meet his salary demands. Accordingly, they settled for Mauer as a much cheaper consolation prize. Prior, chosen next by the Cubs, had one successful season before his career was destroyed by arm injuries, whereas Mauer became a player for the ages — not to mention a rare superstar who chose to remain with a low-budget team rather than choose greener pastures at the first opportunity. A free agent after his 2009 MVP season, Mauer could have signed with a big-market team for Alex Rodriguez–like money ($33 million in 2009), but opted to remain with the Twins, signing an eight-year contract for an average of $23 million a year, not pauper's wages but still representing a sizable hometown discount. Thus the Twins avoided the biggest obstacle facing the low-budget team — the loss of the best players to free agency.

Beyond the luck involved in acquiring and keeping Mauer, the Twins' success provides no particular blueprint for small-market teams. About the only constant during the team's decade-long run of success was its ability to score more runs than the opposition. No other generalizations hold up. And that very fact points to a crucial lesson from baseball history that casts doubt on the viability of sabermetrics' fondest dream: finding the formula for successful baseball.

Baseball History and the Absence of a Championship Formula — Pre- and Post-Sabermetrics

The principal idea behind all the number crunching, certainly the reason teams hire sabermetricians, is that insights gleaned from statistical analysis will help a team figure out how to win. They will be wiser than opponents both in player acquisition and in-game strategy. Their success should predictably breed mimicry, and thus development of an accepted framework — perhaps more pitching strength, more (or fewer) stolen bases, more (or fewer) walks — whatever truths the analyses unveil and experience confirms. Thus, if sabermetrics proved successful, one would expect, over time, reduced variation in the characteristics of winning teams, much as most World Cup soccer teams emphasize a smothering defense.

Had that happened, it would have marked an historical transformation. Traditionally, baseball has been characterized by enormous variety in the nature of championship teams. For example, the early days of baseball produced the "hitless wonders," the pennant-winning 1906 White Sox, whose .230 batting average was last in the American League but whose pitching ranked second. Five decades later, the 1959 champion "go-go" White Sox ranked last in home runs but featured the league's best pitching staff. Fast-forward another several decades and the White Sox did it again, winning the World Series in 2005 despite ranking ninth in the league in runs scored. It isn't just the White Sox who win without big bats; the 1963 World Series champion Dodgers were sixth in runs scored but yielded the fewest runs. So too the pennant-winning Tampa Bay Rays in 2008 — second-fewest runs allowed but only ninth in runs scored.

But baseball history also features examples of the opposite pole; teams that win through dominant offense despite mediocre pitching. The 1982 American League champion Milwaukee Brewers led the league in home runs and runs but were ninth in runs allowed. The 1976 "Big Red Machine" in Cincinnati won the World Series thanks to offensive dominance though their pitching staff was only average. The 1993 pennant-winning Phillies led the league in runs scored but seven teams allowed fewer runs. The 2007 Rockies fit that mold as well — great hitting, average pitching.

Between these extremes lie championship teams with every possible variation of offensive and defensive strength. Moreover, there has been tremendous variation in the individual components of offense — for example, teams that stole tons of bases (the '59 White Sox and '63 Dodgers led the league) and teams that stole very few (the '60 Pirates, '61 Yanks, and '86 Red Sox were last in the league). Quite a few championship teams walked a lot, but the dominant 1961 Yankees finished next to last in the league in walks — the first two guys in the lineup, Bobby Richardson and Tony Kubek, drew the miraculously low total of 57 combined walks in more than 1350 plate appearances.

Thus, when sabermetrics arrived on the scene, baseball history presented highly varied success stories and no single template for teams to adopt. Did sabermetrics' systematic study of the game change that situation? In particular, after *Moneyball* recounted how Billy Beane achieved tremendous bang for his buck by applying saber-insights, did a narrower paradigm develop? We have seen that most of the teams which went out of their way to hire saber-savvy front office personnel fared badly, but could it be that other teams, consciously or not, imitated Beane's early success and experienced similar good fortune?

Oakland's formula was straightforward: pitching and patience. (To be sure, the "pitching" part hardly stemmed from sabermetric insight.) During Oakland's five-year run of excellence, the team was never worse than third in the league in runs allowed. Offensively, the distinguishing features stemmed straight from sabermetrics and were emphasized in *Moneyball*: lots of bases on balls (never lower than fourth in the league) and risk-aversion on the bases (always last or second to last in stolen bases). Did successful teams in the post–*Moneyball* era mimic this (or any other saber-driven) approach? *Moneyball* was published in 2003, so we now have ample evidence to consider.

In 2004, the Red Sox defeated the Cardinals in the World Series, with both teams ranking first or second in runs scored and runs allowed — good teams all around. But their offensive styles differed substantially; the Red Sox finished 13th in the American league in stolen bases and second in walks, much like Beane's successful A's teams, but the Cardinals were close to the opposite in the National League (second in stolen bases, eighth in walks). The 2005 pennant winners were the Astros and White Sox, both pitching-oriented teams that were challenged offensively and drew few walks. The 2006 World Series pitted a Tigers team that won with great pitching and home runs while eschewing both walks and stolen bases, and a Cardinals team which offers no lessons because they won only 83 games in the regular season before catching fire in the post-season. In 2007, the Red Sox were strong both at the plate and on the mound, especially the latter, whereas the Rockies were an offensive juggernaut that struggled on the mound. The repeat-champion Phillies of 2008–09 led the National League in home runs and stole a lot of bases while not walking much, and had good but not great pitching. The 2008 Rays were a pitching-oriented team whose mediocre offense (ninth in the league in runs) featured a generous helping of "small ball" (led the league in stolen bases, second in walks). The 2009 Yankees offered the ideal paradigm — strong in everything — and, not surprisingly, won 103 games. The various pennant winners also spanned the spectrum in terms of defense, ranging from the Rockies and Astros, who led the league in fielding percentage, to the Red Sox and Tigers, who finished near the bottom.

Thus, even after *Moneyball*, sabermetrics has not narrowed the paths to success that teams take. The only valid generalization is that teams win by outscoring opponents. They do so every which way, through scoring a ton of runs or not allowing a lot, with the former predicated on small ball or the power game or a mix. You can win any of many ways, and generally should try to improve your team in as many aspects of the game as possible. But you should also play to your strengths. If you find yourself with good baserunners, steal. If you tend to have slow power hitters, relying on small ball would be foolish. Common sense? Yes, but this common sense refutes the central conceit of *Moneyball* and suggests the misguided nature of much of sabermetrics.

Luck and the Post-Season

If you want to win 95 games and make it to the post-season, you can't just find and follow some saber-formula. But perhaps sabermetrics will afford you an answer to a different question: how can I build a team that, if it does make the post-season, will likely succeed in the playoffs? Sabermetricians have indeed addressed that question. An essay by Nate Silver and Dayn Perry crunched the numbers throughout baseball history to determine which, if any, variables correlate with post-season success. What kinds of teams win the World Series?

First, the authors found that runs scored during the regular season does not correlate with post-season success, and neither do its component parts — home runs, walks or stolen bases. Nothing about how many runs a team scores, or the way it scores them, predicts the team's likelihood to succeed in the post-season. There is a very small correlation between runs allowed during the regular season and World Series victory, suggesting that pitching becomes slightly more important in the post-season. That's about it. No single thing meaningfully correlates with post-season success.

Silver and Perry apparently didn't like the answer they got, because they didn't quite accept it. Sabermetricians being sabermetricians, they concocted arcane technical metrics such as Fielding Runs Above Average (FRAA) and something called Closer WXRL (don't ask). But they used the data generated by these formulae the way the proverbial drunkard uses a lamppost — for support, not illumination. Desperate to find some correlation, Silver and Perry added three factors (quality of the closer, the defense, and the strikeout ratio of the pitchers) together and, while acknowledging that even collectively these factors account for only 11 percent of playoff success, observed that "when these three elements are aligned together, they can become quite powerful."

Sure, whenever several positives are added together, they can become powerful, especially if you call 11 percent powerful. If you look hard enough you'll find that all sorts of things, when arbitrarily combined, correlate with some degree of post-season success. For example, teams that have two left-handed starting pitchers who win 15 or more games, and also an infield that averages well over the league average in double plays, may do very well in the post-season. Which means what exactly? That you should try to put together a team with those characteristics?

In truth, success in the post-season, like success in the regular season, follows no formula. Sabermetrics has uncovered no blueprint to follow in the quest for a championship team. At one point, Silver and Perry almost acknowledged as much, saying that most of the time in the post-season "it's plain old luck that prevails."

They should have stopped there because that's the basic truth; post-season success is largely random and entirely unpredictable. We arrive at this conclusion without fancy formulae, instead using a common sense understanding of the game and looking at what has happened throughout history — not through the prism of FRAA and WXRL but through stories and elementary numbers that anyone with an interest in baseball history can appreciate.

In a sport with inherent parity (where the best teams win only two thirds of their games and even the worst teams win one third), any short series will be hard to predict. This tendency is compounded by the fact that only the top teams compete post-season. Accordingly, each series amounts to a virtual coin flip. If that conclusion seems improbable, consider that through the 2008 season, there were exactly 100 World Series in which the competing teams had non-identical regular season records. The team with the better record won 50.

Luck permeates baseball, but tends to even out over the course of a season (apart from injuries, a major exception that torpedoes teams all the time). It's a different story in a best of five or seven playoff series. There, it would be surprising if luck *didn't* often play a decisive role. World Series history offers numerous examples. The 1924 Series was decided by a catcher missing a pop foul because he inadvertently stepped on his mask in extra innings of Game 7. The Yankees might have won the 1960 World Series but for a routine ground ball striking a pebble and finding its way to Tony Kubek's throat. Then again, they would have lost the 1962 World Series if Willie McCovey's scorched line drive at Bobby Richardson were a few feet higher or to the side. The 1985 series between the Royals and Cardinals may have come out differently but for a terrible call by a first base umpire. And so on.

It isn't just luck that renders post-season series a coin flip, but the normal ebb and flow of the game. Having Babe Ruth and Lou Gehrig on your team yields a significant advantage over the course of a full season, but over five or seven games Ruth and Gehrig may be irrelevant. In 1922, the Yanks lost the World Series as the mighty Ruth hit .118 with no home runs. In the 1962 World Series showcasing Willie Mays and Mickey Mantle, the two wonder boys combined to hit .189 with no home runs in 53 at-bats. These are not isolated examples. You could field a team of immortals who performed poorly in the post-season: an outfield of Willie Mays, Ty Cobb and Joe DiMaggio, an infield of Mike Schmidt, Honus Wagner, Jackie Robinson, and Stan Musial, with Roy Campanella behind the plate. For good measure, you could DH Barry Bonds and bring Frank Robinson off the bench. Not one of these greats batted over .275 in the post-season, and collectively they batted .249 and managed a paltry 39 home runs in 1,158 at-bats. You can have on your roster the game's top players, but that doesn't amount to much if they go flat for one or two weeks.

The converse is equally true; just as superstars often don't play up to snuff in the post-season, ordinary players may vastly over-perform. The 1953 World Series between the Yankees and Dodgers featured a raft of Hall of Famers on both teams. Walking away with the MVP trophy was Billy Martin, a career .257 hitter who bated .500 during the Series. Similarly, the 1978 Yankees featured a wealth of offensive standouts, yet the World Series MVP was Bucky Dent, a lifetime .247 hitter with little power. He edged out Brian Doyle (who batted .438)—the same Brian Doyle whose lifetime slugging percentage of .191 makes him one of the weakest hitters in major league history. Doyle is an extreme example of a common phenomenon. The 1982 Series MVP was Darrell Porter, who that season hit .231. The next year, the Series MVP was another light-hitting catcher, Rick Dempsey, who in the Series hit .385 while superstars Cal Ripken and Mike Schmidt were pathetic. In the 1946 Series, while Stan Musial and Ted Williams barely hit their weight, the famously weak-hitting Joe Garagiola batted .316. When Mantle and Mays struggled mightily in the '62 Series, they were joined in futility by stars Orlando Cepeda, Willie McCovey, Roger Maris, and Elston Howard, none of whom hit more than .200. Light-hitting Jose Pagan and Clete Boyer led their respective teams in batting average. In the 1960 World Series, Bobby Richardson drove in 12 runs—after driving in 26 the entire season! The historic Game 7 of that Series was decided by three home runs. The sluggers of the day were Rocky Nelson, Hal Smith, and Bill Mazeroski, who during the season combined for just 29 home runs. The Pirates had hit just one in the first six games of the Series. What does it mean that they exploded for three in Game 7? It means one thing and one thing only: in a short series, stuff happens.

Stuff happens to pitchers too. Much is made of the performance by Howard Ehmke in Game 1 of the 1929 World Series, when Connie Mack mysteriously started the washed-up hurler and he responded with a complete game victory and 13 strikeouts. Versions of Ehmke's feat have occurred more often than people realize. Everyone knows that Johnny Podres shut out the Yankees in Game 7 of the 1955 World Series, finally bringing a championship to Brooklyn. What's less well-known is that Podres was 9–10 in the regular season. The next year, the Dodgers lost the World Series in seven games, one of them a perfect game by Don Larsen — a sub–.500 career pitcher. (In his previous outing, Game 2 of the Series, Larsen didn't get out of the second inning.)

If journeymen like Ehmke, Podres, and Larsen decide World Series, the flip side is equally true: Hall of Fame pitchers hardly guarantee post-season success. Three of the elite pitchers of the modern era, Steve Carlton, Greg Maddux, and Randy Johnson, were an aggregate 24–29 in the post-season. The formidable Vida Blue was 1–5.

Given all this, it's not surprising that the list of post-season losers includes some of the greatest teams in baseball history. The 2001 Mariners won 116 games and lost in the League Championship Series. The 1954 Indians won 111 games but were swept by the Giants in the World Series. Meanwhile, the 2006 Cardinals won just 83 games, but in the post-season bested the Padres (88 wins), Mets (97), and Tigers (95). That's the nature of baseball.

When it comes to trying to build a team that will win in the post-season, sabermetrics won't be much help (just as it offers no magic formula for building a strong regular season club). You'll do just as well by massaging your lucky feather as by maximizing your FRAA and WXRL.

Sabermetrics Changes Course

The teams that hired saber-savvy general managers do not all play the game the same way. For example, in 2009 the Rays led the league in stolen bases and were third in walks, but managed only 25 sacrifice bunts, whereas Seattle was last in walks, in the middle in stolen bases, but led the league with 56 sacrifices. One reason for this diversity is that, during the third wave of sabermetrics, central tenets, particularly the low priority given to defense and the aversion to risk-taking on the bases, have been revised.

Defense

Sabermetricians took to defense slowly. In his early years Bill James expressed dismay over the absence of good ways to measure fielding and therefore paid comparatively little attention to it. Those second wave sabermetricians who did pay attention to defense claimed it was overvalued. In *The Hidden Game of Baseball*, John Thorn and Pete Palmer asserted that fielding amounts to just 6 percent of baseball.

The devaluing of defense flew in the face of conventional wisdom. To most observers, hot corner defense by Graig Nettles and Brooks Robinson was critical to World Series wins by the Yankees and Orioles respectively. Hall of Fame voters elected Ozzie Smith and Bill Mazeroski primarily based on their glove work. Earl Weaver's formula for success was "pitching, defense, and three-run homers," and neither Weaver nor anyone else thought that the defensive brilliance of Robinson, shortstop Mark Belanger, and center fielder Paul Blair was incidental to the success of the 1960–70s Orioles. Many players in the game's pantheon, including Willie Mays, Joe DiMaggio, Roberto Clemente and Johnny Bench, were revered for their defensive prowess almost as much as their offense.

Sabermetricians began to study defense more closely starting in the early 1990s with the advent of AVM Systems. As noted in Chapter Two, AVM Systems broke the diamond into a matrix of small areas and evaluated fielders by comparing their results dealing with comparable balls hit to specific spots. As discussed, using this system the A's calculated that replacing Johnny Damon with Terrence Long in the outfield would cost them 15 runs. According to *Moneyball*, Billy Beane found that reassuring. He remained convinced that the marketplace overvalued defense, and that the most efficient way to compensate for the loss of Damon was to accept a defensive downgrade and add offense. Though defense could now be quantified to some extent (allegedly), for a time it remained lightly valued.

But eventually the third wave of sabermetrics produced a sea change; defense became highly valued, with the resurgence of the saber-savvy Seattle Mariners and Tampa Bay Rays attributed to their emphasis on glovework. Before the 2010 season, Red Sox General Manager Theo Epstein declared "run prevention" the team's new emphasis, and he put his club's money where his mouth was, acquiring several players known more for defense than offense.

Not surprisingly, the new emphasis on defense coincided with development by sabermetricians of ever more precise measurements of an individual player's defensive ability. One reason sabermetricians traditionally de-emphasized defense was their inability to calculate it. (They correctly considered fielding percentage a primitive gauge of defensive ability.) Those who emphasize quantification could not assert the importance of defense without meaningful data to back it up, nor could they offer much guidance to teams. You can't make a point of obtaining good fielders unless there's a reliable way to identify them. Sabermetrics offered no such measurement. But that has all changed.

At least until something new comes along, the go-to measurement is the Ultimate Zone Rating (UZR), a sophisticated upgrade of AVM created by Mitchel Lichtman. Lichtman credits or debits fielders based on the result of batted balls hit to or near them compared with other players' historical success dealing with such plays. He translates this data into the number of runs per season that a fielder saves or gives up compared with the average fielder at his position. Lichtman's analysis encompasses an impressive array of variables to characterize each play, including the type of ball (line drive, bloop, ground ball, etc.), the speed and power of the batter, the number of outs and base runners, ballpark, weather conditions, and more. This database creates an "expected result of the current play" (for example, over the last six years 65 percent of fielders recorded an out on that kind of play) against which the outcome of the play is measured.

Traditionally, fielding percentage simply looked at errors and plays made. The sensible idea behind UZR is that not all fielding opportunities are created equal. Only by capturing the highly specific characteristics of each play can you evaluate a fielder's performance. UZR marks a dramatic development because it purports to apply the scientific method to baseball. The scientific method involves eliminating (or, in the parlance, "controlling for") all variables other than the single variable being tested. Literally dozens of variables distinguish one batted ball from another and influence the outcome of any given play, but Lichtman attempts to control for all of them. By charting batted balls with the same characteristics, and noting the outcome of the next such ball in relation to the history of such balls, UZR attempts to isolate the fielder's performance (that is, whether he made the play) as the only remaining variable.

The remarkable nature of this approach can be seen by looking at the most valued batting statistics: on-base percentage (OBP) and slugging percentage (SP). Compared to what UZR purports to accomplish, OBP and SP are nearly useless. They lump all at-bats together, taking no account of particular pitches (never mind weather conditions and the like) that a batter faces. A single is a single, a double is a double, an out is an out. The equivalent of the UZR approach with respect to hitting would compare the batter's result on each pitch to the historical results of batters facing the same pitch — for example, a 91 miles-per-hour slider with a certain arc crossing the outside corner belt-high. Capturing all the variables of an activity, as UZR purports to accomplish with respect to fielding, would represent a monumental advance.

But does UZR make good on its claim? The short answer: not even close. Lichtman utilizes generalities that belie precision, such as dividing the speed of batted balls into "slow/soft, medium or fast/hard," and referencing the "estimated position of the fielders." When it comes to assessing the difficulty of making plays on ground balls, he takes into account the "above-average speed" and "below-average speed" of batters, whereas in real life there's a broad spectrum of speeds. More curiously still, the determinations of speed of balls and players are made not by computer or other sophisticated device but rather by the subjective judgments of observers called "stringers." To his credit, Lichtman acknowledges on his website that "we don't know precisely where a ball is hit, we don't know exactly how long the ball was airborne or on the ground before it lands, is touched, or passes a fielder, and we don't know exactly where the fielders were positioned."

Not surprisingly, given all the imprecision, UZR produces inconsistent results, as illustrated by the case of Derek Jeter. Long regarded as an excellent shortstop, winner of multiple Golden Gloves, Jeter routinely scored poorly on the UZR matrix and served as the sabermetricians' poster child for an overrated fielder exposed by the new measurements. His range was allegedly deficient, especially to his left. Though Jeter moved well to his right and made his occasional patented jump throw from deep in the hole, he could not reliably reach balls up the middle. These balls, which other shortstops reached, gave him a poor UZR year after year. But something remarkable happened in 2009; Jeter's UZR soared, placing him well above average among shortstops.

If UZR worked as advertised, the only variable would be how well Jeter reacts and moves compared with other shortstops fielding the same balls. Could he have drastically improved his range at the age of 35 after 14 seasons? That's implausible. Lichtman, who claims that players almost always decline in defensive ability by their mid–20s, does not even suggest a miraculous improvement by Jeter. Rather, he proposes that over one season a player could have a high UZR through luck, just as a batter can have an uncharacteristically high batting average one year because of bloop hits, a favorable ballpark, and other such variables. But likening UZR to batting average, where luck and other variables are acknowledged to play a large role, amounts to a devastating confession, since the raison d'etre of UZR is precisely the aim of eliminating all variables other than the fielder's performance.

Jeter's volatile UZR is not idiosyncratic. Rather, as Lichtman recognizes, Jeter presents a dramatic example of a widespread problem — a relatively weak year-to-year correlation of results. To take another glaring example, outfielder Nate McLouth had a poor UZR of -13.8 runs in 2008 and a strong +3.6 in 2009. In fact, the year-to-year correlation is so weak that Lichtman has devised a system to minimize the random variations, applying a set of "corrections" (which he terms "regressions") to the flawed data. This primarily involves cutting a one-year UZR in half. Obviously if you reduce any measurement by half, the variation will decrease. That such a move makes the UZR data more useful seems unlikely, and this much is certain: a system intended to eliminate variables via precise measurement ends up adjusting the admittedly very imprecise measurements in seemingly arbitrary fashion. In fact, a system designed to replace the subjective judgment of the human eye (the traditional idea that managers and fans know good defense when they see it) ends up relying on the subjective judgment of the human eye (the "stringers" who decide whether to characterize a ball as hit hard or soft, etc.) and then, because the data fail to produce consistent results, applies more subjective alterations — Lichtman's arbitrary "regressions."

Lichtman claims that the problem of year-to-year fluctuation will be reduced when we have data on a player for multiple years. This is surely true (as it is for all statistics), but not terribly helpful. While the additional years supply more data, they render the initial data less relevant. If we consider Derek Jeter's UZR from 2005 to 2010, we reduce the random variation we would get if we looked only at 2005 and 2006. However, by 2010, Jeter is a very different shortstop from what he was in 2005. Indeed, Lichtman notes that defensive ability diminishes so quickly that "almost any player who has been a combined average defender over the last 3 years is likely a below-average defender due to aging." In other words, the shelf life of the UZR data is so short that by the time you accumulate enough data to yield a (perhaps) reliable assessment, you are no longer measuring the same player. UZR is thus stuck with unappealing options; one or two years of data is nearly useless because of random variation, and three or more years of data nearly useless because much of the data is outdated.

And yet, for all its demonstrable failings, UZR and similar defensive measurements are sweeping front offices. More surprising still, some observers credit their use for the recent success of certain teams. From 2008 to 2009, the Seattle Mariners showed incredible improvement, winning 24 more games (61 to 85), despite scoring fewer runs than the previous season. Clearly, their improvement derived from run prevention — they gave up 119 fewer runs. Since they hadn't acquired any significant new pitchers, but did acquire new position players, including excellent defensive outfielders Franklin Gutierrez and Endy Chavez (both scored well on UZR, with Gutierrez off the charts), one might assume that defense accounts for the team's dramatic improvement. The reality is less tidy.

For one thing, some improvement in the team's record figured to result simply from regression to the mean; teams that win only 61 games can hardly get worse and almost always get better. (The notoriously hapless 1962 Mets won 40 games. The still-hapless '63 team improved to 51.) Moreover, despite winning 85 games in '09, the Mariners were actually outscored by opponents. Indeed, their ratio of runs scored to runs given up typically results in roughly 75 wins. How did they manage 85? One likely contributor is that baseball mainstay: luck. The Mariners did uncommonly well in close games, which could conceivably reflect some feature of the team but just as likely reflects the way the ball bounced. In addition, while the Mariners didn't acquire any stellar new pitchers, they did get rid of some notably bad ones. They jettisoned six pitchers and minimized the use of two starters. The eight pitchers, accountable for one-third of the team's innings in 2008, were abysmal. Simply replacing their innings with those of more competent pitchers would figure to bring down opponents' runs.

Of course, we don't dispute that improved fielding played *some* role in the Mariners' improvement. But note that, prior to the 2010 season, the team added two superb infielders (Chone Figgins and Casey Kotchman), yet moved in the opposite direction, plunging deep into the Western Division cellar. The fickle nature of the sport, and improved pitching, helped account for the team's surge in 2009. Moreover, to the extent defense boosted the Mariners, UZR deserves at best limited credit. The naked eye told the baseball world that Gutierrez and Chavez were good defenders without the need for UZR.

The Tampa Bay Rays improved even more than the Mariners, adding a staggering 31 wins (66 to 97) from 2007 to 2008, and, as with the Mariners, some attributed the turnaround to use of new defensive measurements. Once again, there was a superficial basis for that conclusion, since the Rays allowed 273 fewer runs than the year before — the team ERA dropping from an astronomical 5.53 to an impressive 3.82, even though much of the pitching staff remained the same. The saber-explanation is the addition of fine fielders Jason Bartlett and Evan Longoria and the shifting of Akinori Iwamura from third base to second. But, once again, the story is too tidy. After the 2007 debacle the Rays let go of ten pitchers who had accounted for 18 percent of the team's innings and amassed an ERA of over 8.

Again, we don't dismiss the notion that improved defense played a role in the Mariners' or the Rays' improvement. After all, the baseball establishment appreciated the important role of defense long before sabermetricians came along to downplay it (before their third wave reassessment). But the notion that UZR was the catalyst for the Mariners' and the Rays' resurgence is improbable. Clearly other factors besides defense were involved, and UZR was not needed to identify strong defensive players. Indeed, as we have seen, UZR is (to be charitable) a highly flawed system for identifying such players.

From the sabermetric point of view, the solution is more and better data. If UZR is lacking, more complete and precise measurements need to be discovered. And the search is afoot, including plans to place more cameras in ballparks to capture things like the hang time of a batted ball and the player's exact route to it. Interestingly enough, skeptics of this approach include Bill James, who in an April 2010 interview noted, "We've had these cameras pointed at pitchers for several years now and we haven't really learned a damn thing that is useful.... I'd suspect the same thing would be true with respect to fielding."

He's right. The problem with UZR and similar approaches transcends the Derek Jeter example and other inconsistent results. Rather, there's an inherent problem with any undertaking which attempts to eliminate variables, particularly in the sports world. A tradeoff cannot be escaped. If you chart every possible characteristic of batted balls, you do a better job of eliminating variables — you know just which cohort of plays to compare a particular play to. But you'll also find far fewer plays that fit the precise characteristics. In other words, what you gain in precision you lose in sample size. When you look at balls hit to a certain square on the field, at a specific arc and velocity, in a particular weather condition, you may capture enough data to render each batted ball unique, or nearly so. The pool of like balls with which to compare that ball shrivels up. Just consider the size of the grids on the field. At present they are large, which increases sample size but also variability. You could make them much smaller, say one square inch, but then you lose sample size, and the usefulness of any assessment of the expected result on the play diminishes. You can increase the sample size by relaxing the precision of criteria, but then the historical comparison group becomes "reasonably similar" rather than "nearly identical" balls, and what you gain in sample size you lose in quality of comparison. (Lichtman's division of batter speed into two just two categories — above average and below average — illustrates this problem.) In other words, UZR has failed and will necessarily continue to fail to isolate player performance as the only variable.

That the third wave of sabermetrics includes a new emphasis on defense is probably a good thing, bridging the divide between the old baseball establishment trusting their own eyes and the new guys with charts and calculators. But when it comes to defense, like offense, the sabermetric search for precise quantification remains futile. An increased emphasis on defense may have helped the Rays and Mariners to some degree, but UZF and its kin do not and will not provide substantial guidance.

Baserunning

As discussed in Chapter Two, the first two waves of sabermetricians waged war against the stolen base and aggressive baserunning more generally, finding that the attempt to gain an extra base is usually misguided because the risk-benefit ratio is too high. And they may have had an influence, because stolen base attempts dropped steadily during the 1990s.

But, as with defense, something unexpected happened. In the last several years, the trend has reversed itself, with both leagues increasing their stolen base totals. More importantly for present purposes, some of the most saber-minded teams led the way. They have been aided and abetted by sabermetricians calling into question the prevailing saber-wisdom. Most specifically, Dan Fox developed a new formula, Equivalent Baserunning Runs (EqBRR), which, according to an article in *Sports Illustrated* in July 2009, "combines the contributions of all forms of baserunning: SBs, advancement on ground outs, fly balls and hits; as well as passed balls, wild pitches and balks." Fox's formula yielded results suggesting that saber-metricians had underrated aggressive baserunning. Whereas James Click, focusing on stolen bases, concluded that Rickey Henderson barely helped his teams at all on the basepaths, Fox found that guys like Henderson and Tim Raines contributed more than ten runs a season at the peak of their careers and an even better runner, Willie Wilson, almost 20. This conclusion did not even take into account the phenomenon we discussed in Chapter Two — the ways in which a base-stealing threat helps other hitters in the lineup.

The teams influenced by EqBRR included the Tampa Bay Rays, who not only steal bases with abandon but also make a point of taking the extra base at every opportunity — advancing on short passed balls, going first to third on a single, and so forth. Doing so violates the earlier saber-command to avoid unnecessary outs at all cost, but it fits perfectly with the revised thinking championed by Dan Fox.

Surprisingly, another team to accept the revisionist thinking is Billy Beane's Oakland A's. During the A's extraordinarily successful run during the late 1990s and early 2000s, Beane worshipped at the altar of out-avoidance. His A's teams typically finished last in the American League in stolen bases, and *Moneyball* made a virtue of their prudence. But in 2009, Oakland was fourth in the league in stolen bases (more than quadrupling their total from its low point in 2005) and led the league in EqBRR. In 2010, Beane, the man who some years earlier all but preached "thou shall not steal" as the first commandment, hired Rickey Henderson to tutor A's baserunners. Similarly, the Red Sox, previously at or near the bottom of the league in stolen bases, soared to near the league lead. Part of that was the addition of speed demon Jacoby Ellsbury, but once upon a time the team would not have cared for Ellsbury, who lacked power and whose on-base percentage was not particularly high, nor let him run so often. And he wasn't the only Red Sox player to run. Dustin Pedroia, not especially fleet of foot, stole 20 bases in both 2007 and 2008.

Revisionist thinking had taken hold. In an interview in April 2010, Beane explained his newfound attachment to aggressiveness on the bases:

> The thing about stealing bases is that it helps create that mentality of aggressiveness and [manager] Bob [Geren] has done that well. A guy like

Raj [Rajai Davis] is going to steal bases no matter where he's at. He's a pretty unique talent, speed wise. What it does from a mentality standpoint is that guys who might not run as well as Raj get into a more aggressive mindset. It's not just stealing bases, but going first to third and taking the extra base on a base hit. I think creating that mentality is as big a positive as anything. Ultimately, having guys like Ryan Sweeney and Kurt Suzuki, who runs very well for his position, you create a mentality of not waiting around for things to happen. It's not just the stolen base in a vacuum. It creates a mentality of aggressiveness throughout the club. Bob did a great job of instilling that in the guys and ultimately guys get confident on the bases as they do at bat. The best way to do it though is to have those guys at the top of the lineup and then get the power guys and then you have a dynamic club. Nobody wants to be one-dimensional where the only way you can score runs is by hitting home runs and the only way you can score runs is by stealing a base.

As with defense, sabermetrics was arriving at a position everyone else had long held. But there's something noteworthy about Beane's reversal. It does not lean on a reassessment of the numbers. Beane may have been influenced by EqBRR, but notice that his analysis above revolves around non-quantifiable factors — an "aggressive mindset" helping produce a "dynamic" offense. Is Beane coming to appreciate that baseball cannot be reduced to a social science? Regardless of his precise thinking, it is important that the second-most famous man associated with sabermetrics, one who formerly regarded risk-taking on the bases as anathema, has come to embrace the pre-saber wisdom on the subject.

Where Are We Now?

Sabermetricians' reversals with respect to defense and baserunning could be seen as progress. Surely, that's how they see it; more study yields more refined ideas. Science works this way, so why not the science of baseball? Sabermetrics remains a young field, baseball a complex game. It stands to reason that there were wrong turns early on. Each new wave of sabermetrics yields better data, hence deeper and more reliable insights. That, at any rate, is the sabermetric self-perception.

But this optimistic narrative is subject to challenge. The latest wave of sabermetrics uses complex formulae and ends up verifying what the common sense and experience of the baseball establishment always taught: defense and aggressive baserunning are important. Best-case scenario, the number-crunchers caught up with the old conventional wisdom. (If so, sabermetricians, who routinely deride old-timers' established wisdom, should be humbled.) But we fear an alternate scenario; the current takes on defense and stolen bases are just way stations on the path to different valuations guided or misguided by different formulae. We are, needless to say, not opponents of data. To the contrary, as should be clear, we're prone to traffic in numbers ourselves. But one needs to do so with a healthy dose of skepticism and awareness of limitations. One senses sabermetrics careening almost randomly from one pole to another. Baserunning and defense are overvalued, then undervalued. What next? Surely we will hear about ever more esoteric formulae, backed by more and better technologies producing more and allegedly better data that will offer different assessments in every direction.

None of this would matter so much were it not for a phenomenon we might call intimidation by data. How odd that some front offices accept UZR even as its creator describes its unpredictability and imprecision, uses subjective observers to characterize the data, and arbitrarily modifies the data himself. Just because formulae are complex and difficult to understand does not mean they are accurate or useful.

The idea that valuations of baserunning and defense can be continually improved is appealing. To children of the Enlightenment, the notion of progress through increased information seems unassailable. Can this idea possibly be mistaken? Yes, at least in the sense that it's far from absolute. Apropos the micro-study of batted balls, we noted the tradeoff between precise data and sample size. This problem applies across the board. The basis of the universe's physical structure — our sub-atomic underpinnings — is shrouded in doubt. Heisenberg's Uncertainty Principle holds the impossibility of knowing simultaneously the position and momentum of an atomic particle. Knowledge of the one varies inversely with knowledge of the other. Even in the hard sciences, more data does not necessarily yield more knowledge.

The 2000 presidential election offers an easily accessible illustration of this principle. When the nation argued about the propriety of a recount in Florida to resolve the virtual dead heat between George Bush and Al Gore (Florida's pre-recount tally had Bush 537 votes ahead out of millions cast), a key question tended to get short shrift: could a recount actually get us closer to the truth of exactly how many votes each candidate received? Temple mathematician John Allen Paulos wrote a perceptive op-ed piece in the *New York Times* that answered that question emphatically: no. There was a strong *legal* basis for the recount (Florida law authorized one), but no reason to expect the recount to be useful. For every ballot more accurately assessed during the recount, there might be another less accurately assessed. For example, chads would fall off during the handling of the ballots, sometimes reflecting voter intent, sometimes not. You could not improve on the original count with any degree of confidence. Looking carefully at every ballot was akin to studying the nuance of every batted ball — the returns would diminish to the point of zero.

Sabermetricians keep wading into ever-deeper statistical waters without appreciating that more data and more complex formulae will not necessarily yield progress in understanding or playing baseball. As sabermetricians change their view of defense or baserunning, what they consider progress may amount to meandering. Too many variables tend to escape measurement. As noted, we doubt sabermetrics can capture the effect that Rickey Henderson's baserunning has on a game, the extent to which Mickey Mantle's presence in the lineup helped Roger Maris, the ability of a fielder based on mapping the characteristics of each batted ball, and perhaps most of all, the workings of the human heart. The latter is what we'd need to understand to appreciate why one prospect succeeds and another fails, what allows Bob Gibson in the 1964 World Series or Kirk Gibson in the 1988 World Series to defy normal expectations of the human body. How and why did Enos Slaughter score from first on a single to win the 1946 World Series and why did Johnny Pesky hold the ball too long before firing home? You can chart that play on a UZR grid, factoring in wind and sun and God knows what, but you will surely be missing the point.

The very goal of reducing baseball to a social science, rather than accepting, indeed embracing, the irreducibly mysterious element, strikes us as wrong-headed — and, in any event, unachievable. But when it comes to the futility of much of what third wave sabermetricians do, don't take it from us. Listen to this assessment by a shrewd front office person known for his attachment to sabermetrics: "If people like me were working on it for a thousand years, we'd make a little bit of progress but not much." That's Bill James talking (in a recent interview) and he's right, just as he's right about the futility of adding more cameras to ballparks to produce ever more esoteric measurements of player performance.

If sabermetrics maintains its current course, where will it be in 2025? Perhaps with a reversal of the previous reversals and a renewed devaluation of defense and small ball, only this time the case made with even more hyper-sophisticated formulae that even fewer people can understand. We doubt that's progress.

CHAPTER 4

Two Cheers for Sabermetrics

The first three chapters have focused on sabermetrics' flaws. At the same time, we have acknowledged that sabermetrics has advanced baseball understanding. For various reasons, however, even sabermetrics' keenest insights have had only a limited impact. In this chapter we focus on two undeniable saber-contributions, showing how they are less impressive than sabermetricians think and have changed the game far less than they expected.

On-Base Percentage

Probably the most significant achievement of sabermetrics comes down to this: enhancing appreciation of the base on balls. Historically, media and fans focused on a player's batting average, but that can be misleading because it fails to tell us how often he reaches base. The player who bats .300 but rarely walks may be less valuable to his team than the player who hits .250 but, because he walks a lot, reaches base more and makes fewer outs. Batting average matters much less than on-base percentage (OBP). The relative importance of OBP was an early theme of Bill James, an emphasis of the second wave of sabermetricians, and a focal point of *Moneyball*.

While raising the profile of OBP marked a legitimate advance, it needs to be kept in perspective. For one thing, the ballyhooed saber-insight about OBP amounted to something obvious and not really novel. Almost since the days of Alexander Cartwright, little leaguers have chanted: "A walk is as good as a hit." To be sure, the chant usually occurs with a weak hitter at bat, subtle encouragement not to swing, but it also reflects recognition that a walk, no less than a base hit, puts you on base. Bill James was hardly the first to appreciate that basic point. Certainly no one needed James to understand that a key aspect of Rickey Henderson's greatness was reaching base often owing to his uncanny ability to draw walks. Henderson couldn't have stolen all those bases and driven pitchers crazy if he didn't find a way to reach base in the first place.

More importantly, while sabermetricians were correct that walks were traditionally undervalued, some of them erred in the opposite direction — overvaluing walks. As noted, sabermetricians obsess over the importance of not wasting outs. As long as you don't make three in an inning you remain at bat, and good things can happen. Since you're given only 27 outs in a game, each must be treated as precious. This insight fuels their worship of walks (the batter avoids the dreaded out) as well as their misgivings about sacrifice bunts, which give away an out, and stolen base attempts, which risk doing so.

But the value of an out can be easily exaggerated — it depends on the nature of the game. For example, if baseball had much higher scoring (suppose there were 20 runs in a typical game), each out would be particularly costly. If the next several batters usually get base hits, the third out of an inning likely costs a team many runs. On the other hand, in a 1–0 or 2–1 game, in which almost all batters make out, the cost of each out decreases tremendously — the batter who reaches base is likely to be stranded anyway. In that circumstance, where multiple hits are rare, strategy should change. The offensive team should be less inclined to treat each out as precious, and instead should be more willing to swing for the fences (though increasing the chance of an out), sacrifice outs (with bunts) or take risks (through aggressive baserunning) that might give away outs in order to get into scoring position. In other words, outs become more or less precious depending on the characteristics of an individual game, and also depending on the era. Outs were more harmful in the slugging 1930s than in the low-offense '60s.

This point has direct implications for walks. Walks tend to be a good thing, but not indiscriminately. Their value depends on numerous variables, including the nature of a game or era. Closely related, in their worship of walks sabermetricians overlook real-world baseball factors that can't be captured by mathematics in a vacuum. They criticize players who are too impatient at the plate, failing to recognize the inevitable tradeoffs if a player consciously seeks more walks. Some players seem so intent on drawing walks that they rarely swing at the first pitch, often missing their best opportunity to drive a fat fastball. In certain situations (depending on inning, score, number of outs, runners on base and the quality of the hitter on-deck), this is particularly unwise.

The career arc of Kevin Youkilis illustrates the perils of over-valuing OBP. Youkilis surfaced in *Moneyball* as a minor league player whom Billy Beane craved because of his ability to draw walks. Beane was right to appreciate Youkilis, who became a star for the Red Sox, but Youkilis's development reveals something curious. From 2006 to his breakout season in 2008 (when he finished third in the Most Valuable Player Award voting) his walks decreased from 91 to 77 to a modest 62. Over the same time, his home runs increased from 13 to 16 to 29. From decreasing walks and increasing home runs we can reasonably infer that Youkilis became more aggressive at the plate, choosing to value power over patience. In other words, Youkilis achieved stardom by sacrificing walks for aggressiveness, the very approach that, according to *Moneyball*, drives Billy Beane and sabermetricians crazy. Youkilis no doubt understood that the catchphrase "a walk is as good as a hit" is generally false. A walk is as good as a hit with no runners on base, and even then, only as good as a single. A walk is not as good as an extra-base hit, nor as good as a single that advances runners more than one base.

There's an additional problem with trying to build a team around high OBP, quite apart from the fact that it may lead you to discourage players like Youkilis from doing the right thing. *Moneyball* emphasizes Billy Beane's interest in players who are underrated because the non-saber world fails to appreciate their capacity to draw walks. We will call such a player an "Eddie" because the paradigm is a pair of 1940–50s era players with that name: Eddie Yost and Eddie Stanky. Neither could hit very well (Stanky's lifetime batting average was .268, Yost's .254, and they lacked power), but miraculously they each walked so often that they actually led the league in OBP several times. Yost's career OBP was a superb .394 and Stanky's a staggering .410.

Moneyball suggests that Beane's appreciation of Eddies, such as Jeremy Giambi and Scott Hatteberg, was a major ingredient in his ability to succeed on a shoestring budget. But something unexpected happened in the post-

Moneyball years; few Eddies found their way to the A's roster, and the team's walk totals actually declined steadily. It wasn't just the A's. Despite quite a few teams hiring front office personnel from the sabermetrics ranks, there was no increase in Eddies around baseball. How is that possible?

For two reasons. First, the Eddie is a rare commodity — very few guys who don't hit particularly well manage to draw many walks. Players walk a lot for one of two reasons (or, more typically, the combination): they have a good batting eye or pitchers fear them. As a rule, a good batting eye correlates with good hitting. Players who swing only at pitches in the strike zone generally hit well. Guys known for a great batting eye, like Rickey Henderson, tend to be good hitters. And, of course, players who are feared are, well, fearsome. Guys like Barry Bonds and Albert Pujols can't help walking a lot because pitchers are afraid to throw them strikes. The list of the top 50 players in lifetime walks consists of almost all great hitters. (Yost is the most notable exception.) So, as a rule, players who draw many walks tend to be high quality all-around and valued by all teams, not just the saber-savvy. They are not Eddies, meaning not available cheap.

But don't feel sorry for Billy Beane that there aren't many Eddies for him to pluck from obscurity — he may be lucky. You see, Eddies, despite their walk totals, tend not to be very good. They may be undervalued by the rest of the world, which undervalues walks, but they are overvalued by sabermetricians, who overvalue walks. For example, one of Beane's Eddies, Jeremy Giambi, walked a lot but couldn't run (he managed just one stolen base his entire career), had only modest power, and was poor defensively. A team of players like Giambi and Jack Cust (one of the few Eddies acquired by Beane post–*Moneyball*) might lead the league in walks but also losses.* As discussed in Chapter One, Beane famously drafted

---

*Cust holds the American League single-season record for strikeouts, and also walks constantly. In his first two full seasons, he either struck out or walked well over 50 percent of the time, making him a candidate for most boring player in baseball. Yet Cust was the principal figure in perhaps the most exciting play ever to end a game. In a 2003 Yankees-Orioles games, Cust, then with the Birds, was on second base in the 12th inning with the Orioles down a run. He tried to score on a single, and made it halfway down the line before slipping and falling flat on his back. When he got up, he found himself in a run-down, a dead duck. Somehow the Yankees screwed up and left home plate unoccupied, so Cust triumphantly sprinted home with the dramatic game-tying run ... except on the way home he fell on his face. Game over.

Jeremy Brown, the portly college catcher whose principal virtue was drawing walks, but Brown couldn't make the Show. Walking is not enough. (In addition, professional pitchers make a point of not walking guys who can't hit.* Brown's walk totals were far less impressive in the minors than in college.)

All of which explains why Beane failed to continue his run of success by loading up on Eddies — there aren't many and they usually aren't very good. But it doesn't explain why walks have not increased across baseball in the last decade. As noted, a number of teams hired front office personnel versed in sabermetrics, and *everyone* inhaled the idea that OBP was undervalued. One would have expected that players who walked a lot would be drafted more often and kept around longer, that all players would be encouraged to narrow their strike zones or alter their swings to draw more walks, and OBP would increase substantially across the board. In fact, overall OBP barely fluctuated (between .330 and .337) from 2001 to 2009. The number of walks per game stayed between 3.1 and 3.42, which was actually a slight decrease from the 1990s. Thus perhaps the single biggest contribution by sabermetrics to baseball understanding had no discernible impact. Why?

To a large extent this non-development was a function of points already noted; OBP is not the be-all and end-all and you can't fill your roster with Eddies both because there aren't enough to go around and, if you somehow managed, you'd realize the ineffectiveness of this strategy. There's also another factor; those teams which understand that walks and OBP are undervalued presumably apply this insight to defense as well as offense. If they aim to increase walks at bat, they emphasize decreasing walks when in the field.

---

*They also make a point of not walking guys who are dangerous on the basepaths. Critics of players like Jacoby Ellsbury and Jose Reyes complain that these speedsters, unlike Rickey Henderson, don't draw many bases on balls. The fallacy is the idea that batters can will themselves to walk. The pitcher must throw four pitches out of the strike zone. With few exceptions, the players who walk most are the ones pitchers pitch around. Alex Rodriguez and Alex Pujols draw numerous walks because pitchers don't mind seeing them at first base — sure beats a likely alternative if they throw them strikes. By contrast, pitchers desperately want to *avoid* walking Ellsbury or Reyes. They are not major long-ball threats, but put them on first base and they won't remain there long. The genius of Rickey Henderson was that he walked constantly despite pitchers' desperate desire to avoid that result.

Even if the saber-revolution had produced a sharp increase in walks, this development wouldn't have lasted. Baseball exhibits an accordion-like tendency to react against sharp swings away from the norm. Since the end of the deadball era in 1919, the overall major league batting average has varied around a mean of about .260. It reached a high of .296 in 1930 and a low of .237 in 1968, but in each case quickly regressed toward the mean. Over this 90-year period, parks changed size, a livelier ball was introduced, the strike zone changed, the mound was raised, steroids made an appearance, and so forth, yet the deviation in batting average has always been transient, eventually returning towards .260. (It was .262 in 2009.)

It isn't just batting average. Since 1920, baseball has maintained a relatively stable equilibrium with respect to virtually every major batting and pitching statistic. (The main exceptions are strikeouts and complete games, which have persistently increased and decreased respectively.) Even the general increase in home runs, which peaked during the age of steroids, seems to be abating; in 2010, the rate of home runs per game returned to 1955–1962 averages.

As a result of the game's natural tendencies, even if sabermetrics' emphasis on OBP had significantly changed the way baseball is played in the short term, the change wouldn't have lasted. If general managers located more Eddies, and batting coaches worked with hitters to become more selective, and this indeed resulted in teams scoring more runs, a reaction would have ensued; teams would have placed greater priority on finding pitchers with good control and pitching coaches would have emphasized this feature more with all their pitchers. The initial increase would revert back towards the usual equilibrium, in much the same way that batting average, after swings in both directions, reverts back towards .260.

In sum, even though sabermetrics contributed to baseball knowledge by emphasizing the undervaluation of walks, saber-inspired teams generally failed to capitalize on this insight and the game itself remained relatively unchanged. As we shall see, this phenomenon carries over to other areas where sabermetricians successfully challenged the conventional wisdom.

Billy Beane and his sabermetric friends think like the revolutionary Thomas Paine, who proclaimed that we have the power to begin the world anew. But at least when it comes to baseball, Paine's antagonist, Edmund

Burke, tends to rule the land. Burke insisted that societies are too complex, and too driven by unseen forces, to be mastered and remade. When it comes to OBP, sabermetricians deserve credit for identifying a flaw in conventional thinking. But their insight failed to have the anticipated impact because baseball, like society, is a complex organism. It generally changes through evolution, not revolution, and certainly resists the master plans of mathematicians.

Closers

If we had a dollar for every time someone declared Mariano Rivera the greatest relief pitcher of all time, we would be wealthy enough to purchase the Yankees. And if we did, the first thing we would do is entertain trade offers for Rivera. Make no mistake, he is freakishly effective; throwing just one pitch, he somehow breaks more bats than he allows base hits. There's no one you'd rather have on the mound protecting a ninth-inning lead. But also make no mistake: Mariano Rivera is wildly overrated.

Bill James understood this first and best. Note that Rivera is considered a lock for the Hall of Fame and has on several occasions finished in the top five of the Cy Young Award or MVP Award voting. Many commentators claim he was the most valuable Yankee during the team's impressive run from 1996 to 2010. Yet James does not rank him — or any relief pitcher — in his top 100 players of all time. Non-Hall of Famers like Ron Santo and Minnie Minoso make the cut but not Mariano Rivera. How is that possible? What does Bill James know that the rest of the baseball world does not?

For one thing, he appreciates the truth behind Woody Allen's quip that 90 percent of life is just showing up. Rivera (like the other elite closers today) rarely shows up. From the time he became a closer in 1997, Rivera has pitched 80 innings in a season only once. In a typical season he pitches 70, which means he is on the field less than 5 percent of the time. How valuable can a player be when his team makes do without him 95 percent of the time?

Suppose a basketball team employed a defensive specialist solely to block shots or take away lay-ups in the last few minutes of games in which the team leads. This hypothetical player — let's call him Manute Bol, who could have been used that way — plays in 40 games a season, and is so effective that he helps his team maintain the lead in 35 of those games. Will anyone nominate Bol for the all-star game based on his 80 minutes all season? Or, perhaps a better comparison, think of football's greatest field goal kickers. They, too, are on the field for a very limited time, but it's usually important when they are and they almost always do the job. When was the last time a field goal kicker finished high in the MVP voting?

Moreover, quite a few of Rivera's 70 innings are insignificant. Roughly a third of his work involves protecting a three-run lead — something virtually no closer fails to do. In any given season, many teams do not blow a single three-run ninth-inning lead. When we subtract those and other trivial outings, we're left with roughly 35 meaningful performances in a typical Rivera season. He succeeds in 32 or 33. This level of success is typical not only for Rivera but also for the top half-dozen closers in any given year. (It's not the same guys every year. Rivera and a few other elite closers are extraordinarily consistent. That speaks to their career value, but does not make them more valuable in any given year.) There is a second sizable tier of closers who blow four to six saves instead of two or three. When we factor in that teams go on to win some of those games anyway, the difference between the top closer and the 20th-best amounts to a few games at most.* The analogy with field goal kickers hold true. They, too, operate within a very narrow range of performance — the 20th-best barely separable from the top few.

It wasn't always that way with relief pitchers. When Jim Konstanty won the MVP Award in 1950, he pitched 152 innings. Whereas Rivera may pitch two innings in an outing a few times all season, Konstanty *averaged* more than two innings per outing. Mike Marshall pitched a staggering

---

*One response is to trot out horror stories of a particular team that blew ten or more saves in the ninth inning. These teams exist — there are a few every year — but they are outliers. There are also football teams which miss 35 percent of their field goals, but that doesn't mean that the field goal kickers who make 90 percent are as valuable as quality quarterbacks or running backs, players who are on the field much more often.

208 ⅓ innings of relief in 1974. Three different seasons Goose Gossage pitched more than 130 innings in relief, Rollie Fingers pitched over 100 innings in seven consecutive seasons, Sparky Lyle topped the century mark six times, and Bruce Sutter five. These guys routinely pitched two or three and occasionally even four or more innings a clip. In 1975, Gossage recorded at least 10 outs in 17 games, and pitched *seven* innings of relief on three occasions. Equally important, the closers of that era, far more often than today's, faced a "high difficulty" save — coming in with the tying or go-ahead runs on base. Today's closers usually begin the ninth inning rather than come in with trouble brewing.

That is a major reason why the gap between Rivera and the 20th-best closer is small — the job all closers are called upon to do is relatively easy; record three outs starting with no one on base. Roughly 65–70 percent (with some variation across eras) of all innings are scoreless, and that figure includes starters who have to pace themselves, who tire and give up more runs in later innings, and who have to go through a lineup several times and face hitters who adjust. It also includes middle and long relief pitchers, generally the worst pitchers on a staff. In the ninth inning, when you bring in your best reliever fresh, when he knows he has to get through just one inning, the number of scoreless innings naturally rises to near 90 percent. Rivera may get his three outs easier than his counterparts, but most of them succeed at a very high rate. And, again, more often than not they have a two- or three-run cushion and "succeed" even if they give up one or two runs.

Successful closers include guys like Armando Benitez, who throw hard but have little else going for them. You can throw 20 straight 97 mph fastballs in an outing. Few pitchers can throw much more than that without losing something (and losing their arm) and, even if they could, by the second time around the lineup hitters will adjust to the pitcher who throws only heat. The relatively easy task facing closers is why pitchers get pulled off the ash heap and succeed in that role. Dustin Hermanson foundered as a mediocre starter for three teams when the White Sox decided he might be effective at getting three outs. In 2005, Hermanson recorded 34 saves and posted an ERA of 2.04. When Hermanson was injured the next year, the Sox pulled up Bobby Jenks, a hard thrower who had been kicking around the bushes for years. The idea was simple: a flamethrower, even an unheralded and non-savvy minor leaguer, can get three outs. Sure enough, Jenks thrived in the role. And so, the White Sox plugged the closer hole twice without bringing in a proven pitcher or top prospect. Similarly, after Kerry Wood accomplished nothing in four injury-plagued seasons, the Cubs made a shrewd move; instead of cutting him loose, they converted him into a closer. Wood saved 34 games in 2008.

Journeymen succeed as closers because the role has been defined into triviality. The main culprit is Tony La Russa. La Russa generally reserved his closer for the ninth inning, and made a point of bringing him in to start the inning. Worse still, he *automatically* used his closer in that situation if his team led by three runs or less. Coincidentally or not, that usage conformed to the official definition of a "save." (If the team leads by four or more runs, the reliever who finishes up is not credited with a save.)

The adoption of La Russa's approach did not result from some carefully thought-out plan. Rather, it stemmed from a combination of whim (of La Russa's pitching coach Dave Duncan) and happenstance. This is La Russa's description of what took place during the 1988 season:

> Dunc says to me, "Do we have anyone better than Eck [Dennis Eckersley] to pitch the ninth?" I say no, we don't. He says, "Doesn't it make sense to use him as often as possible?" And the way to do that is not to bring him in with men on base before the ninth, just pitch him one inning, the ninth. He starts the ninth, and that's it. Then you could use him four or five times a week. But the only reason it caught on is that it worked. Eck was good. We were good. And we also had a great setup man in Rick Honeycutt. If it failed, that would have been the end of that.

Indeed, success breeds imitation, so when La Russa's A's won three consecutive pennants, other managers mimicked his approach. This knee-jerk reaction was silly. Every year a few teams succeed, and they do it different ways — with their own approach to scouting, trades, free agency, game preparation, and in-game tactics. Without careful study, one cannot conclude that a team won *because* they did X, Y, or Z. It can't hurt to comb box scores and films for approaches worth adopting, but there can be no more obvious fallacy than for a manager to reason as follows: (a) La Russa used closers in a newfangled way; (b) his team won; (c) therefore, I should use closers the way he did. Yet such "reasoning" is exactly what transpired, despite the fact that no rational analysis would support La Russa's approach (which we will call, with props to *Boston Globe* sportswriter Bob Ryan, "LaRussaization").* At a bare minimum, an approach that appears to defy common sense should not be followed without probing.

Sabermetricians did such probing. They argued, most notably in an essay by Keith Woolner aptly titled "Are Teams Letting their Closers go to Waste?" that LaRussaization is dumb on several grounds. We will never know how many games the Yankees lost in the eighth inning when other relievers failed to maintain the lead for Mariano Rivera. It may be thought that Rivera, whose cutter exacts a toll on the arm, simply cannot pitch more than one inning. But that's demonstrably false. Come the post-season, Rivera routinely records saves of four or more outs. In Game 7 of the 2003 League Championship Series, he pitched three shutout innings without noticeable strain. Now it may be that the Yankees, who tend to make the post-season anyway, have the luxury of using their dominant relief pitcher sparingly all season so as to preserve his strength for the post-season. But that hardly speaks to the wisdom of other teams following suit — teams which do not make the playoffs, perhaps in part because they lose games in the eighth inning while their best pitcher sits tight solely because Tony La Russa did it that way in 1988.

Besides, if you need to limit the usage of your closer, there's a far better solution than refusing to use him for more than one inning — refrain from wasting him in games where you lead by three runs. On any team with a decent relief corps, the odds of your second- or third-best reliever blowing a three-run lead in the ninth inning are exceedingly small. At a minimum, you can start the inning with them. If they allow a few runners to reach base, bringing the tying run to the plate, *then* bring in your Rivera or Trevor Hoffman.

The related point is that the decisive juncture of a game can be in any inning. The ninth inning may be critical, but often matters hardly at

---

*Ryan uses the term to refer to La Russa's use of relief pitchers more generally, particularly the tendency to use several each game, but we will borrow the term as one of convenience referring solely to his use of closers.

all — the game is already won or lost. Put differently, LaRussaization involves holding back your best relief pitcher for a situation that usually doesn't arrive, rendering him irrelevant to the outcome of most games.

As Keith Woolner argues in his aforementioned essay, there is an obvious alternative; you can "leverage" the appearances of your best reliever to make them matter more. For example, suppose the other team rallies in the seventh inning of a close game. Quite likely, this is the key moment of the game. A big inning will make the eighth and ninth innings anticlimactic. Why not bring in your best reliever now? And why not use him when the game is tied, or when your team trails by a run? Why use your best relief pitcher only to *protect* a lead, if that approach means you'll get fewer leads to protect? Let's suppose, just for the sake of argument, that Rivera or Hoffman cannot pitch more than 70 innings in a season without endangering their arms or crippling their effectiveness in the latter portion of the season. If 25 of those innings are spent protecting a three-run lead, and you instead give those low-risk innings to someone else, you'd preserve Rivera and Hoffman to pitch in 25 games which were tied, or where you trailed by a run — a vastly greater contribution.

This alternative approach entails using your closer in many non-save situations. Because they would often enter games in non-save situations, elite relievers pre–La Russa, while amassing fewer saves, *won* quite a few games. Mike Marshall won 14, 14, and 15 games in relief during a three-year sequence, and Goose Gossage and Rollie Fingers both reached double figures in wins four times. By contrast, Mariano Rivera has never won more than seven games in a season. These numbers don't even begin to capture how often Marshall and crew contributed to victories by keeping their team close, something today's closers are almost never called upon to do.* Note that previous generations of elite relievers were called *firemen*,

---

*While discussing the role of Seattle Mariners closer J.J. Putz in the 2007 season, sportswriter Jim Capel captured the insanity perfectly: "Putz 'saved' 40 games last year with a 1.38 ERA, was named the team's best pitcher by the local writers and the Reliever of the Year by the league. Yet when Seattle was in the midst of losing 13 of 14 games in late August and early September to tumble from the wild-card lead to hopelessly out of playoff contention, Putz pitched only twice. So when the team was floundering at a make-or-break point of the season, its supposed best pitcher — the league's alleged best reliever — was of no help because the Mariners were not in official and proper 'save situations.'"

because they got you out of trouble whenever it brewed. Today, they are just *closers*, relegated to a far more limited role that often could be performed by someone else.

Just as teachers hinder education by teaching to the test, LaRussaization diminishes the value of relievers by managing to the save. How much does it diminish their value? When Woolner studied the matter, using a series of charts and crunching the numbers in typical saber-fashion, he reached the following specific conclusions: At the high end, teams could add 4.5 wins if they abandoned LaRussaization and used their relief pitchers more judiciously, whereas the average team would secure an additional 1.6 wins.

Sabermetricians' work on closers represents a legitimate contribution, but far less than one might think. For one thing, their number-crunching established what thoughtful observers already knew. Consider the straightforward closing sentence of Woolner's essay: "Rollie Fingers or Goose Gossage would be called upon whenever the game threatened to get out of hand." In other words, Woolner's insight merely takes us back to an understanding that governed in previous eras. The folly of LaRussaization was apparent long before sabermetricians claimed to prove and quantify the matter. It defied common sense to lose games in the seventh or eighth inning while your lights-out reliever idled in the bullpen, unable to pitch more than one inning because the day before he preserved a three-run lead that anyone else could have preserved or because you arbitrarily determined that he can only pitch in the ninth.

The folly of LaRussaization was always apparent because it is subset of a basic point applicable beyond baseball; almost any approach that treats all situations exactly alike is sub-optimal. Consider all of the "decisions" involved in LaRussaization: (1) The starting pitcher will not complete games if the team leads by three runs or less (this includes games in which the starter is dominating and his pitch count low); (2) The team will designate one relief pitcher as its closer rather than determine who will finish games based on who is pitching well or who might be better suited to the particular situation; (3) The designated closer will not pitch in any inning but the ninth, nor (4) in a game his team doesn't lead, and (5) will enter at the start of the ninth rather than the middle. Moreover, LaRussaization means sticking to this rigid formula from April to October, regardless of a team's place in the standings, the opponent, or any other variable that might call into question its effectiveness.

In certain walks of life, such a rigid approach is justified. McDonald's succeeds in part because of an obsessive quality control which ensures that all of its franchises make every hamburger and french fry identically. That makes sense because the same foodstuffs respond uniformly to circumstances. It makes good sense (putting aside the wastefulness) to throw out all french fries that have not been sold within five minutes of being cooked, because they all begin to lose something at that point. But baseball players are not hamburgers and french fries. No two are identical, and they go through good spells and bad, have days and weeks when they feel strong or weak, have different success rates against different opponents, and so forth. Yet LaRussaization imposes the McDonald's approach on ballplayers and ballgames.

The problem transcends the rigidity of the approach. Let's posit for the sake of argument that this rigidity actually made sense for the 1988 Oakland A's because of some unique feature of that team. LaRussaization means that *every* team applies that same approach, regardless of personnel or even how well it is working. And, to circle back to sabermetrics, recognizing the folly of such rigidity did not require a complex numerical probe featuring tables with names like "Expected Runs Matrix for Different Base-Out Situations." Again, in debunking LaRussaization, sabermetricians did little more than state the obvious.

Did their charts and calculations add anything to the unremarkable insight that a cookie-cutter approach to relievers is unwise? On its face, they added precision. During the quarter century when we and others railed against LaRussaization, we were able to explain why it made no sense but we could not quantify the effect — could not prove that the approach costs teams on average 1.6 wins and at the high end 4.5 wins. In reality, though, neither can Keith Woolner or anyone else. The precision of his conclusion is illusory, for the many steps in his analysis involve what might charitably be called "estimations" and less charitably called arbitrary assertions. (Woolner himself admits to "educated guesses.") To take one example, consider his analysis of how his formula "of allocating responsibility of runs" treats a hypothetical situation where Yankees set-up man Tom Gordon comes in with runners on first and third and nobody out and allows one to score:

> An average pitcher would be expected to allow 1.8367 runs to score during the remainder of the inning. Of that total, 1.3195 are due to the runners on base that Gordon has inherited.... We credit him with 1 run allowed minus 1.3195 runs expected due to inherited runners = -0.3195 runs for that appearance.

On the surface, this may seem like an admirable effort to evaluate a reliever's performance. In reality, it foolishly treats fundamentally different situations identically. Consider two games in which Gordon enters with runners on first and third and nobody out in the eighth inning. In Game 1, the Yankees lead by two runs. Gordon will mostly concern himself with the runner on first and not the runner on third. If he keeps the trail runner from scoring, he turns over a lead to Mariano Rivera and the game is secure. The Yankees ignore a possible squeeze bunt — they'll gladly accept the tradeoff of one run for an out. For the same reason, Gordon will be delighted to induce a ground ball or fly ball out while the run scores. Let's imagine this is exactly what happens; he yields a sacrifice fly, then gets out of the inning with just the one run scoring. He has done the job, and returns to the dugout to high-fives. Now let's take Game 2, in which Gordon comes in with the game tied. He must worry about the runner on third and the possibility of a bunt, and he needs a strikeout first and foremost. He pitches differently, and must be evaluated differently. Let's suppose he again yields a sacrifice fly and then escapes further damage. Just as in Game 1, he allowed one of the two inherited runners to score. But this time he will not be hailed, because he failed to accomplish his goal and the team lost as a result. Yet in evaluating Gordon, Woolner's formula treats Game 1 and Game 2 identically.

The imprecision of Woolner's formula for "allocating responsibility of runs" triggers other errors, since he uses this statistic to generate additional statistics that ultimately lead to his claims of 1.6 or 4.5 extra victories if closers are used properly. Every step of his analysis involves additional instances of treating different cases alike or ignoring relevant variables. When Woolner speaks of this exercise as involving educated guesses, the noun trumps the adjective. It is impossible to calculate with precision the value of using closers in particular situations.

Woolner certainly can't be faulted for lack of effort. He actually reviewed every plate appearance for each game from 2000 to 2004 to help develop a chart which assigns a "leverage" value to every conceivable situation based on baserunners, score, outs, and inning. The chart is more than two pages long and includes almost 1,000 numbers. Then he determined what leverage number should trigger insertion of a team's best reliever into a game. Woolner compared actual results with what would have happened if managers followed his chart — that's how he arrived at his conclusion that proper leveraging would secure on average an additional 1.6 wins and as many as 4.5.

But the conclusion borders on fantasy. The reality is that his formula provides no better a basis for deciding when to bring in a closer than the more general knowledge traditionally used by managers. Everyone always knew that close games and situations with runners on base are highly leveraged. Billy Martin preferred using Goose Gossage or Sparky Lyle with the bases loaded in a one-run game than with no one on and a four-run lead. But there are far too many variables to generate specific guidance of the sort Woolner claims to provide. He acknowledges that everything changes if a reliever pitched the day before, but the problem lies much deeper. Not all relievers recover equally quickly, and time between appearances is not the only consideration when it comes to potential fatigue. Managers must consider whether it's too early in the season for an ace reliever to pitch two days in a row, or too late in the season with cumulative innings having taken their toll. They must consider how rapidly a particular pitcher can warm up, because a leveraged situation may develop quickly, and how many times the pitcher has already warmed up — not only in the current game, but previous games as well. The wise manager will also consider the other team's batters. You might hold back your top reliever, even with men on base, for the next inning and the heart of the lineup. A prudent manager will leverage not only the situation and the lineup, but the opponent and time of year. Do you bring in Mariano Rivera to face Kansas City in the seventh inning with the bases loaded, if a series with the Red Sox begins the next day? How much does this calculation change from

April to August? If the Yankees are comfortably in first place or trailing the Red Sox?

In other words, if one can actually imagine a manager consulting Woolner's leverage chart, there are any number of reasons why he might reject its recommendation. Managers should use the leverage *concept* but, like all managers pre–La Russa, they must rely on instinct and educated guesses to sort out countless factors that Woolner's staggeringly detailed analysis ignores. At the end of the day, Woolner tells us what we already knew and "adds" a bogus element of precision.

Finally, like it or not, it's La Russa's world — closers just live in it. Regardless of whether it made sense in 1988 to manage to the save, it's now been done for two decades and closers are accustomed to it. They are measured by their save totals, which affects the praise and awards and ultimately the salaries they receive. Good luck to the manager who tells his ace reliever that he will henceforth be used in many non-save situations and not used in many save situations.

Yet, for all that, we acknowledge that sabermetrics made an important contribution by challenging LaRussaization. That isn't the only way in which saber-knowledge pertaining to closers has born fruit. One of Billy Beane's best insights (culled from Bill James) is that top-flight closers need not actually be top-flight *pitchers*, and thus could be had on the cheap. Here is *Moneyball*'s description of Beane's approach:

> It was more efficient to create a closer than to buy one. Established closers were systematically overpriced, in large part because of the statistic by which closers were judged in the marketplace: "saves." The very word made the guy who achieved them sound vitally important. But the situation typically described by the save — the bases empty in the ninth inning with the team leading — was clearly far less critical than a lot of other situations pitchers faced.... You could take a slightly above average pitcher and drop him into the closer's role, let him accumulate some gaudy number of saves, and then sell him off. You could, in essence, buy a stock, pump it up with false publicity, and sell it off for much more than you'd paid for it.

Over the years, Beane has used a succession of closers for one or two years (Jason Isringhausen, Billy Koch, Keith Foulke, Huston Street, Octavio Dotel, Alan Embree, Andrew Bailey), generally trading them in for someone who cost less without sacrificing much if anything in terms of effectiveness.

But, once again, a situation suggesting the value of sabermetrics also reflects its limitations. At one point Beane abandoned his approach to closers, offering Foulke a lucrative long-term contract after the 2003 season. Foulke declined, opting for Boston's greener pastures. His odyssey was doubly curious; why did Beane and the saber-savvy Red Sox engage in a bidding war over a closer, seemingly violating the saber-insight that closers are overvalued? Why, for that matter, did these teams employ a single closer at all? Wouldn't it be more flexible and cost-effective and in keeping with saber-insight for teams to use different pitchers to close, depending on the situation, rather than insist on one specialist?

There are good explanations as to why Beane and Theo Epstein and the other saber-inclined general managers have by and large treated closers conventionally. First, conformist pressures can restrain even the most innovative thinkers. In 2003, the Red Sox did indeed experiment with "closer by committee," using several relievers to close depending on who was pitching well, or was rested, or what batters were due up. The experiment failed—the Sox blew several ninth-inning leads, Red Sox Nation went berserk, and Epstein acquired Byung-Hyun Kim to be the team's exclusive closer. Of course, the experience hardly discredited the idea of closer by committee. The problem wasn't the committee concept, but the particular committee. Indeed, what Red Sox Nation and most of the baseball world conveniently forget is that Kim failed too and the Sox had to replace him with Foulke. But because the public and media reflexively buy in to the single closer concept, Kim's failure was treated as his own rather than Epstein's, whereas the committee's failure somehow indicted the very concept of closer by committee.

In opting for free agent Foulke, Epstein showed he'd learned a lesson, but it wasn't the lesson everyone assumed. For him to ignore the overwhelming sentiment of media and fans, and seek to patch together a different committee to close, would have invited venom and not been worth the trouble. Every time the team blew a save, half of Boston would call for his head, and the ensuing controversy would consume both Epstein personally and the clubhouse. General managers and managers cannot ignore public relations (not if they want to keep their jobs), and some battles are not worth fighting. Epstein tapped Foulke and turned to other affairs.

There are, to be sure, also substantive reasons to prefer a single closer, which may help explain why Beane tried to sign Foulke to a long-term contract at some expense rather than continuing to "create" inexpensive closers. The latter is a cheap solution, but unreliable. Although Beane rightly realized that many unheralded closers perform nearly as well as the elite closers, there are two problems with relying on journeymen to close. First, not all teams succeed in finding or creating the low-cost closer. Every year, a handful of teams simply cannot close games — they suffer ten or more blown saves in the ninth inning. When you have a proven guy like Foulke, you're set for closing games.* Given Foulke's consistency, not to mention popularity, Beane was willing to compromise his usual frugality. For the same reason, Epstein has kept Jonathan Papelbon for years, though a strong case can be made for trading his coveted ace reliever for a field player or starting pitcher and turning over the closer role to hard-throwing Daniel Bard or someone else.

In other words, when the saber-savvy general manager attempts an outside-the-box approach, real-world complications may force him to relent. Sabermetrics teaches that closers are overrated, and Billy Beane and Theo Epstein shrewdly extrapolated from the saber-insight; Beane recognized that inexpensive closers present an opportunity to get bang for his limited buck and Epstein realized that you can succeed without a single high-profile closer. Good thinking, but the numbers failed to convey the full complexity of the situation facing a general manager. Team-building requires consideration of other factors, some of which (including the headache of dealing with an uncomprehending media and fan base, and the psyche of your players) cannot be quantified.

With closers, as with OBP, sabermetricians deserve credit for identifying the flaw in the prevailing approach (even if their "insight" was hardly stunning or novel). But, once again, Edmund Burke prevails over Thomas Paine. It is one thing to recognize a deficiency in baseball tactics, quite another to correct it, particularly without unleashing unanticipated

---

*As noted, this is the sense in which Rivera and the other elite closers deserve the high praise they receive. Their accomplishments tend to be wildly overvalued, equaled by several journeymen, but they succeed year after year, whereas the journeymen, the Dustin Hermansons and Kerry Woods, often succeed for only a year or two before flaming out.

negative consequences. Focusing on numbers, while overlooking the nuances and subtle forces that can't be quantified, sabermetricians fail to appreciate the complexity of the game they seek to transform.

In our view, they miss not only the game's complexity, but also the features that make it most appealing. We now take up the challenge of presenting a vision of baseball that illuminates the beauties of the game that sabermetrics has obscured.

CHAPTER 5

What Makes Baseball

Baseball has always been the sport of choice for intellectuals, a fact brought home by the 1989 hiring of Bart Giamatti, former president of Yale and scholar of medieval literature, as the game's commissioner. Its principal competition in this regard comes from boxing, which inspired the devotion of Ernest Hemingway, Norman Mailer, and Joyce Carol Oates, among others. But however much these pugilistic scribes may fancy boxing "the sweet science," surely much of the sport's appeal lies in the morbid fascination of watching homo sapiens knock each other silly. While there's been some good writing about the finer points and history of boxing, you're unlikely to find even the intellectuals who love the sport debating just what makes it so captivating.

The year 1990 treated fans to a particularly delightful and vigorous dispute between two of baseball's brilliant rhapsodists: George Will and Yale classics professor Donald Kagan. The occasion was Kagan's scathing review of Will's bestselling book *Men at Work: The Craft of Baseball*, and Will's equally scathing response. The pair of essays, along with Will's book that sparked them, amounted to a debate about what makes baseball great. These two heavyweights offered fundamentally different visions of the game.

Men at Work champions the preparation and performance of three superstar players and an accomplished manager: Tony Gwynn, Cal Ripken, Orel Hershiser, and Tony La Russa. Will traces Gwynn's hitting prowess to a combination of practical intelligence and a relentless work ethic. Gwynn seemed to spend every waking hour taking batting practice, viewing videotapes of his swing, or just plain thinking about hitting. In Will's telling, Ripken's defensive brilliance at shortstop and Hershiser's success

112

on the mound likewise derived from ceaseless preparation and thought. In each case, Will emphasizes the player's physical skills, critical though they are, less than his mental approach. And by comparison to the hypercerebral manager La Russa, these players are downright thoughtless. La Russa obsesses over nuggets of knowledge that might spell the difference between victory and defeat. As should be apparent, a theme of Will's book is baseball as the thinking man's sport, where "games are won by a combination of informed aggression and prudence based on information." Will sees baseball in Enlightenment terms — progress through knowledge.

Men at Work enjoyed a long run on the best-seller list and received overwhelmingly positive reviews. Then along came Donald Kagan, in a lengthy review in the journal *Public Interest*, to declare that Will missed the boat. To Kagan, baseball is not an Enlightenment sport for rationalists but a Romantic sport for dreamers. It resembles a Homeric epic in which god-like figures achieve a degree of immortality through extraordinary feats, not a chess match in which one side outfoxes the other through subtle machinations. Baseball is Babe Ruth delivering on his promise of a home run to a hospitalized kid, not Tony La Russa calling for a timely pitchout; Nolan Ryan overpowering batters with a blinding fastball, not Cal Ripken shrewdly shading a batter toward second base.

In a comment that presages complaints about *Moneyball* more than a decade later, Kagan laments that Will's book is "not for humanists, poets, or hero worshippers — but for system analysts, social scientists, and computer programmers." Even the title of Will's book receives a going-over from Kagan. "The very name of the book is ominous for Will's approach to the subject: *Men at Work: The Craft of Baseball*. It is not a game but a *craft*; the participants do not play, they *work*." Will's choice of players follows the folly of his title: a finesse pitcher, a singles hitter, a slow shortstop who compensates through clever positioning, and the manager with the law school diploma on his wall and laptop on his desk. Why not the overpowering Ryan or Roger Clemens rather than the crafty Hershiser? Why not a slugger instead of Gwynn, or the acrobatic Ozzie Smith instead of Ripken? Why not a gritty old school manager like Sparky Anderson or Tommy Lasorda rather than La Russa? In each case, says Kagan, Will's choice arose from a profoundly mistaken idea of what makes baseball great.

Kagan goes for the jugular, calling Will's book "the fantasy of a smart, skinny kid who desperately wants to believe that brains count more than speed, power, and reckless courage."

What Will misses, according to Kagan, is the true stuff of Romantic heroism. Will reserves his highest praise for those with the distinctly anti-heroic instinct not to reach beyond their grasp. Kagan scoffs, "If Mighty Casey came to bat at a crucial moment today, George Will would want him to punch a grounder to the right side to move the runner to third and leave things up to the next batter." True heroes, Kagan insists, "must far outdo ordinary mortals, to the point where their actions give rise to song, story and legend." True heroism is Babe Ruth and Joe DiMaggio managing feats that inspire tales for the ages (Ruth's "called shot") and transcend the world of sports (DiMaggio as symbol of greatness in a Hemingway novel and Simon & Garfunkel song). Will's book, Kagan concludes, "missed what baseball is all about."

Will responded in kind (also in *Public Interest*), chiding Kagan for being "uninterested in anything more subtle than a three-run home run." He took the bait on Mighty Casey; if Casey had advanced the runners with a ground ball, "he would have earned no praise from Kagan. But there would have been joy in Mudville." Will mocked Kagan for all the Romantic claptrap about heroism, explaining that he wrote *Men at Work*, in part, "to rescue baseball from the fell clutch of a certain kind of person who writes about it" — the Kagan kind, that is, who gives us "a lot of clotted talk about the 'potentially tragic' and 'dramatically heroic' and 'Homeric' and 'poetic' facets of the game.... Spare me. Spare it."

Who won this great debate? They both lost. Kagan's blind spot is captured by the clash over Mighty Casey. Kagan pays short shrift to the fact that the objective of a baseball game is to outscore the opponent, and Romantic heroism means something only in that context. Babe Ruth provided superhuman feats *and* victory, but the two do not always go hand in hand. Dave Kingman supplied monster home runs and Casey-like whiffs, but wasn't much of a player. Baseball Romantics worship Nolan Ryan, he of the seven no-hitters and 5,714 strikeouts, conveniently ignoring his unimpressive won-lost record. The success rate of an athlete can no more be dismissed than that of a general or surgeon. By hyping feats of greatness, and downplaying the little things that Will trumpets, Kagan loses sight of the goal of the game.

That's not to say Will does much better. One of the shrewder responses to the Will-Kagan face-off came from Chris Mead, who's as qualified as anyone to wade into deep baseball waters. While an honors student at Yale, Mead wrote a history thesis on Joe Louis that he later turned into an acclaimed book. When he wasn't studying, Mead was on the diamond, where he played second base behind a pitcher named Ron Darling who would later star for the Mets. Mead's take on Will-Kagan? They *both* miss the boat. The greatness of baseball, says Mead, has little to do with either heroism or brains. Those who play the game understand that its specialness turns on something else altogether: instantaneous precision execution.

Baseball players cannot jump like NBA players or run like NFL players. What they can and must do is execute remarkable feats of hand-eye coordination in a heartbeat. The batter must react to a fast-moving pitch in the instant he decides to swing. The middle infielder must catch the flip and pivot, leap, and throw in one motion to turn the double play. That kind of execution, Mead insists, is what baseball is all about. Rather than casting a vote for the Enlightenment or Romantic school of baseball greatness, he proposed a third: the Execution school.

But Mead, too, missed the boat. Will, Kagan and Mead evoke the legend of the blind men who touch different parts of an elephant and reach radically different conclusions about the nature of the beast. Baseball gives us the superhuman achievements of Babe Ruth *and* the crafty positioning of Cal Ripken; *and* the precise split-second execution of Ichiro Suzuki at bat or Ozzie Smith in the field. That multitude of riches helps explain its appeal. Fans do or should appreciate all of the features trotted out by Will, Kagan, and Mead as representing the game's essence. The three go wrong by downplaying or dismissing other important aspects of the game.

That said, none of them has located anything unique to baseball. The "informed aggression and prudence based on information" that Will sees as at the heart of baseball applies equally to football. To the casual observer, football may resemble, as Jacques Barzun put it, a riot occurring at a distance, but in reality professional football is a game of headsets, complex diagrams, and strategic intricacy. Tom Brady and Bill Belichick study tapes as much as any baseball player and manager, looking for every little edge in positioning and play calling. Indeed, most sports are turning high-tech and analytical. National Hockey League coaches, too, dissect videotape in search of nuggets of information. Basketball teams hire assistant coaches and analysts to chart each player's movements on every play.

Nor is Kagan-style heroism unique to baseball. Michael Jordan elevated his body and game to superhuman heights. By any objective measurement, Pele, Wayne Gretzky, and Walter Payton are as heroic as baseball's greats. Each demonstrated, in Kagan's phrase, "ability beyond mortals" that took them and their teams to the summit. Kagan compares baseball to *The Odyssey*, with the batter, like Odysseus, embarking on a journey among hostile forces before he can return triumphantly home. Such metaphors can apply to other sports, too. Basketball's shot-blockers, the towering last line of defense, evoke Hector defending his home city of Troy under siege. Ditto the defensive line in football making a goal-line stand or the soccer keeper who must keep the ball from the net at all cost.

The same holds true for Mead's split-second execution. The basketball player who must move his feet to prevent an opponent from driving, the tight end who must make the catch while enduring a crushing blow, the goalie who must move his pad to block a 100 mph slap-shot — all of them face challenges of instant execution similar to those so impressive in baseball.

Of course, the fact that other sports share features that contribute to baseball's greatness is cause for celebration, not lamentation. And we don't mean to suggest that nothing distinguishes baseball from other sports. To the contrary, if the major team sports are looked at as a group, baseball clearly seems out of place. Every sport has its unique features; football players spend half the game in huddles, soccer players can't use their hands, hockey players are on ice skates, and so forth. But baseball has a more fundamental difference from the others, even apart from the oft-remarked absence of a clock. All other major team sports are essentially territorial. The contest rewards penetrating to the furthest reaches of the other team's territory and repelling it from your own. In baseball, by contrast, you wish only to whip around your opponent's territory without getting caught.

Related, in baseball alone there is no fight over possession of the ball — a feature at the heart of every other major team sport. In fact, in baseball the offensive team wants to get rid of the ball, to knock it far away. In all other team sports, you need the ball in order to score.

These differences suggest a larger distinction; baseball is the most contrived, unnatural sport. Imagine that cavemen stumbled on a ball and decided to break up into two teams and engage in some contest. They might have come up with a version of football or soccer rather quickly, but it's inconceivable that they'd have devised anything resembling baseball. There is something elemental about territorial sports; they resemble military conflict, and history teaches that war comes naturally to our species. If viewed afresh, through the eyes of a caveman or child, baseball seems impossibly perplexing. Why do baserunners run in circles? Odd rules have evolved in all sports, but rarely something so central.

To emphasize baseball's unnaturalness hardly amounts to criticism. Another way of putting it is that it's the most created, meaning most artistic sport. The sound of thunder is more natural than the thunderous opening of Beethoven's Fifth Symphony, but not to be preferred on that account. Like the symphony, and more than other sports, baseball presents an elaborate design reflecting the guiding hand of a creator (we don't mean a deity), not an offshoot of human nature. We suspect that George Will, Donald Kagan, and Chris Mead would all agree on one point: Whether baseball is seen as an Enlightenment project, Romantic phenomenon, or display case for brilliant execution, it marches to its own drummer.

All of this is prelude to what *really* lies at the heart of this great game and distinguishes it from other sports. You've heard a million times that every baseball game features something you've never seen before. The triteness of the sentiment doesn't make it less true. A less cliché-ish formulation is that baseball presents an uncommonly rich narrative.

A number of factors contribute to baseball's reservoir of narrative richness. Part of it is the simple fact that we can see what happens. Other sports, like football and soccer, may present all sorts of narratives that get missed amidst the fog of war. In football, after all, the bulk of the action involves a dozen helmeted men jostling in close quarters. It takes a couple of replays and an expert commentator just to understand how a hole was opened up for a runner to sneak through. In addition, with the partial exception of football (with its structure of huddle, play, huddle, play), other sports involve continual action whereas baseball involves very discrete plays, invariably followed by ample time to digest and discuss what has transpired. Thus, baseball lends itself to being seen in narrative terms, whereas in other sports particular moments blend together. Also, baseball features multiple stations (bases), with the possibility for action at more than one on any given play. Baseball is simultaneously easier to follow and more complex than other sports.

In addition, each unique playing field adds an element of narrative. In most professional sports, the dimensions are stipulated by rule and the playing surfaces tend to be the same. Not baseball. Think Fenway Park with its Green Monster, Oakland with the enormous expanse of foul territory, Houston with its strange hill in center field, and domes where balls crash into speakers. Each ballpark adds potential mischief not available in other sports. In his book that amounts to an extended love letter to baseball, ESPN's Tim Kurkjian captured this aspect of the sport and its narrative richness more broadly:

> Baseball is the funniest game because it presents so many opportunities for humor; it has props that other sports don't. It has walls to run into, mounds to run over, ... and fans that are nearly in play. In what other sport could Larry Walker toss a baseball to a kid in the stands after making a catch, realize that there were only two out, grab the ball back from the startled child, and throw it to the plate? There is Ivy on the outfield fence in Wrigley Field; Michael Jordan never had to frantically search for a basketball in the Ivy before taking a jump shot. There's a hill in play in centerfield at Houston's Minute Maid Park; Jerry Rice never had to climb a hill to make a catch.... The funniest bloopers come from baseball. The clip of third baseman Lenny Randle on his stomach, *blowing* a bunt into foul territory, will live forever. As will the fly ball that hit right fielder Jose Canseco in the head and bounced over the fence for a home run.

Kurkjian does a real service by pointing out the prominence of weird plays in baseball. Comcast Television produced a hilarious show, "The 50 Comcast Most Bizarre Damn Plays Ever," covering all sports. Twenty-one of the 50 plays were from baseball, by far the most of any sport. It was no accident. In other sports, the plays most remembered are defined by the game's story-line — which players and teams performed best. If you attend a handful of basketball games, you're apt to remember the individual games (if you do) in just that way — the game Kobe scored 45 points, the one where the Celtics couldn't miss, another featuring a buzzer beater. In baseball, you're just as apt to remember something unrelated to the outcome: the player pinch-run for in the middle of a play, or the player who stole first base, the battle of beanballs, fan interference, or the time four outs were recorded on a single play.

Other sports have their bloopers and highlights, but these mostly amount to particularly good and bad plays, perhaps spiced by an element of improbability, such as the half-court shot in basketball or players taking a nasty spill. By contrast, baseball history offers a compendium of genuine Believe it or Nots. Believe it or not, a player (turn-of-the-twentieth-century star Fred Clarke) stole home *accidentally* when he, along with the catcher and everyone else, believed that the batter had walked, forcing him in from third. In fact, the umpire had called the pitch a strike, but gone momentarily speechless. Clarke strolled across the plate, with a leisurely, uncontested theft of home.

Believe it or not, in a game in 1927, as the ball rolled toward the Cardinals dugout and a Phillies baserunner streaked home, Cardinals *coach* Jimmy Austin grabbed the ball and hurled it home to nail the runner at the plate. (The umpires somehow missed his intervention, the sort of oversight one normally associates with professional wrestling.) We don't know how the official scorer recorded this coach-catcher putout.

Believe it or not, in 1979 Cubs outfielder Larry Biittner lost a ball in his cap. Biittner's cap flew off when he made a diving attempt to catch a line drive by the Mets' Bruce Boisclair. Biittner searched frantically for the ball while Boisclair circled the bases. All's well that ends well, and Biittner located the ball under his cap just in time to nail Boisclair at third.

Believe it or not, Lou Gehrig was deprived of winning his only home run title outright in 1931 (he had to share it with Babe Ruth, each hitting 46) because a would-be round-tripper of his bounced back onto the field where it was grabbed mid-air by Senators outfielder Harry Rice. The umps weren't fooled, but the same can't be said for Gehrig's teammate, Lyn Lary, who was on base at the time. Thinking the third out had been made, Lary returned to the dugout, crossing paths with Gehrig, who was called out for passing a runner.

That's nothing compared to the legendary potato play. Catcher Dave Bresnahan threw a peeled potato into left field, luring the unsuspecting runner to race home, where Bresnahan was waiting to tag him out with the actual ball. You can look it up. It happened August 31, 1987, in a Class-A game in Williamsport, Pennsylvania.

Twenty-eight years earlier (June 30, 1959), a Major League game featured something oddly similar but wholly spontaneous. Stan Musial took ball four and headed to first while the ball sailed passed the catcher to the backstop. The pitcher and catcher protested that the ball had grazed Musial's bat for a strike, and while they argued at home plate, Musial rounded first and headed for second. Third baseman Alvin Dark streaked to the backstop to retrieve the ball, which for some reason (don't ask) had ended up in the hands of field announcer Pat Pieper. Dark grabbed it from Pieper and threw to second to try and nail Musial. As this was happening, the umpire, forgetting that the ball was still in play, handed a new ball to the catcher. The pitcher, Bob Anderson, saw Musial racing towards second, so he grabbed the ball from the catcher and fired the second ball in that direction. Dark's ball arrived too late to get Musial, and Anderson's throw sailed into center field. Musial instinctively headed for third, where he was tagged out with the original ball. This "believe it or not" becomes a "believe it or *not*" — the umpires decided that, because Musial was tagged with the original ball, he was indeed out. Kind of like the potato play, but unplanned.

Four years later, in July 1963, the major leagues featured a more "normal" play that strains credulity to the breaking point. On a hit-and-run, Willie Mays raced for second while Orlando Cepeda tapped a ground ball to Phillies second baseman Tony Taylor. Mays never broke stride rounding second, figuring he could make it to third by the time the Phillies completed two throws. But Taylor read Mays' mind and never threw to first. Instead, he threw to third, where he had Mays by a mile. Mays turned back and got into a rundown while Cepeda raced to second. Just as Cepeda arrived, so did Mays — chased back to the bag by the third baseman. Two players arriving at a base simultaneously is amusing but far from unique.

But in this instance the third baseman dropped the ball before he could tag Mays and/or Cepeda. That set off a chain reaction, with Mays and Cepeda each figuring he'd better depart the base and leave it to his teammate — Mays headed back to third while Cepeda returned to first. Taylor retrieved the ball and, for the second time in a single play, threw to third to trap Mays, who for the second time in a single play got into a rundown between second and third. If you're scoring, that's ... time for an aspirin.

There's plenty more where this sort of thing is concerned, including a doozy from baseball's early days. On June 27, 1893, a player improbably named Con Daily was chased back to third in a rundown, where he noted that the base was already occupied by his teammate, the improbably named Oyster Burns. Daily took an unusual approach to this unfortunate circumstance, rounding third in reverse and heading for second. The puzzled catcher continued his pursuit of Daily, then threw to second where the puzzled ump called Daily safe. Until the men in blue straightened things out, Daily and Burns stood on second and third respectively — having switched bases from the previous play!

Some years later, a player registered an inside-the-park home run in Washington when the ball he smacked to deep center rolled into a little doghouse that stood at the base of a flag pole in the outfield. Unable to retrieve the ball by reaching in, the delightfully named center fielder Socks Seybold poked his head in the doghouse, where it (his head, that is) got stuck. The batter circled the bases, achieving the oddest field-assisted home run in baseball history.

In a modern version of that play, in 1998 Ray Durham scampered home on a passed ball while the poor catcher could not locate the ball — stuck, it turned out, in the umpire's shirt pocket. On a play even more bizarre, Toronto's Lloyd Moseby slid into second with a stolen base, as the catcher's throw sailed way over everyone's head into center field. Seeing the flight of the ball, Moseby understandably determined that it had been hit rather than thrown, and feared he'd be doubled off first. He scrambled to his feet and sprinted back to first. The center fielder's throw sailed over the first baseman's head, and Moseby turned tail and raced back to second. He covered 270 feet on the play to progress one base — a one-man relay team.

As Tim Kurkjian noted, fans become involved in baseball plays in a way that doesn't happen in other sports. Steve Bartman is widely blamed for the Cubs' loss in the 2003 League Championship series, for impeding Moises Alou's attempted catch of a foul ball in the fateful eighth inning of Game 6. A 12-year-old boy named Jeffrey Maier (who later became a star player at Wesleyan University) is famous in Baltimore and New York for interfering with a ball hit by Derek Jeter and helping the Yankees defeat the Orioles in a post-season game. Does any other sport have its Bartman and Maier—fans who played a role in the outcome of key games?

The two most improbable plays in baseball history involved fans. On August 17, 1957, in Philadelphia, Richie Ashburn drilled a line drive into the crowd, striking and breaking the nose of a woman named Alice Roth. A stretcher was summoned to carry Roth off. On the very next pitch Ashburn hit another line drive into the crowd, which hit poor Ms. Roth (lying on the stretcher) on the hip. Believe it not, Alice Roth was not the unluckiest spectator ever. On May 14, 1939, in Comiskey Park, Bob Feller pitched in front of a large crowd that included his parents, who'd made the 250-mile trek from their home in Iowa. Early in the game, a foul ball off Feller's fast-ball brained ... his mother. She had to be taken away, although thankfully she wasn't seriously injured. The really weird thing is that Mrs. Feller's ill-fated visit to the ballpark didn't happen any old day, but rather on Mother's Day. The *really, really* weird thing is that this stranger-than-fiction history repeated itself in a spring training game in 2010, when Denard Span's line drive struck his mother in the chest. The incident took place on March 31, which meant it was reported in newspapers around the country on April 1. April Fools? Nah, just baseball displaying its boundless imagination.

Of course, not every baseball game produces such craziness, or we wouldn't dip back decades to recount particular plays. Still, according to the adage, you see something new every game. We decided to put the adage to the test, a nice excuse to watch 162 Red Sox games in 2009. We also watched as many games as possible involving other teams, and of course got our fill of *Baseball Tonight*. We kept a "narrative richness" diary, focusing on the unique occurrences in each game.

In the next two chapters, we don't merely describe bizarre happenings in 2009, but in some cases use them as springboards to muse about base-ball, life, or whatever else seems worth musing about. For example, an unprecedented play on the bases in a Nationals-Mets game leads us briefly to revisit a play Mickey Mantle made in the 1960 World Series that has somehow been lost to history. A steal of home leads us to discuss and reject the conventional wisdom on why that play so rarely occurs. A strange play in the outfield triggers our argument that Willie Mays' famous catch in the 1954 World Series was wildly overrated. (We're braced for brickbats.) Other events lead us to profile some of the game's most vivid personalities, past and present. We deal mainly with the 2009 season, but baseball always invites a conversation with history.

Without further ado, we bring you the 2009 season, focused on the game's inexhaustible capacity for surprise and the other non-quantifiable qualities that sabermetrics fails to capture and, worse, tends to block out.

CHAPTER 6

One Normal Crazy Season

When we commenced watching every Red Sox game in 2009, and many other games from around both leagues, we had no way of knowing how well a single season would capture baseball's delightful spontaneity and quirkiness. We began the diary in an experimental mindset, figuring we had nothing to lose. If worst came to worst, we had "wasted" time by watching a few hundred ballgames. As it turned out, baseball kept its end of the bargain. In more than 50 games, we saw something remarkable that we had never seen before and in many cases would be shocked ever to see again.

We weren't the only ones. It was striking how often an announcer remarked that he had just seen something he'd never seen before. Often it was Dennis Eckersley or Jerry Remy, who have been playing or watching baseball for decades and seen thousands of games. Yet time and again they saw something novel. It was also striking how often they made that observation in a ho-hum voice. It has long since ceased amazing them when they see something for the first time in a sport they've been watching forever. We hope you readers are not that jaded, that as you encounter the wild and unprecedented occurrences produced in just one season, you soak up baseball's narrative richness with an appropriate sense of wonder.

4/12

Against the Diamondbacks, the Dodgers had runners on second and third with one out when Randy Wolf's shot was snared in mid-air by pitcher Dan Haren. Haren tossed to second baseman Felipe Lopez, who tagged Juan Pierre for the third out. After the Diamondbacks left the field, Dodgers manager Joe Torre came out to argue that Andre Ethier, the Dodgers runner on third, had crossed home before the tag on Pierre for the third out. The umpires agreed and awarded the Dodgers a run. But wait. Ethier had not tagged up. He left on contact. The solution was for the Diamondbacks to make an appeal play at third. (Oddly, that would get them a *fourth* out in the inning. A team can indeed record four outs in an inning — when they need to in order to prevent an improper run from scoring.) Except it was too late for the Diamondbacks to make an appeal play because they had left the field. The run counted because of a crazy technicality; the Dodgers convinced the umps to recognize their run after the Diamondbacks had left the field, and the Diamondbacks had no opportunity to challenge that run because they had left the field.

So it came to pass that, in the Dodgers' 3–1 victory, one of their runs was awarded ex post facto after a line drive double play. The Associated Press account of the game included this nugget: "Ethier knew he had crossed home plate, but he didn't realize he had scored until he took his position in the outfield for the bottom of the second. 'I still wasn't aware, running out to right field,' Ethier said. 'I see some people talking, and I'm not understanding. And you see a run go up. It was kind of shocking.'"

4/14

A gusting Fenway wind made every fly ball an adventure and contributed to back-to-back zany plays. With Kevin Youkilis at first, J.D. Drew lofted what seemed like a routine fly to left. The A's Matt Holliday staggered around trying to follow the ball's wind-blown flight, and eventually made a sliding catch. Lured by Holliday's journey into thinking the ball would drop, Youkilis had reached second. He turned tail and sprinted back to first, barely beating the throw, but his momentum took him past the base and towards the dugout. He was tagged out, having overrun first in the wrong direction. Youkilis's embarrassment was matched on the very next play when A's right fielder Travis Buck attempted an all-out, airborne dive on a ball hit to right by Jason Bay, and missed ... by five feet.

4/17

Royals second baseman Alberto Callaspo's full-length dive corralled a grounder up the middle, but left him in no position to flip the ball to the shortstop for the force play. He improvised brilliantly. While fully prone, face in the dirt, and without moving his torso, he flipped the ball behind his neck — on the money and in time for the out. It resembled a Magic Johnson no-look behind-the-back pass more than anything ever seen on the baseball diamond, but Magic never made such a play while flat on his face.

4/21

In the fourth inning of the Giants-Padres game, with runners on first and second, a long extra-base hit sent both runners scampering home. Because the lead runner, Adrian Gonzalez, held up to see if the ball would be caught, the trail runner, Chase Headley, almost overtook him, and the two Padres arrived at the plate along with the relay throw home. Gonzalez slid wide, evading the tag of catcher Bengie Molina but also missing the plate. The umpire properly made no call — to that point Gonzalez was neither safe nor out. A split-second later, Headley found the plate blocked and tried leap-frogging Molina. He was unsuccessful and was called out. Now, both Gonzalez and Molina lay sprawled on the ground, Gonzalez's fate unresolved. He dove back toward the plate, while Molina dove to tag him. Gonzalez was safe by a hair. Thus the baserunner from first was out at the plate before the baserunner from second scored. (As bizarre as this play was, it could have been even more so. If Headley had slid in "safely" under the tag, he presumably would have been declared out for passing Gonzalez.)

4/22

In Toronto, Texas pitcher Darren O'Day was brought in to face the Blue Jays' Kevin Millar with runners on first and second in the 11th inning. O'Day had been claimed on waivers earlier in the day and arrived at the ballpark mid-game. With Texas short on pitching, he was rushed out to pitch before the team could get him his own jersey. He borrowed Kason Gabbard's top, which threw Millar for a loop as he watched the new pitcher warm up. "I thought [Gabbard] was a left-handed pitcher. He came in throwing a sinker ball, side-armed, right-handed. I was a little confused." (Millar nevertheless laced a game-winning base hit, providing O'Day a rude welcome to town.)

4/26

In the fifth inning of a Yankees–Red Sox game, Jacoby Ellsbury was on third with one out, J.D. Drew at bat and the Sox ahead 2–1. Drew had struck out in his two previous at-bats, and looked overmatched by Andy Pettitte. Ellsbury must have taken notice. As Pettitte went into his high-kick delivery, Ellsbury streaked down the line — a straight steal of home! He was easily safe. Arguably, the play changed the game, quite apart from the extra run. The crowd went ballistic, and Drew promptly pounced on a Pettitte pitch for a double to extend the Sox's lead to 4–1. While the Red Sox seemed to strut from that point on, the Yankees went flat, managing just one hit in the last four innings. Of course, to credit Ellsbury's dare with Drew's double or the Yankees' subsequently quiet bats is guesswork. We'll never know what would have happened if Ellsbury hadn't electrified Fenway, and it's better that way. As the poet Edwin Arlington Robinson wrote, "The best of life ... is in what we do not know."

If you are old enough to have seen Jackie Robinson play, you may be scratching your head over the idea that we've never before seen a straight steal of home — Robinson pulled the trick at least a dozen times. (He stole home 19 times, but some of those were on delayed steals or the back end of a double steal.) Today, though, the play is rarely even attempted. Occasionally someone mourns the "lost art" of stealing home. Nonsense. Over time, teams realized that a pitcher pitching from the stretch and the third baseman playing closer to the bag eliminate the steal of home. No one steals home anymore because the game has gotten better, not worse.

5/1

In the Tigers-Indians game, Detroit's Josh Anderson chopped a ground ball to first. Victor Martinez knocked it down but it bounded away, several feet in front of the bag. Martinez chased it down, arriving at the same time as Anderson. The first baseman attempted to scoop the ball and tag Anderson in one motion, and Anderson attempted to leap-frog the tag. Neither player fared well. The ball squirted out of Martinez's glove, rolling towards home plate. Meanwhile, Anderson lost his balance and flew through the air head over heels, landing past the first base bag. Pitcher Carl Pavano raced to retrieve the ball while Anderson tried, unsuccessfully, to get to his feet. Now ensued an amazing sight — a play at first in reverse — with Pavano flipping to Martinez while Anderson dove to the bag from the right field side. The throw clearly beat him, but the umpire called him safe, perhaps unconsciously thinking that Anderson's crash landing merited reward.

5/9

With the bases loaded in the bottom of the seventh, Diamondback Josh Whitesell lined a base hit to right field — or so it seemed. The Nationals' Aaron Kearns fielded it on a hop and, seeing that the runner on third, Felipe Lopez, had held up thinking the ball might be caught, threw home. Catcher Jesus Flores did a stretch worthy of a first baseman, and Lopez was out. In the books, it goes down as just another force-out, albeit a 9–2 force-out — right field to catcher — which can't happen more than once a decade.*

---

*But just two months later, it happened again! In the sixth inning of the Royals–Red Sox game on July 11, with the bases loaded and one out, Ryan Freel lined a base hit to right field. Well, not technically a base hit, because a charging J.D. Drew one-hopped the ball and threw home ahead of the runner Miguel Olivo. In this case, the baseball gods were particularly cruel. Freel, whose clean "hit" goes down in the books as just another 9–2 force-out, was hitting .169.

5/10

Outfielders sometimes attempt to fool baserunners by pretending they are going to catch a ball they know they won't reach. It rarely works, but it's worth the try. Jason Bay played a variation on this theme, and it actually worked. With Carl Crawford on first and two out, Pat Burrell lifted a towering fly to left. Bay never stirred, as if the ball were an obvious home run. He stared straight into the infield, hands on knees, until the ball hit the wall, at which point he raced into action. He held Burrell to a single, which isn't shocking — wall balls at Fenway often result in singles and Burrell runs like he's under water. The surprise was that the speedy Crawford, who with two outs was running on contact, didn't cruise home. He did score, but on a play at the plate so close that it baffled — until replays showed Crawford jogging towards second while admiring the flight of the ball. He thought the ball was gone, no doubt influenced by Bay's ruse.

5/13

In Baltimore, Melvin Mora lofted a foul pop near the Orioles dugout and Rays catcher Dioner Navarro and first baseman Carlos Pena gave chase. Pena made a lunging catch, then flipped over the dugout rail, clinging to it for dear life. He seemed headed for a scary plunge, but for Navarro's quick reaction, grabbing Pena's leg and righting him. It looked like a gymnast spotting a teammate on the uneven bars more than anything you see at a baseball game, and gave new meaning to infield assist.

5/16

On a ground ball up the middle with a runner on first, Oakland shortstop Orlando Cabrera didn't have time to catch the ball and flip for the force at second. He improvised, swatting the ball toward the bag with the outside of his glove. Amazingly, the play worked, the ball rolling into the outstretched bare hand of second baseman Adam Kennedy in time for the out. The 6–4 force normally proceeds from the throwing hand of the shortstop to the glove pocket of the second baseman. Cabrera and Kennedy pulled off a backwards variation — outside of shortstop's glove to second baseman's throwing hand.

5/17

Seems something was in the air — four games produced plays off the probability charts. In the sixth inning of the Red Sox–Mariners game, with Wladimir Balantien on first, Rob Johnson bunted in front of the plate and Balantien dashed to second. Jason Varitek threw to first, but players on both teams thought the ball was foul. The exception was shortstop Nick Green who, seeing Balantien returning to first, alertly called for first baseman Jeff Bailey to throw him the ball. Or maybe not so alertly, since his alarm clued in Balantien, who reversed course and returned to second. Bailey's throw nipped him, and the play went down as a sacrifice bunt (since Balantien had reached second before voluntarily departing) and a double play. After the game Dustin Pedroia said, "I don't think we'll ever see that again."

We're even less likely to see a repeat of a play from the Nationals-Phillies game. With the Nats up 6–5 in the eighth inning and runners on first and second, Pedro Feliz of the Phillies bunted down the third base line. Third baseman Ryan Zimmerman and pitcher Jesus Colome both went to field the ball. Zimmerman's glove arrived first, it looked as if he came up with the ball, and he cocked to throw before realizing he'd come up empty — the ball had somehow ended up in Colome's glove. Colome made a perfect throw to first, but Anderson Hernandez, apparently looking for a throw from Zimmerman, let the ball sail into right field. The tying and winning runs scored on the play.

With one out in the ninth inning of a Twins-Yankees game, speedy Brett Gardner was at second as the potential winning run. Francisco Cervelli hit a comebacker that pitcher Jose Mijares knocked down. The ball rolled between the mound and home, where catcher Joe Mauer pounced on it. Out of the corner of his eye Mauer saw Gardner rounding third aggressively, so he faked a throw to first, inducing Gardner to continue his sprint home. What followed was a scene out of a Matt Christopher novel. After three hours, the game came down to a foot race between the Yankees' speed demon and the Twins' athletically gifted catcher, culminating in simultaneous head-first dives toward the plate. Mauer won the photo finish, applying the sprawling tag just before Gardner (impeded by Cervelli's bat) touched the plate with the game-running win. (A walk-off homer by Johnny Damon in the tenth nullified Mauer's effort.)

Finally, a defective line-up caused a 13-minute delay during the first inning and could have cost the Rays a game. The Rays handed in a lineup card with both Evan Longoria and Ben Zobrist penciled in at third base. After the Indians batted in the first, their manager Eric Wedge pointed out the double-dipping to the home plate umpire. After a lengthy conference, the men in blue determined that the Rays had to forfeit the designated hitter and bat their pitcher, Andy Sonnanstine, in the third spot where they had put Longoria (their intended DH). This being the American League, Sonnanstine never bats, meaning the Rays were saddled with a near-automatic out in a key lineup spot. Wouldn't you know it, Sonnanstine doubled in a run in the Rays' 7–5 win.

5/22

Minnesota's Michael Cuddyer hit for the cycle — single, double, triple, home run. The cycle is a contrived accomplishment,* but there was something compelling about this one; Cuddyer completed the feat with a *broken bat ground ball triple.*

---

*Consider that a player who hits a home run, triple, and two doubles — which is better than the cycle — misses the accolades. He's punished because his redundant second double comes at the expense of a cycle-completing single. This can lead to strange behavior. In the seventh inning of a game against the Rangers on August 17, 2001, Toronto's Jeff Frye drove a ball to right-center field that rolled to the wall. He could have cruised to second, but stopped at first instead. The Associated Press story the next day quoted Frye: "I was rounding first and I said 'What do I do, what do I do?' And [first base coach Garth Iorg] goes, 'Stay here, stay here.'" But the most bizarre quote, which really captures the folly of the cycle, was supplied by Frye's teammate, Jose Cruz. "I saw him looking at Garth, asking him what to do, but I would've stayed as well," Cruz said. "How many times do you get a chance to stop at first base to complete the cycle?"

5/23

A base hit by Boston's Nick Green sent the ball into center field and the splintered bat flying in multiple directions. A close-up of Green at first base showed an inch-long fragment of the bat lodged in his sleeve. Green was blissfully unaware.

5/24

What do you call a hailstorm in May? New England. The Red Sox and Mets were delayed by a storm that left the warning track strewn with hailstones, a situation not covered in the grounds crew's manual. The game itself supplied a comic moment. In the sixth inning, as he started his delivery, Mets rookie Ken Takahashi dropped the ball — but didn't realize it. Takahashi continued his full motion, follow-through included, while the ball rolled behind him toward third base. As reward for this delightful pantomime, Takahashi was called for a balk.

In the sixth inning in New York, Cole Hamels jammed Mark Teixeira so effectively that a chunk of Teixeira's bat flew toward third base. Another piece fell in front of home plate, and only the handle remained in Teixeira's hand. Meanwhile, the ball sailed well over the wall in left — a broken-bat home run.

5/28

May has been the month of broken battiness, producing a broken bat triple, broken-bat home run, and broken bat lodging in a player's uniform, but what happened to David Ortiz takes craziness honors: his bat broke on a swing and miss. Ortiz struck out and found himself holding only the knob of the bat. The rest somehow snapped off and flew behind him — a broken bat strikeout.

6/1

In the seventh inning of the Yankees-Indians game, Jacobs Field seemed overtaken by an Old Testament plague. First came bugs, which swirled around the mound. Rain followed. Next came birds, an army of seagulls decamping in center field. Curiously, no attempt was made to move them, even though center fielder Ben Francisco would have had to traverse an avian minefield had a ball been hit his way. Instead, Nick Swisher banged a double to left, breaking the game open. Suddenly the gulls took off, like fans rushing for the exits after the game is out of reach (but with no trouble beating traffic).

6/5

Trailing 5–1 in the ninth, the Red Sox mounted a bit of a threat, putting runners on first and third. Texas pitcher Darren O'Day then attempted an old silly trick that just wastes time ... and it worked. O'Day faked a throw to third to lure J.D. Drew from first, and Drew indeed broke for second. He'd have been a dead duck, but the Rangers' middle infielders were even less alert than he, and no one covered second.

6/6

With Luis Castillo on first for the Mets, Emil Brown drove the ball to right field, where the Nationals' Elijah Dukes made a sliding catch. The umpire ruled the ball a trap, but Castillo didn't see that and returned to first, crossing paths with Brown who headed for second and implored Castillo to do the same. Castillo, who by this point was almost all the way back to first, reversed course and headed back toward second. Meanwhile, from flat on his back, Dukes threw the ball in to the infield, where first baseman Nick Johnson scooped it up and threw to second in time to get Castillo. Brown was called out for passing Castillo, and a seeming fly out became a seeming base hit that became a strong candidate for the strangest double play in major league history.

The play received a lot of media attention, but one aspect of the situation was overlooked: Castillo messed up by returning to second. Once Brown passed him, he (Brown) was automatically out, thereby eliminating the force on Castillo at second. He could have and should have remained at first. Of course, Castillo cannot really be blamed for failing to realize, in the heat of the moment, that Brown passing him on the bases eliminated the force. His understandable mistake calls to mind one of the great unsung moments in World Series history.

Everyone knows that Bill Mazeroski hit a walk-off home run in the ninth inning of Game 7 of the 1960 World Series. What has been lost to history is that Mazeroski's blow was made necessary by a brilliant piece of baserunning by Mickey Mantle in the top of the ninth. The Yankees trailed by a run with one out, Gil McDougald on third, Mantle on first, and Yogi Berra at bat. Berra hit a one-hop shot to first basemen Rocky Nelson that looked like a Series-ending double play. Nelson stepped on first and turned to throw to second to nail Mantle, but the slugger known more for brawn than brains instantly recognized that the force was lifted by the out at first. Mantle dove back to first, barely beating Nelson's tag. McDougald scored on the play, tying the game and setting the stage for Mazeroski's dramatic home run.

6/7

The Red Sox–Rangers game produced two things we've never seen before — one on the field, one in the dugout. With the bases loaded in the fourth inning, Jacoby Ellsbury's one-hopper got past second baseman Ian Kinsler and rolled into right-center. Ellsbury took a wide turn, and when center fielder Marlon Byrd lobbed the ball to second, he charged. The throw arrived at the base while Ellsbury was still a good ten feet away — he had made a reckless gamble and was out by a mile. Except he caught Texas by surprise and the roaring Sox crowd drowned out efforts by Rangers players to play Paul Revere. Shortstop Omar Vizquel, who received Byrd's throw, somehow didn't notice Ellsbury's approach. Standing at second, he held the ball chest high, attempting no tag until Ellsbury had already slid in safely.

As it turned out, the crazy non-tag hurt the Red Sox more than the Rangers — Ellsbury was injured, because he couldn't anticipate Visquel's obliviousness. "It was like, 'Oh, where'd this guy come from?'" Ellsbury explained after the game. "That's kind of how I landed on it weird. I thought it was going to be a bang-bang play, so I was going to try to get around the tag. I landed kind of on my right shoulder."

While an Ellsbury injury is anything but funny to the Red Sox, his removal from the game produced high comedy. With J.D. Drew unavailable because of injury, the new Red Sox center fielder would have to be either Rocco Baldelli or Mark Kotsay. Both are right fielders who almost never play center. Rather than decide which player was better suited for the new position, Terry Francona told the players to figure it out for themselves. Which they did, though surely not the way Francona envisioned. An alert cameraman took us inside the dugout, where Baldelli and Kotsay were playing rock/paper/scissors to determine their positions. Baldelli pumped his fist in celebration of his victory, then marched out to right field. Kotsay, the loser, took center.

6/11

Once again the seagulls perched in their seats out in center field in Cleveland, but this time not content to be spectators. With the Indians and Royals tied 3–3 in the tenth inning, Shin-Soo Choo singled to center and Mark DeRosa raced home with the possible winning run. A charging Coco Crisp seemed to have a play on DeRosa, but the ball struck a gull and deflected past the chagrined center fielder. The bird lost a feather, but managed to fly away — a unique walk-off/fly-off victory for the Tribe.

6/17

Jeremy Hermida drilled a ball at Brad Penny so hard that the Red Sox pitcher's glove never moved, the ball striking him squarely in the chest. Six inches higher and Penny's life, or at least his season, would have been in jeopardy. Yet Penny not only escaped injury, but got an inning-ending out. The ball smacked off his chest and rolled straight to Kevin Youkilis at first. That's 1–3 if you're scoring, but without a throw.

6/20

In Colorado, Pirates left fielder Nyjer Morgan may have pioneered a new way for players to outfight fans for foul balls in the crowd. As he approached the railing down the left field line, Morgan eschewed the normal face-first leap into the crowd. Instead, he pirouetted in mid-air, so that by the time he caught the ball his back was to the crowd — essentially boxing out the fans as if he were a basketball player going for a rebound (except no basketball player has ever attempted a 180 mid-air box-out). For good measure, as he came down Morgan found himself seated on the railing, a fitting finish to a catch that required a combination of athleticism and improvisational skills.

6/24

Trivia question: when is a ground ball through the shortstop's legs not an error? In the Red Sox–Nationals game, Elijah Dukes reached base on a bad-hop, broken-bat single — but it was the bat, not the ball, that took the bad hop. Both the top half of Dukes' bat, and the ball, went directly at shortstop Nick Green — the bat airborne, the ball on the ground. The bat dropped just in front of Green and bounced over his shoulder. He recoiled in self-defense, and thus was in no position to field the ball. It rolled between his legs — a routine grounder turned into a base hit by a bat that played the role of a pulling guard in football. To make the play even more bizarre, the bat became impaled in the outfield grass, standing upright. When Green ran to chase the ball down, he had to spread-eagle the bat, barely avoiding the nasty thing for the second time.

7/2

In San Diego, the Astros and Padres, poised for the ninth inning, had to wait 52 minutes as a brave beekeeper contended with thousands of bees swarming around the ballgirl's chair in left field.

7/10

In the seventh inning in Anaheim, the Angels' Chone Figgins popped a ball near the plate, then became tangled up with Jorge Posada, who was trying to position himself to catch the ball. As the Yankees catcher wrestled himself free, his glove flew off. So he caught the ball bare-handed.

7/11

In Oakland, Rays catcher Michel Hernandez committed an odd infraction — using his mask to gather the ball which lay a few feet away. He gained no advantage by doing so — the runner on second, Matt Holliday, was going nowhere — but rules are rules and the catcher is not allowed to use his equipment to gain control of the ball. Home plate umpire Jeff Nelson advanced Holliday to third. For his alertness, Nelson was treated to a torrent of nose-to-nose abuse from Rays manager Joe Maddon. Nelson ejected Maddon, who after the game said this: "That was the right call by Jeff Nelson. I didn't see it at first, but when I watched the replay, he was right."

7/17

In the Boston-Toronto game, Sox reliever Daniel Bard retired all four batters he faced while hitting one. You read right. Bard hit Dave Dellucci on the foot with a slider, but the umpire ruled that Dellucci swung at the pitch for strike three. *That's* a bad at-bat, made worse by the fact that the ball ricocheted off Dellucci's foot to the backstop; he easily could have made it to first, but he didn't believe he had swung and refused to budge.

Oddly, a similar misfortune befell Nick Green in the fourth inning. He got creamed on the hand, but the umpire thought the pitch hit the knob of the bat and ruled it a foul ball. This led to an incongruous scene around home plate: two extended meetings a few feet apart. While the Sox trainer tended to Green, Terry Francona demanded that the umpire explain why his player needed medical attention if the pitch didn't hit him.

7/18

After the Dodgers scored on a close play at the plate, the catcher handed the ball to Astros pitcher Mike Hampton. As the veteran pitcher strolled to the mound, he went to slam the ball into his glove in disgust and ... missed. The ball rolled into foul territory, and another Dodgers run scored. By unofficial count, pitchers have slammed balls into their mitt 4,876,793 times but, so far as anyone knows, this is the first time the move misfired and led to a run.

7/19

In the Blue Jays–Red Sox game, Alex Rios stole second, easily beating Jason Varitek's throw, but home plate umpire Eric Cooper marched out onto the field and returned Rios to first. This is commonplace in Little League, where the runner is not allowed to leave the base until the ball crosses the plate and violators are sent back to the bag from whence they came. But in the Major Leagues? It turns out Varitek's arm brushed against Cooper on the throw, and the umpire called interference on himself!

7/20

Kevin Youkilis's line drive in the first inning sent Rangers left fielder David Murphy scurrying back to the warning track, where he raised his glove and waited for the ball to arrive. It landed roughly 100 feet in front of him in shallow left. That's a tough Texas sun.

7/24

At Wrigley Field, Cubs left fielder Alfonso Soriano turned to play a ball off the ivy-covered wall and was surprised to see two balls emerge: the game ball and one that apparently lodged in the ivy during warm-ups. Soriano grabbed the one nearest at hand and threw into the infield.

7/27

With a runner on second, the Giants' Randy Winn lined a ball to right field that bounced off Pirates right fielder Garrett Jones' glove, then his shin, followed by his foot, which inadvertently punted the ball back towards the infield. Second baseman Delwyn Young, moving to shallow right on the play, saw the ball flying by and made a spectacular, diving bare-hand grab. Perhaps not believing what he'd seen, the umpire ruled base hit, though the ball clearly never touched the ground. Despite the missed call, the Pirates retired Winn, who apparently couldn't believe his eyes either and was tagged out while meandering between first and second. But the umpire's error meant that a run scored on the play. It also meant that perhaps the craziest catch in baseball history went down as a base hit — a single followed by a 9–4–3 put-out. The box score fails to capture the unique nature of the play and all the body parts involved.

7/28

On Cubs Kosuke Fukudome's grounder back to the mound, the ball bounced inside the shirt of Astros pitcher Jeff Fulchino. Fukudome sprinted to first while Fulchino frantically tried to retrieve the ball from himself. Fukudome won the race and was credited with a base hit. Fulchino, for his part, offered the following account after the game. "I looked down, and I was like, 'Where is it?' Then I felt it right over here to my side, and I was like, 'You gotta be kidding me.'"

8/9

In Philadelphia, home plate umpire Ed Rapuano took the taboo against arguing balls and strikes to a new distance, ejecting Shane Victorino for protesting from *center field*. (Victorino's replacement, Jayson Werth, made two errors before the inning was over.) After the game, Victorino said of Rapuano, "I love the guy.... I mean that sincerely." As for the gesticulations that earned his ejection, Victorino said, "It's not something you should be doing but I've done it a thousand times."

8/14

"There's more to baserunning than speed." Terry Francona should be forced to write that on the blackboard 1,000 times after today's fiasco in

Texas. With the Red Sox trailing the Rangers by a run in the ninth inning, Francona inserted pitcher Clay Buchholz to run for Jason Varitek, the potential tying run at second. Varitek is slow, but Buchholz has not scored a run in his professional career and had not run the bases a single time this season. On Dustin Pedroia's shot off the left field wall, it showed. Unable to get a read on whether David Murphy's leaping attempt at the catch succeeded, Buchholz hesitated, staggered, then stumbled rounding third, and actually took the trouble to adjust his helmet as he struggled to maintain his footing. He was nailed at home — out from second on a double.*

8/20

In the fourth inning of the Red Sox–Blue Jays game, Jason Bay drew a walk. With David Ortiz at bat, catcher Rod Barajas' throw back to the mound got past pitcher Brett Cecil. Cecil scrambled to retrieve the ball near second base, then held up the scuffed ball, signaling the home plate umpire that he wanted a new one. But the flustered pitcher didn't call time out, nor throw the ball home for the exchange. Instead, he tossed it into the Jays dugout. Bay was awarded third for this gratuitous throwing error (E-1—"pitcher's decision to remove live ball from game"), the most effortless two-base advance in baseball history.

8/21

After banging a ball off the Green Monster against the Yankees, Dustin Pedroia was thrown out trying to stretch it into a triple, violating the tenet never to make the last out of an inning at third base. In fairness to Pedroia, when the ball caromed off the wall, flew back over the head of left fielder Eric Hinske, and bounced a good ways toward the infield, he had every

---

*Buchholz did not run the bases again until June 26, 2010, this time through no choice of Francona's. In the first at-bat of his Major League career (an interleague game against the Giants), he singled. But just as his batting average is 1.000, his track record for baserunning futility remains perfect as well — he pulled a muscle rounding first, placing him on the disabled list and costing him his first All-Star Game appearance.

reason to expect an uncontested triple. But the ever-alert Derek Jeter raced to shallow left and in one motion retrieved the ball and fired to third. If you're scoring, that's 6–5, a player thrown out attempting a triple without any involvement by an outfielder.

Meanwhile, in the Cardinals' loss to the Padres, Albert Pujols cruised into second with what he thought was an uncontested stolen base. But his teammate, Brendan Ryan, already occupied the bag and didn't budge. Catcher Nick Hundley raced from behind the plate all the way to second to tag them both. Ryan was entitled to the base, so Pujols was caught stealing ... without a throw. An unassisted putout by a catcher at second base.

8/25

In New York, Angel Pagan led off for the Mets, popped harmlessly to second, then circled the bases for a run. Second baseman Chase Utley somehow dropped the routine fly, then compounded his error with a hurried throw to try to nail Pagan at second base. The throw sailed into foul territory in left field, allowing Pagan to score. Utley was assessed *two* two-base errors on the play, not the best way to start a game.

9/4

When Reds pitcher Bronson Arroyo spun around after his delivery, Yunel Escobar's line drive struck him squarely in the back. Arroyo pounced on the ball and fired to first, but his throw hit Escobar ... in the back. Back to back, on a single play. But the Braves did not find the play amusing. Escobar, who twisted his ankle on the bag and had to be removed from the game, was ruled out for running in fair territory — insult added to injury. And Bobby Cox was so incensed by the call that he earned his 150th career ejection.

9/5

A player reaching into the opposing dugout attempting to catch a foul ball can expect no help, but the anti-hospitality principle was taken to an extreme by White Sox coach Joey Cora. After Victor Martinez's failed attempt at a catch took him into the enemy dugout, Cora yanked on his glove. And kept on yanking until the glove came off. All in good fun, but what possessed Cora to initiate the hijinks? Martinez was using his first baseman's glove to catch Tim Wakefield. Maybe Cora was offended by the idea of a catcher using a first baseman's glove?

9/15

A key blow in the Yankees' 5–3 win over the Angels was Mark Teixeira's first triple in two years. Teixeira managed to reach third even though, as he ran to first, he turned back to yell at the home plate umpire. He was screaming that his bat hit the glove of catcher Mike Napoli, so catcher's interference should have been called. Somehow, the impeded swing still sent a ball off the center field wall, where the mischief continued. As Torii Hunter attempted the catch, his foot became wedged in the wall and his shoe came off. Teixeira coasted into third with a perhaps unprecedented catcher's interference triple.

9/16

On Eric Byrnes' long double, the Padres threw home trying to nail the runner from first. The throw bounced off catcher Nick Hundley and rolled towards the Diamondbacks dugout. Had the ball made it to the dugout, Byrnes, now racing towards third, would have been awarded home. Hundley sprinted after the ball and arrived just in time to corral it while he slid. However, his momentum was taking him into the dugout. Before sliding down the dugout steps, he flipped the ball from his glove onto the field. Then he climbed the steps, retrieved the ball, and threw home. To get the charging Byrnes, the Padres needed a second alert play and creative slide. First baseman Adrian Gonzalez raced in to cover the plate, arriving at the same time as Byrnes, but Hundley's rushed throw short-hopped him. Gonzalez made a sliding pick-up and slap tag in one motion, a fittingly dazzling end to a play featuring the catcher sliding into the dugout and first baseman sliding into home.

9/28

The Astros-Phillies game featured a play at the plate in which Phils catcher Paul Bako failed to tag Lance Berkman but Berkman failed to touch the dish. Berkman had run way past the plate almost to the backstop by the time teammates alerted Bako to the situation. The catcher turned around to pursue Berkman, who bobbed and weaved, trying to elude the catcher near the on-deck circle. After Bako won the game of tag, Astros manager Dave Clark came out to protest that Berkman had in fact touched the plate. It was a moot point. The umpire wasn't about to call Berkman safe after the player desperately tried to return to the dish. Clark might better have spent his time explaining to Berkman that, in that situation, whether or not you touched the plate you make a beeline for the dugout and, if the catcher's still looking for you, the clubhouse.

10/8

Catcher's interference is rare enough, but is there ever a case of mistakenly called catcher's interference? The batter's instant reaction lets you know whether his bat hit the catcher's glove, and without that reaction, no call. But Jacoby Ellsbury was awarded first after grounding out even though he ran to first and gave no indication that his swing was impeded by Jeff Mathis's glove. Indeed, Ellsbury was heading for the dugout when he received the good news. The replay revealed no contact — a phantom call.

The umpiring crew made another error, this one contributing to an extremely unusual double play for the Red Sox. With the bases loaded and no outs, Mike Lowell fielded a sharp ground ball and came home for the force. In that situation catchers always throw to first if they're looking double play, but Victor Martinez fired back to third instead. Although Torii Hunter clearly beat Lowell's tag, the umpire called him out: a 5–2–5 twin killing. The second out would have been easy if Lowell had stepped on the bag rather than tagging Hunter, as the out at home did *not* eliminate the force at third. But Lowell can be forgiven for not realizing that; in his long career, he probably never received a return throw from a catcher.

Not Unprecedented, But....

The 2009 season produced quite a few plays that, while not unprecedented, reflect the sport's quirkiness. Some of these plays actually recur from time to time precisely because of baseball's uniqueness. For example, only baseball provides a foul territory where play takes place but non-players (coaches, ballboys and ballgirls, photographers) are permitted to roam, producing strange occurrences with no counterpart in other sports. What follows are instances of non-player participation and assorted other oddities.

4/25

The 16–11 slugfest between the Red Sox and Yankees featured a subtle play on the bases that backfired. Caught in a run-down between third and home, the Yanks' Jorge Posada delayed capture long enough so Hideki Matsui cruised into third. As the Sox chased Posada back to third, you knew what would come next: Matsui and Posada would meet at third, the Sox would tag them both and the umpires would determine which player was out and which would remain on base. But Posada had other ideas. He knew that, as the lead runner, he was entitled to the bag — Matsui would have been the one sent packing. Posada, a 37-year-old catcher, considered himself a poor option to remain on base. He stopped short of third, forcing the Sox to tag him out. The sacrifice bunt is commonplace, but how often does a *runner* deliberately give himself up for the good of the team? But beware the law of unintended consequences. Matsui, no speed demon in the best of times, was coming off knee surgery. He runs no faster than Posada, and keeping him at third (setting up a possible sprint home and even collision with the catcher) is the last thing the doctor ordered. Posada outsmarted himself.

4/27

It must have seemed to the Indians as if home plate umpire C.B. Bucknor was on the Red Sox payroll. With two outs in the fourth, Mike Lowell appeared to strike out swinging on a low offering from Cliff Lee. But as the Indians marched off the field, Bucknor signaled that Lowell tipped the ball and it skimmed the dirt before being corralled by catcher Kelly Shoppach. Indians manager Eric Wedge protested, but mildly. As he growled after the game, "We left that one alone."

On the next pitch, Lowell topped a ground ball over the third base bag. Mark DeRosa fielded it and stepped on third for the force. Again the Indians started off the field, and again Bucknor belatedly bid them stop, ruling that the ball was foul, overruling the third base ump who'd signaled it fair. This one Wedge did not leave alone. He stormed out to Bucknor and said something like, "Screw me once, shame on you. Screw me twice and I'm in your face like a nasty sunburn." Wedge got tossed, concluding a sorry sequence for the Indians: two pitches, two outs, no outs, no manager. When the dust cleared, Lowell was *still* at bat. He eventually struck out, arguably his third out of the at-bat, an inning onto himself.

But Bucknor wasn't done impeding the Indians. The Tribe rallied in the ninth inning, putting runners on first and second with no outs and bringing to the plate Jhonny (that's spelled correctly) Peralta as the potential tying run. Bucknor rung up Peralta on a pitch so far from the plate that Sox announcer Jerry Remy insisted it was a waste pitch.

4/28

In Kansas City, the ballboy cleanly fielded a hard-hit ball down the right field line and flipped it into the crowd, providing a grateful fan with a souvenir. Just one problem: it was a fair ball.

5/15

In New York, Brett Gardner hit a 200-foot home run. What should have been a bloop single to shallow left took a bad hop past Twins left fielder Denard Span and rolled and rolled while the speedy Gardner rounded the bases for an inside-the-park round-tripper. When people cite home run totals to demonstrate that balls fly out of the new Yankee Stadium, Gardner's "blast" will be included — a lazy pop fly that wouldn't have cleared the fences at some Little League parks.

5/29

In Anaheim, the Angels' Juan Rivera made a spectacular leaping catch to rob Seattle's Russell Branyan of a home run. The next batter, Jose Lopez, sent a ball to almost the identical spot, and Rivera made the identical attempt, this one eluding his glove by inches. Mariners manager Don Wakamatsu, who's been in the game for a quarter century, remarked, "Never in my years have I ever seen back-to-back robbed home runs, but that was awfully close."

6/4

Jason Varitek slugged two home runs, but was deprived of a chance for his first career three-home-run game by a short-fused umpire in an inning from *The Twilight Zone*. Three batters after Varitek's second blast, Jeff Bailey was called safe at home on a close play, prompting a spirited reaction from Twins catcher Mike Redmond. Home plate umpire Todd Tichenor ejected Redmond, prompting a vehement protest from manager Ron Gardenhire. Tichenor ran Gardenhire too. In the bottom of the inning, when Beckett and Tichenor exchanged unpleasantries over a called ball, Varitek turned around to take up his pitcher's cause. Tichenor ejected him, prompting Terry Francona to storm out of the dugout and get *himself* tossed. In a single inning, both teams' catchers and managers were sent to the showers.

6/14

Josh Beckett led off the fifth inning after being touched by the Phils for four runs in the fourth. With the Sox trailing 5–4, and Beckett unlikely to last much longer in any event (on account of pitch count and poor performance), Terry Francona figured to pinch-hit. The decision seemed especially easy given that Beckett was a weak hitter in the National League and now hardly bats. For some reason, Francona chose to let him hit. Perhaps stunned by the decision, Beckett tripped climbing the dugout steps. He then proceeded to crush a home run to tie the game.

7/1

In the first inning, the Orioles' Felix Pie tried to stretch a single into a double. Dustin Pedroia made a lunging tag with his glove, while he held the ball in his bare hand. The umpire, focused on the tag at the bag, didn't notice Pedroia's trickery and called Pie out.

Pie played because yesterday Adam Jones lost a collision with the wall. Later in today's game, Pie got hurt on a freakier collision. On Pie's ground ball to first, Josh Beckett covered the bag. But Beckett tripped over the bag, which sent the strapping pitcher sprawling into Pie, knocking the Orioles player senseless. Pie was taken into the clubhouse for repairs, but had to stay in the game — the Orioles were out of center fielders. (It's been that kind of a decade for Baltimore.)

7/5

Jon Lester allowed an infield hit when he lost Franklin Gutierrez's high bouncer in the sun. Lester is not the first to suffer this fate. The Yankees squeaked by the ill-fated Dodgers in Game 6 of the 1952 World Series thanks to Billy Loes losing a ground ball in the sun. Loes was famous for that, and for explaining that he didn't want to win 20 games because "then they expect you to every year."

8/2

There was a five-minute delay in the second inning of the Red Sox–Orioles game when Sox outfielder Josh Reddick sprinted into the dugout. Reddick needed emergency medical attention for ... a nosebleed. He's fresh up from Double A and apparently unaccustomed to the big league's macho ethic. The trainer must have patched him up well; Reddick came to bat in the next inning and smashed his first career home run.

Later in the game, with the Sox leading by a touchdown, 14–7, the team's dugout resembled summer camp. Someone placed a huge gum bubble atop George Kottaras' cap, and the catcher struggled to figure out why the cameras honed in on him while his teammates cracked up. An alert cameraman caught the culprit who planted the gum on the unsuspecting Kottaras. The man who set in motion the sophomoric hijinks was 42-year-old John Smoltz. As Roy Campanella observed, "baseball is a man's game, but to play it you've got to have a lot of little boy in you."

8/28

After blasting a homer in the first inning, San Diego's Kyle Blanks completed his trot, then headed for the clubhouse, done for the day. He had stumbled rounding first base and injured his foot.*

9/2

Clinging to a 5–4 lead in the eighth inning against the Red Sox, Rays pitchers walked the bases loaded. Alex Gonzalez struck out, but the Sox scored anyway on a wild pitch. In the inning, six Red Sox came to bat; three walked and three whiffed. The team tied the score without a single player so much as putting the ball in play.

9/9

Mike Lowell is so slow that he needs three traffic light changes to cross the street, but today he stole a base. The play was a hit-and-run, and the pitch bounced before home plate, giving Jason Varitek no chance to hit it. Intent on protecting Lowell, Varitek desperately half-hacked at the ball *after* it bounced. It resembled an attempt to chip a moving golf ball, and he missed, but the ball ate up catcher Matt Wieters and Lowell coasted into second with his first stolen base of the year.

9/27

Yankee Nick Swisher surprised everyone by tagging and going to third on a fly to medium right-center. The Red Sox appealed, claiming Swisher left too soon, and the umpire agreed. Replays showed that Swisher didn't

---

*He was outdone in 2010 by the Angels' Kendry Morales, who broke a leg when celebrating his walk-off home run at home plate.

budge until the ball was caught. Bad calls happen, but this one was astonishing. Because it's impossible to gauge whether a runner leaves a split-second before ball hits glove a few hundred feet away, umpires grant the appeal only when the violation is obvious. Yet Swisher, who did nothing wrong, was called out. The explanation? The same reason the Sox appealed in the first place: It seemed impossible that Swisher, no speed demon, could reach third on such a play *unless* he left early. Talk about a good deed punished. Swisher was penalized because he made such a fine play that no one could believe he'd made it.

Exceptional Performances

The season produced any number of exceptional performances, good and bad, either on a single play or during the course of a game, that warrant acknowledgement.

4/29

The Brewers' Yovani Gallardo pitched an eight-inning shutout against the Pirates, allowing just three baserunners and striking out 11. But the Brewers couldn't score either, and Gallardo and the Pirates Ian Snell seemed poised to produce neutralizing shutouts that left neither man the winner. So Gallardo took matters into his own hands, blasting a home run in the seventh inning. The Brewers won 1–0, and their manager Ken Macha opened his post-game press conference with a terse statement: "Hitting? Gallardo. Pitching? Gallardo. Any questions?"

On the same day, Orioles relief pitcher Koji Uehara experienced one of the worst innings of all time. With the score 1–1 in the seventh inning, he gave up a pair of home runs and then got hit smack in the chest by a line drive.

5/2

Detroit outfielder Ryan Raburn supplied a week's worth of lowlights on a single play. Raburn misjudged a fly ball, then stumbled and fell while chasing it. He managed to spring to his feet in time to track the ball down and ... drop it. Then, as he retrieved the ball, he lost his balance and crashed into the wall. Looking dazed, he again dropped the ball. By the time the carnage was complete, three runs had scored.

5/8

In the Indians-Tigers game, Detroit center fielder Curtis Granderson made a play involving a collision between baseball's most exciting offensive and defensive moments: the robbed home run and the walk-off home run. He robbed the Tribe of a walk-off home run. With one out in the bottom of the ninth, a runner on first, and Detroit leading 1–0, Grady Sizemore lofted a shot that had the Indians poised to shoot out of the dugout to congregate at home for the victory celebration. Granderson's perfectly timed leap took his glove a few feet over the center field wall for the catch. For good measure, Granderson scored the game's only run.

5/11

In the seventh inning against the Dodgers, the Phillies' Jayson Werth singled and proceeded to steal second, third, and (on a delayed steal) home. Werth benefits from strong athletic genes. His mother, an Olympic quality sprinter, is the daughter of major league ballplayer Ducky Schofield. But before giving Schofield credit for his grandson's prolific base-stealing, consider this: In a career spanning 19 seasons, Schofield stole just 12 bases. He was caught stealing 29 times for a scandalously low percentage of .293.

5/18

The Mets committed five errors against the Dodgers, including two decisive ones in the 11th inning, and that wasn't their biggest sin. The game would have been over by then except Ryan Church, scoring from first on a double, somehow missed third base. The Mets' performance evoked their 1962 team, the club that prompted manager Casey Stengel to agonize, "Can't anyone here play this game?" The team's lovable buffoon, Marv

Throneberry, hit a triple but was declared out for missing second base. Stengel raced out to argue but was intercepted by his first base coach, who sadly informed him that Throneberry missed first, too.

5/23

In Houston, the Rangers' Omar Vizquel, a Gold Glove shortstop playing second base for just the second time in a career spanning three decades, made a fine over-the-shoulder catch — the genre made famous by Willie Mays in the 1954 World Series. But Vizquel offered a twist; while in pursuit, he deliberately tossed off his cap (shades of a catcher shedding his mask), presumably not wanting the brim of his cap interfering with his vision as he looked skyward to track the ball. Mays' catch may be the most talked about play in baseball history (and we will make some startling claims about it in the next chapter), but Vizquel's version triggers a few new observations. Despite running as far as he ever would for a ball, Mays, who was famous for running out from under his cap, did *not* lose his cap on the signature play of his career. (The cap fell off only when Mays spun on the throw.) And he might have been better off if he had.

5/27

George Kottaras catches only when Tim Wakefield pitches. Life presents few more demanding and less desirable specialties than catching a knuckleball pitcher. You can't predict the destination of any pitch, requiring a complete focus that usually isn't enough; even on a good day, there figure to be balls that get away and constant scuffling. To make matters worse still for the poor catcher, opposing teams find it easy to steal bases against the knuckleball.

Terry Francona presented Kottaras with a rare treat: the opportunity to catch someone other than Wakefield. Daisuke Matsuzaka throws a number of pitches, but none of them knuckle. Compared to the usual mad scrambling to keep Wakefield's pitches in front of him, the game figured to be a piece of cake for Kottaras. Wouldn't you know it, Matsuzaka threw four wild pitches. That's more than Wakefield has ever thrown in a game, and tied a Red Sox record set in 1929. Mercifully for Kottaras, Matsuzaka was removed after five innings. His replacement, Manny Delcarmen, threw a wild pitch in the sixth. In the seventh, Justin Masterson threw wild pitch number six, tying a major league record. The Twins' speedy Carlos Gomez scored all the way from second but was sent back to third when the ball bounded into the Twins dugout. Even that good break for the Red Sox was bad news for Kottaras. The next batter hit a ground ball to Dustin Pedroia, whose throw home arrived just in time for Kottaras to be run over by a stampeding Gomez.

It gets worse. The Twins stole two bases. On one, Kottaras bounced his throw to second. On the other, the flustered catcher air-mailed the ball to center, allowing the runner to reach third. For good measure, he went 0–4 at bat, whiffing twice, including the final out in the Sox's 4–2 loss. Kottaras no doubt sees Wakefield's dancing knuckleballs in his sleep and yearned to play in a game or two with someone else on the mound. Be careful what you wish for.

6/1

Against the Indians, the Yankees set a major league record with their 18th consecutive errorless game, and saved themselves from defeat with an unlikely sparkler in the field. In the fifth inning, the Tribe had runners on first and second with no out when Kelly Shoppach popped a bunt towards third. If it dropped, the bases would be loaded, but Joba Chamberlain was determined not to let it. The hefty pitcher made a soaring catch that would have done an NFL receiver proud, though he more closely resembled a fat man belly-flopping off a diving board. His bounce when he crash-landed evoked Joe Garagiola's observation that "Pete Rose just took a bad hop off the AstroTurf." The Indians' Ryan Garko thought Chamberlain had no chance and was doubled off second.

6/12

In Chicago, the Twins had runners on first and third in the eighth inning when Joe Mauer lofted a fly ball to Milton Bradley in right field.

After catching the ball, Bradley casually turned around and threw it to fans in the right field bleachers. His generosity was misplaced, however, since his catch was only the second out of the inning. The runner on first was allowed to advance to third on the play. After the game, Bradley pled not guilty on account of sun exposure. "I turned my back to shade the sun some. I caught it. I exhaled, and I was still seeing purple and green spots because I was looking into the sun. I sensed that something wasn't right. My heart was in the right place, I tried to give a souvenir. It was messed up." While acknowledging the right of Cubs fans to boo, Bradley pled further mitigating circumstances. "They have high expectations. I have high expectations for myself. I've never made that mistake in my life." That puts Bradley in the same boat as virtually every other major leaguer ever to play the game. The only difference is they can *still* say they've never made that mistake.

On the same day, Mets second baseman Luis Castillo made a mistake he may never live down. In their intra-city showdown with the Yankees, the Mets took an 8–7 lead into the bottom of the ninth after plating the go-ahead run against Mariano Rivera. Francisco Rodriquez came in to nail things down. With two outs and two on, came the dramatic showdown with Alex Rodriquez — K-Rod vs A-Rod. K-Rod won, inducing a game-ending infield pop-up. A-Rod slammed his bat to the ground in disgust, breaking it, and the Yankee Stadium crowd collectively groaned. Castillo camped under the ball and ... dropped it. The odds of anyone dropping an easy infield pop are remote, and Castillo isn't anyone. Just two years ago, the three-time Gold Glove winner set the major league record for second basemen with 143 consecutive errorless games.

6/17

Pudge Rodriguez broke Pudge Fisk's record for appearances behind the plate, and celebrated by committing two errors in a game for the first time in five years. One of the errors was a throw to third that one-hopped ... the left fielder.

7/27

On a hit-and-run, Oakland's Eric Patterson over-slid second base. That shouldn't have been a problem, because the batter, Adam Kennedy, lofted an outfield fly. Patterson scrambled to his feet and retreated to first, but in the process did not re-touch second. The Red Sox appealed, and Patterson was called out — a strange piece of baserunning that involved over-sliding and over-striding a base on a single play.

The A's Mark Ellis matched his teammate for double futility. In his first at-bat, Ellis swung and missed and the bat flew out of his hands and into the stands. In his second at-bat, same thing except the bat flew into the Oakland dugout.

9/6

The Brewers turned a 5–4–3 triple-play against the Giants on a ground ball. The rally-killer kept the Brewers close, and they went on to win the game in 12 innings. In another 12-inning affair, Cincinnati's Micah Owings was the winning pitcher and "knocked in" the winning run the hard way — getting conked on the head with the bases loaded.

9/19 and 9/20

The first three at-bats by Orioles rookie phenom Matt Wieters produced line drive base hits to center, right, and left. The next day Wieters produced another three hits — again one each to all three fields. Even more remarkable, whereas his first day of all-field hitting came from the right side of the plate against lefty Jon Lester, the next day it came from the left side against right-hander Daisuke Matsuzaka.

9/21

A pitch from the Royals' Jamey Wright to Dustin Pedroia was right out of *Bull Durham* — so far and wide that it brushed back Victor Martinez ... in the on-deck circle.

9/23

After managing just one hit and no runs against Kansas City's Luke Hochevar in the first four innings, the Red Sox punished him in the fifth, slamming seven hits and plating six. But not every Red Sox batter fared well in the inning; Mike Lowell made all three outs.

9/29

Toronto's Kevin Millar, who has played first base for the last six years, played third instead and showcased his *middle-infield* defense. Because the David Ortiz shift had him playing near second base, on Ortiz's ground ball to the right side Millar had to cover second and turn the double play. He looked like someone who'd never done that before (he hadn't — what career first baseman gets stuck in that position?). Even so, his awkward pivot got the lumbering Ortiz at first. Millar also covered second (the Ortiz shift again) on a stolen base attempt by Kevin Youkilis that turned out comically. When the throw in the dirt squirted away from Millar, Youkilis noticed no one covering third. But as Youkilis started to dart there, Toronto collectively noticed the vacancy and pitcher, catcher, and shortstop all sprinted to the bag. Youkilis returned to second, or we might have witnessed a baseball version of rugby.

9/30

Sox pitcher Dustin Richardson, making the second appearance of his career, entered the game with two runners on and promptly threw a wild pitch. He's no doubt done that before. A few batters later, he committed a balk when the ball squirted out of his hand and rolled a few feet toward first base. That he's surely never done before. Welcome to the big leagues, kid.

10/9

The Yankees took an ALDS game from the Twins with the help of two strange blunders. In the fourth inning, Minnesota had runners on first and second with two outs when Matt Tolbert singled to right. Carlos Gomez fell down rounding second and, when Nick Swisher threw behind him, was caught scrambling back to the base for the third out. Such things happen. What made the play creepy for Minnesota was that Gomez was tagged out just before Delmon Young crossed home plate uncontested. The run would have scored if Gomez had taken the trouble of getting into even a brief rundown. After the game, Gomez offered this not-very-reassuring assessment: "It was the only mistake I made."

In the 11th inning, Joe Mauer's fly ball down the left field line hit Melky Cabrera's glove while Cabrera was in fair territory, then bounced onto the field in fair territory — a fair ball for two reasons. Umpire Phil Cuzzi inexplicably called it foul. Missed calls will happen, but this kind of miss is deeply perverse in the post-season, where the umpiring crew expands to include an umpire down each outfield line whose main responsibility is to call a fly ball down the line fair or foul. Cuzzi hung around watching for four hours yesterday without doing a thing. Then came the one play that justified his existence — the key fly ball that virtually fell in his lap — and he got it egregiously wrong. Cuzzi was unavailable for comment after the game, or he might have opted for Carlos Gomez's defense: "It was the only mistake I made."

The Twins' defeat was painless compared to the NLDS loss the Cardinals suffered in Los Angeles. Behind a run, the Dodgers were down to their last out, with no one on base, when James Loney lined the ball right at left fielder Matt Holliday. Holliday somehow took the ball in the stomach rather than glove, and it fell to Earth. With the done deal undone, pitcher Ryan Franklin came undone himself, allowing the next four batters to reach base. Game over, Dodgers up 2–0 in the series. But the fiasco produced a grace note prior to the first pitch of Game 3. When the players were introduced, Matt Holliday received a rousing ovation. Holliday may take his place next to Bill Buckner as a post-season goat, but the Cardinals fans apparently approach these things differently from Boston fans, whose hostility to Buckner after his World Series gaffe drove him to seclusion in Idaho for nearly two decades.

Just Plain Quirky

On April 14, the Braves' usually reliable outfielder Garret Anderson, who had made just two errors in his previous 450 games, *dropped two routine fly balls*. Fast-forward sixth months, to October 4, when Toronto and Baltimore closed out their seasons with an extra-inning affair. In the bottom of the 11th, the Birds scored the winning run thanks to throwing errors on consecutive plays by pitcher Brandon League — his first two errors of the season. League pitched in 67 games and was flawless in the field until the last two plays of the year. In a similar vein, the first home run yielded by Red Sox pitcher Justin Masterson was a grand slam by Evan Longoria. To that point in the season, Masterson had faced 85 batters, throwing roughly 350 pitches, and given up no home runs. There's always a first time. And a second — which, in this case, came two pitches later (courtesy of Carlos Pena).*

On April 18, the Indians bombed the Yankees 22–4, rewriting the record books with a 14-run second inning in which all nine Indians got at least one hit. Yankees fans suffered another disappointment beyond the two-touchdown second inning that put the game out of reach before some fans found their seats. The last time the Yanks lost by a football score, a few weeks earlier, they brought in outfielder Nick Swisher to pitch an inning. He held the Rays scoreless. Accordingly, faced with an even bigger deficit against Cleveland, the fans chanted "We Want Swisher." But manager Joe Girardi didn't oblige, preserving his outfielder's perfect pitching record. In fact, well into April, Swisher was the Yankees' odd triple crown winner, leading the team in home runs, RBI, and ERA.

On April 29, in the top of the second, with two outs and none on, Fausto Carmona faced the bottom of the Red Sox lineup. With the Sox riddled with injuries, that meant Jeff Bailey, Jonathan Van Every, and Nick Green, guys Carmona's supposed to attack. Instead, he committed one pitcher's sin after another, walking Bailey and Van Every and hitting Green

---

*The 2008 World Series produced the ultimate in this genre. In Game 2, the Rays became the first team in 105 years of World Series history to score two runs on RBI groundouts in one inning. Believe it or not (and we'd understand if you didn't), in Game 3 the Rays did it again. Once in 105 years, twice in two days.

to load the bases. He retired Jacoby Ellsbury to avert self-imposed disaster. A weird inning that in retrospect got weirder; in the bottom of the eighth, Sox reliever Manny Delcarmen replicated Carmona's struggles. Delcarmen, too, retired the five and six hitters in the lineup, then walked the seven and eight and hit the nine. Just as Carmona escaped by retiring the Sox's leadoff hitter, Delcarmen retired Grady Sizemore to strand the three runners.

On May 5, Yankees starting pitcher Joba Chamberlain got Comeback Player of the Year ... within a game. He began the day by yielding base hits to the first three Red Sox batters, followed by a towering home run by Jason Bay, then another base hit. Five batters, five hits, four runs. From that point on, he gave up just one scratch single in six innings and struck out 12 overmatched Red Sox. After the first inning, the Sox failed to hit a ball out of the infield. In his next outing against the Orioles, Chamberlain gave up base hits to five of the first six hitters, and three runs in the first inning, before abruptly turning things around and pitching six innings of shutout ball. Someone ought to work on this guy's warm-up routine.

David Ortiz went more than 150 at-bats without a home run, sending Red Sox Nation into a two-month panic. The nadir was May 19, when Astros pitcher Russ Ortiz slugged a home run and David Ortiz fell to second place in home runs by guys named Ortiz.

At one point in mid–May, Bengie Molina's batting average (.310) surpassed his on-base percentage (.308). Impossible? No. Sacrifice flies count against a batter's on-base percentage but not his batting average. Molina had three sac flies and zero walks.

On May 12 in Toronto, Roy Halladay smothered the Yankees, allowing just one run and five hits in a complete game victory that raised his career record against the Bombers to 16–5 — the second-best record in history of any pitcher against the Yankees. The best is 17–5 by a guy named Babe Ruth. You can't make this stuff up.

April produced injuries to superstars in both leagues, and May was the month of the triumphant return. Josh Hamilton, Joe Mauer, and Alex Rodriquez all came back in style, hitting home runs in their first game. (Mauer and Rodriguez did the trick on their first at-bat.) But there was one notable exception. Angels ace John Lackey, whose arm injury had kept him on the sidelines since September, made his return against Texas on May 17. The first batter he faced was Ian Kinsler. Lackey's first pitch sailed behind Kinsler and his second plunked Kinsler in the ribs. Lackey insisted it was a matter of rust, but because Kinsler hit two home runs the day before, home plate umpire Bob Davidson didn't buy it. Davidson ejected Lackey, whose long-awaited return to the mound lasted exactly two pitches.

On May 25, the Rays took 20 consecutive pitches (16 of them balls) in the second inning against Cleveland's Fausto Carmona.

On July 9, the Nationals and Astros completed a game that was suspended because of rain more than two months earlier after the Astros batted in the top of the 11th inning. When the game resumed, the Nationals quickly scored to end it in the bottom of the 11th, making the winning pitcher Joel Hanrahan ... of the Pirates. Hanrahan, who pitched the top of the 11th back in May, was traded to Pittsburgh in early July. The winning run for the Nats was scored by Nyjer Morgan, whom the Nats acquired in the trade for Hanrahan.

On July 12, Jason Bay managed a memorable performance just by showing up. Bay's first three at-bats all produced four-pitch walks. The first pitch to Bay in his next at-bat hit him on the arm. He reached base four times without swinging the bat or seeing a strike. His fifth at bat? He was hit on the shoulder on what would have been ball four. When a batter is hit by what would have been ball four, it's officially scored as hit by pitch rather than a walk. Still, Bay is now the answer to a trivia question for the ages: "Who drew four walks and was hit twice in five at bats?"

On August 27, with the Red Sox trailing the White Sox 9–2 in the eighth inning, Terry Francona decided to rest his relief corps, summoning shortstop Nick Green to pitch. Throwing 90 mph fastballs, Green set down the heart of the White Sox lineup. The Red Sox scored two in their half of the eighth to close the gap, but Francona nevertheless sent Green out for the ninth. He mowed down the White Sox again. While it seems remarkable to use a field player on the mound in a game that remains competitive, Francona is the man to think players capable of such flexibility. Amidst a ten-season career as an outfielder and first baseman, he pitched an inning in 1989 — setting the side down in order on just 12 pitches. More curious still, Francona, who throws left-handed, played four innings at third base in 1985. He handled three chances flawlessly.

The Angels, known as masters of small ball, took that approach to a ridiculous extreme in September. In three consecutive games they scored with the help of a missed third strike.

On October 1, all eyes were on Jon Lester who, less than a week earlier, had to be helped off the field after taking a line drive just over his right knee. Lester missed no starts because, despite the scare, he suffered only a bruised quadricep. But would he be fully recovered? Unfazed mentally? Lester looked good as new, pitching six shutout innings against Cleveland. But in the fourth inning, all eyes were on Tribe hurler Carlos Carrasco, who had to be helped off the field after taking a line drive just over his right knee. Tonight x-rays came back negative on Carrasco. The diagnosis? Bruised quadricep. (Really, you can't make this up.)

Wacky Games

We have, to this point, highlighted notable plays, events, and performances. On a number of occasions during the 2009 season, the narrative richness was cumulative, with wackiness characterizing the game itself more than one or two individual plays.

4/11

The Red Sox's pulsating 5–4 victory produced three bizarre catches. In the bottom of the fourth inning, the Angels' Torii Hunter drove a long fly to left. Jason Bay drifted to the wall, reached over his shoulder and at first seemed to make a snow-cone catch, but the ball popped out. It appeared to hit the wall, then the back of Bay's mitt, and was falling to Earth when Bay snagged it with a basket-catch knee-high. Maybe you had to see it. Which Fox's nationwide audience did, at least ten times. But the umpire doesn't have the benefit of replays, and didn't see the ball hit the wall, so Bay's juggling adventure was ruled a catch.

Fans had to wait less than one inning to see an even more improbable catch. The top of the fifth featured a belief-defying *bare-handed, back-handed* grab. Fortunately for Mike Lowell, his blast was still a home run — the catch was made by a fan in the left field bleachers.

The game also featured five home runs, with Bay's second giving the Sox a two-run lead going into the ninth. With lights-out closer Jonathan Papelbon on the mound, the game was as good as over. Except Hunter greeted Papelbon with a home run, and the Angels proceeded to load the bases with two outs. The game came down to an epic showdown between Papelbon and Howie Kendrick. With nowhere to put the Angel, Papelbon threw eight consecutive strikes — the last six fouled off. On number nine, Kendrick flied to right for what should have been a routine out. But Rocco Baldelli had to battle a sun so nasty that he actually twisted away from the ball as it plopped into his glove — a suitable ending to a game featuring improbable catches.

In terms of craziness, the next day's game picked up where the previous one left off. In the bottom of the first, as Josh Beckett was about to deliver a pitch to Bobby Abreu, the umpire jumped in front of the plate and called time. Beckett let fire anyway, a screaming fastball over Abreu's head. Abreu gestured angrily, Beckett walked toward the plate, the benches emptied, and the Angels communicated their contempt for Beckett so forcefully that two players and a coach were ejected. In the next inning, still steaming over the injustice, Angels Manager Mike Scioscia got himself ejected for barking from the dugout. He came on the field and protested at length. No sooner did he depart than Kevin Youkilis and J.D. Drew slugged home runs on consecutive pitches. We're not sure if this was injury added to insult or vice versa, but either way the Angels came away from an altercation started by the opposing team with a depleted roster and a two-run deficit. The Angels laughed last, winning 5–4.

5/20

In the third inning against Toronto, Jacoby Ellsbury squared to bunt, which was surprising and disappointing — surprising because the Sox had zero sacrifices on the year, disappointing because Ellsbury came into the game with a 14-game hitting streak and could ill afford to waste at-bats.

But baseball has more imagination than we do. Ellsbury popped up his bunt and the charging third baseman Scott Rolen seemed to have a play, but pitcher Brett Cecil dove in front of Rolen and failed to make the catch. Thus Ellsbury's hitting streak reached 15 thanks to a bad bunt intended to give himself up.

Cecil smashed his shoulder on the play and lay prone for several minutes while the Toronto bullpen sprang into action. But the rookie stayed in the game, which meant facing the heart of the Sox lineup with runners on first and third. He got Dustin Pedroia to hit into a double play and struck out David Ortiz. The next inning he fanned Jason Bay and Mike Lowell and got Rocco Baldelli on a nubber in front of the plate. Cecil had been on the ropes until he hurt his shoulder, then suddenly became dominant. But talk about feast or famine. In the fifth inning, Jason Varitek homered. Later in the inning David Ortiz hit his long-awaited first home run. Two batters later, Jason Bay went yard as well. Mike Lowell followed with yet another home run. Manager Cito Gaston finally removed the rookie pitcher, who could have reprised the line "What took you?"

6/3

Two batters into the game, the Red Sox had two runs on two hits (a single by Pedroia and home run by Drew). After six innings, the Tigers had zero runs on zero hits. A rather one-sided affair. When Curtis Granderson broke up Josh Beckett's no-hitter in the seventh, and the Sox spanked Detroit for six runs in the eighth to extend the lead to 10–0, the game seemed drained of suspense. Pity those Tigers fans who departed early.

In the eighth, the Red Sox committed errors around the horn — a Mike Lowell boot, Nick Green bobble, and Dustin Pedroia throwing error. When Granderson cleared the bases with a triple, the Sox's lead had been halved, and the crowd morphed from comatose to manic. That wasn't all. Kevin Youkilis, the only Sox infielder not to commit an error in the inning, suffered a worse fate; Josh Anderson, hustling down the line on Green's bobble, took a leaping last step and came down on Youkilis's ankle. The Sox's first baseman had to be removed from the game, punctuating the team's Inning from Hell.

Still, they led 10–5 going into the ninth. But Takashi Saito walked the first two batters and, two outs later, plunked Placido Polanco. With the bases loaded for slugger Magglio Ordonez, and the fearsome Miguel Cabrera on deck, the prospects of the Sox blowing a ten-run lead seemed real. Except for one detail. Ordonez was not up because he was no longer in the game. When the Sox held the touchdown and field goal lead in the eighth, Tigers manager Jim Leyland removed him. Like the early-departing fans, Leyland paid the price for lack of faith. Ordonez's replacement, Anderson, skied out, and Boston breathed a huge sigh of relief.

Meanwhile, in this wild affair, the spiking at first base wasn't the game's strangest collision. In the fifth inning, with Green on second, Pedroia grounded to Brandon Inge at third. On Inge's throw to first, Green tried for third, and Cabrera's throw sailed into left field. Green headed home, but en route collided with pitcher Armando Galarraga, who was mysteriously hanging out by the third base line. Green fell down, got up, and stumbled home, but was tagged out. However, the umpires ruled interference on Galarraga and allowed the run. Pitcher's interference on the bases? About as likely as around-the-horn errors in an inning.

6/30

In the fourth inning, Orioles pitcher Matt Albers brushed back Jason Varitek with a fastball. Varitek took off for first base as if the ball had hit him, and the umpire concurred. Replays showed that the Red Sox captain had bluffed — the ball never touched him. But with the Sox leading 9–1 and ominous rain clouds hovering, Varitek may have been too clever by half. His ploy brought Orioles manager Dave Trembley out for an extended argument, increasing the chance of a deluge that could cause postponement of the game and wipe out the Sox's comfortable lead. Indeed, heavy rains came, and the umps ordered play stopped just before the Orioles were to bat in the fifth and make the game official.

More than an hour later, the rain ceased and the game resumed, so Varitek's ploy didn't hurt his team. But it may have cost John Smoltz his first win as a Red Sox, since he couldn't continue and was one inning short of the five requisite for a victory. Miraculously, as things turned out, the

Red Sox would have been better off if the rain never relented and the game was called after four innings.

Justin Masterson replaced Smoltz and pitched a perfect fifth inning to make the game official. In the sixth, Masterson induced a ground ball to short. Julio Lugo threw to first baseman Jeff Bailey for the out, and the Red Sox infield marched into the dugout — Lugo, Bailey, Youkilis and Dustin Pedroia, followed by Masterson. The Sox seemed to be doing a weird drill of some kind, because catcher Jason Varitek and the outfielders remained on the field. With good reason — there were only two outs.

Perhaps the infield collectively lost concentration because of the team's eight-run lead. That lead vanished, as the Orioles batted around in both the seventh and eighth innings to score ten runs, and held on to win 11–10. Maybe the fiasco was condign punishment for Varitek pretending to be hit by a pitch or for five players losing track of the number of outs. This much we know: the Sox fell victim to the biggest comeback in Orioles history.

8/23

Trailing the Phils by three runs in the ninth inning, the Mets scored one and put the tying runs on base thanks to a pair of miscues by second baseman Eric Bruntlett. The Mets put the runners in motion and Jeff Francoeur drove a live drive at Bruntlett, who snared the ball, stepped on second, and tagged the approaching Daniel Murphy for the game-ending unassisted triple play. In a matter of seconds, Bruntlett went from goat to assuming a place in history — the second player ever to end a game with an unassisted triple play.

Curiously, the game that ended so serendipitously for the Phils started with a play equally improbable but disastrous. Angel Pagan's drive to left-center lodged underneath the fence. Phils center fielder Shane Victorino turned to the umpire and raised his hands, appealing for a ground-rule double. However, before the umpire granted the request, left fielder Raul Ibanez foolishly retrieved the ball, keeping the play alive. Pagan resumed his sprint and made it home for an inside-the-park home run.

Yes, the game began with an inside-the-park home run and ended with a triple play. From alpha to omega....

9/24

The Red Sox's 10–3 win was an unfair fight after the Royals' Cy Young Award candidate, Zack Greinke, was ejected in the third inning for arguing balls and strikes. Okay, we exaggerate the effect of the ejection — Greinke wasn't pitching. He was ejected by home plate umpire Greg Gibson for grousing from the dugout. Gibson, known for his quick trigger, didn't stop there. The next inning, he issued a warning to Anthony Lerew for throwing at Mike Lowell, though the pitch in question was a 76 mph change-up. When manager Trey Hillman pointed out this absurdity, Gibson ran *him*.

The Royals neither helped themselves (five errors) nor received help from the men in blue, including a strange play in the sixth inning. Seeing the catcher's throw sail into center field on his steal of second, Alex Gonzalez awkwardly aborted his slide, bounced up and ran to third — seemingly stepping over second base in the process. The Royals appealed, but the umpire ruled that Gonzalez nicked the bag. When was the last time you saw an appeal play claiming a runner missed a bag on a stolen base?

10/6

The Twins' 13-inning 5–4 win over the Tigers in Game 163 for each team, to win the Central Division crown, takes its place alongside the other tie-breaker classics: Dodgers-Giants '51, Yankees–Red Sox '78. One could devote a book to the game's twists and turns, but we'll settle for a few items that illustrate baseball's capacious imagination:

- In the third inning, a high fly by Curtis Granderson landed harmlessly in foul ground. Three Twins players (third baseman Matt Tolbert, left fielder Delmon Young and shortstop Orlando Cabrera) appeared to lose the ball against the Metrodome roof. So much for the "home dome" advantage that commentators had been trumpeting.
- The game should have been over an inning earlier and with a different champion. In the 12th inning, with the bases loaded,

Bobby Keppel's pitch brushed Brandon Inge's shirt. Except the ump missed the brush. Inge then grounded into a force at home and Keppel fanned Gerald Laird on a 3–2 pitch with three runners in motion and 54,000 fans on their feet.

- When the dust cleared, the Tigers found themselves out of first place for the first time in five months and 132 games. And for Keppel, the winning pitcher in the game that displaced them, it was career victory number one. Baseball has a wicked sense of humor.

10/11

The Red Sox season, too, ended in wacky fashion. In Game 3 of the ALDS against the Angels, with the Sox leading 5–2 in the eighth inning, Bobby Abreu bounced a chopper to first that kicked off Kevin Youkilis's glove and sailed into the photographers' well next to the dugout — an infield double. Later in the inning, Juan Rivera greeted Jonathan Papelbon with a two-run single that pulled the Angels within one. When Mike Scioscia sent the speedy Reggie Willits in to run for Rivera, the tying run was as good as in scoring position; the Red Sox throw out few base stealers and Papelbon doesn't even try to keep runners close. So Papelbon picked Willits off. Talk about a rally-killer!

The Sox had added an insurance run in the bottom of the eighth and Papelbon retired the first two Angels in the ninth, then got ahead of Erick Aybar 0–2. At that point, they took the game off the board in Las Vegas. Papelbon, who had not allowed a post-season run in 26 innings spanning 17 appearances, had a two-run lead to work with, no one on base, and needed just one strike — against the Angels' number nine hitter. But Aybar stroked a single, the first of five consecutive Angels to reach base. The last was Vlad Guerrero, whose bases-loaded single pushed across the tying and go-ahead runs. The Sox went quietly in the ninth, and New England had seen its last baseball for six months.

Two-run lead, two outs in the ninth, no one on base, two strikes, suddenly followed by a parade of batters reaching base and an unthinkable defeat? Red Sox fans were understandably reminded of the 1986 World

Series, probably not the best way to end a season. But Red Sox diehards are old hats at handling pain. They do so by counting down. In just 150 days, pitchers and catchers report.

Compelling Personalities

We noted in the introduction that some sabermetricians are more drawn to Strat-O-Matic Baseball than to the actual sport. That mindset reflects a failure to appreciate not just the bizarre and unpredictable occurrences we've been describing, but something equally rich: the compelling personalities of those who play the game. On a number of occasions during the 2009 season, events on and off the field placed the spotlight on someone who deserves it. Below, we briefly visit five of baseball's unique personalities.

Mark Fidrych

Tragedy struck the baseball world on April 12, with former Tigers pitcher Mark "The Bird" Fidrych found dead beneath a dump truck on his Massachusetts farm. Fidrych burst on the scene like a meteor in 1976, and crashed almost as quickly. During his dream season, he went 19–9 and earned unanimous selection as American League Rookie of the Year. He was injured the next year, and spent that season and the following three desperately trying to regain his form, before mercifully calling it quits. From 1977–80, he was 10–10 during his limited time in the majors. He spent the bulk of those seasons in the minors, enduring long bus trips and pitching poorly before modest crowds, his brilliant success in '76 both keeping him going and haunting him.

Fidrych captured the public's imagination in '76 not so much with his dynamic pitching as his incandescent personality. He talked to the baseball, groomed the mound, and raced across the diamond to salute teammates who made good defensive plays. It took awhile for opponents to accept these antics. When the still relatively unknown rookie pranced around and beat the Yankees in May, Thurman Munson vowed that, if

Fidrych acted out when the teams played again, "we'll blow his ass out of New York." The remark was relayed to Fidrych, who innocently asked, "Who's Thurman Munson?" Told that Munson was the Yankees' all-star catcher, Fidrych (still innocently) inquired how his antagonist had done that night. Informed that Munson missed the game with an injury, Fidrych said, "See what I mean?" Not exactly, but his pitching and body language were always more eloquent than he.

As often happens when someone passes away, decorum or wishful thinking dictated that his life be rewritten. Less than 24 hours after Fidrych's death, Jason Beck wrote on ESPN.com that "He treated his post-baseball life, many said, with the same upbeat nature that helped make him so popular during his playing days. Instead of regretting what he had lost, he was grateful for what he had gained." In a terrific article in *Sports Illustrated* in 1986, Gary Smith told a different story of a bitterly nostalgic athlete who might have been better off dying young. Fidrych, then several years removed from his last futile comeback attempt, had found nothing to replace the spirit of '76. His arm was feeling a little better, and though he hadn't thrown in a few years, he clung to the dream. "I won't count baseball out. I won't."

Like the young Magic Johnson, a fellow Michigan sports legend, Fidrych displayed an infectious and utterly unaffected puppy-dog love for the game. He was also compared to Dizzy Dean, another brash, colorful star pitcher in his day. But there's a better comparison, a contemporary of Fidrych who, while less known, has a personality, career, and life that parallels the Bird's. The year before Fidrych dazzled the baseball world, the National League Rookie of the Year was Giants pitcher John "The Count" Montefusco. The Count was very good, and liked to say so. He made outrageous predictions ("I'm going to shut out the Dodgers"), then made good on them. But like Fidrych, he spent the rest of his injury-plagued career trying to re-bottle the rookie magic. After his glorious first year, Montefusco kicked around for ten more seasons in which he won exactly one more game than he lost.

Off the field, Montefusco's story took a turn even more depressing than Fidrych's. A divorce from hell landed him in prison for two years. The book *Giants: Where Have You Gone?*, published in 2005, reported that

Montefusco hasn't lost the swagger. "'I've got a dream again,' he said, imagining a return to baseball in some capacity. 'Hopefully it will be with the Giants.'" Unlikely, but we can at least hope that The Count enjoys a less tragic ninth inning than the Bird.

Rick Ankiel

On May 4, a compelling image was supplied by Cardinals outfielder Rick Ankiel, who made a great catch but couldn't maintain his footing and stumbled hard and awkwardly into the wall, his neck snapping back as he went down in a heap. Ankiel didn't move for a long time, as players from both teams nervously gathered around. Eventually, he was strapped onto a stretcher and carted off.

Ankiel has that certain something. "Charisma" comes closest to capturing it, but it's less a matter of personality than persona. It's the gift for attracting attention without trying. Bo Jackson had it. Bo didn't find the limelight; it found him. He was never really a great ballplayer, just one destined to absorb our gaze. Ditto Ankiel. He started out as a highly promising pitcher, finishing second in Rookie of the Year voting in 2000. But in the post-season, he couldn't throw the ball near the plate. In his first start, he walked four batters and threw five wild pitches in a single inning. In his next start, he threw five pitches to the backstop and didn't get out of the first inning. Sent down to Triple A the following season, in just five innings he walked 17 batters and threw 12 wild pitches.

Ankiel kicked around the minor leagues for several years, but at a certain point he gave up on pitching and re-invented himself as an outfielder. Like Babe Ruth. And when he finally made it back to the big leagues as an outfielder in August 2007, he did it in Ruthian style, blasting three home runs in his first three games and receiving repeated standing ovations from Cardinals fans. This feel-good story prompted the usually cheerless pundit Charles Krauthammer to gush in print, "Just two days after Barry Bonds sets a synthetic home run record in San Francisco, the Natural returns to St. Louis."

But it turned out that Ankiel was more echo of Bonds than counterpoint. In the off-season, just a few months after his triumphant return to

169

baseball, he admitted to using Human Growth Hormone. Say it ain't so, Rick. But seen a certain way, Ankiel didn't disappoint — youthful stardom, the sudden collapse, the Hollywood return, and the big letdown — everything in the Grand Style.

Now, in his post-steroids phase, Ankiel routinely finds his way into our living rooms, a Human Highlights Film who seems to make a sensational catch every other day. The one today just happened to produce a scary collision with the fence. Showing the instinct of someone with that certain something, as he was carried off Ankiel flashed a thumbs up, making the entire image — the catch, collision, and departure — all the more indelible.

Ozzie Guillen

The 2009 season (like the 2008 season and 2007 season, and hopefully many seasons to come) was spiced with delightful rants by the nutty White Sox manager, who was actually ejected from one game for disputing a call that favored his team. Guillen saw his player, Jermaine Dye, tossed for arguing a strike call, but said nothing. When the Indians came to bat, Jhonny Peralta took a called strike. Guillen complained from the dugout and was ejected for arguing balls and strikes. After the game, the irrepressible skipper explained, "They thought I was crazy because I wasn't protecting J.D. [Dye.] I was protecting the opposition.... I was going to send the message that I wasn't here to protect my players. I was here to protect baseball."

Ozzie's analysis triggers several thoughts. First, it's fun to imagine an alternate universe in which players and managers really want the umpires to get things right even if it means hurting their own team, and actually fess up (and ask for a correction) if the ump blows a call in their team's favor. That's not done even in honor-bound Japan. Second, it's not clear who Ozzie was referring to when he says "they" thought he was crazy. Third, whoever they are, they're right.

On June 5, during the first game of a doubleheader against the Tigers, Ozzie watched his White Sox commit three errors, strand runners all game long, and stagger to their sixth loss in nine games. Between games, Ozzie unleashed a tirade featuring his characteristic combination of passion, illogic, and mangled syntax. "If this was the 1980s, none of these guys would be in the big leagues right now because if you hit between .210 and .230 and you don't execute, I don't think you should be out here." In fact, no one on the Sox was batting between .210 and .230, and such low averages were more common in the 1980s than today. Facts be damned, Ozzie may have fired up the troops. In the second game, the Sox whipped division-leading Detroit 6–1, playing flawlessly behind Jose Contreras, who entered the game 0–5 with an ERA of 8.50 and pitched eight innings of one-hit ball.

But Contreras's success didn't last. In late August after a lost dropped the White Sox to .500, 4.5 games behind Detroit for the Central Division crown, Ozzie was asked whether Contreras might return to the rotation by the end of the year. He replied, "I don't want to get a heart attack before my time."

Ozzie seemed on the verge of a heart attack all season. On September 8, the White Sox allowed seven runs in the first two innings in a drubbing by Oakland. The battered pitcher was Carlos Torres, who had pitched seven scoreless innings in his previous outing. Observed the merciless manager, "It's a shame in five days how people can change."

Nine days later, the White Sox lost a heartbreaker to Seattle, their two-run lead in the ninth evaporating when closer Bobby Jenks yielded a pair of home runs. In the 14th inning, Ichiro Suzuki's single gave the Mariners a walk-off win. After the game, Ozzie summed things up, "Two and a half hours of satisfaction and two and a half hours of horseshit baseball. What the fuck am I going to say? They're horseshit." For good measure, he added a threat to his horseshit players. "They give up on me, I give up on them."

You can understand Ozzie's frustration, especially knowing that his team's failure to turn the season around could cost him his job. The manager's hair-shirt existence calls to mind Casey Stengel's sage counsel on the secret to success: "Keep the players who hate you away from the ones who aren't sure." Ozzie does not heed this advice. He seems quite willing to alienate all of his players at once.

All his harassing failed to light a fire under his team. The White Sox fell out of contention, but still got a chance to play spoiler. The Twins and Tigers battled down to the wire, and in the last series of the season, Ozzie's boys beat the Tigers twice to create a tie atop the Midwest division going into the last day of the season. In their losses, the Tigers seemed as tight as you'd expect from a team in the midst of a devastating collapse, so prior to the season finale Ozzie offered them this advice: "Just relax." Sound advice, but why was Ozzie counseling his opponent?

Perhaps benefitting from his counsel, the Tigers whipped the White Sox on the last day of the season, forcing a playoff with Minnesota. The hero for Detroit was Magglio Ordonez, with four hits and a home run. The finale must have been especially sweet for Ordonez since it came against Ozzie, his ex-manager. The two feuded when Ordonez played for the White Sox, with Guillen once offering this assessment of his slugger: "He's a piece of shit. That's what he is. He's another Venezuelan mother-fucker." Guillen hails from Venezuela.

Kevin Millar

On May 19, the Blue Jays' only run against Tim Wakefield came on a mammoth home run by former Red Sox Kevin Millar. Oddly, it was Millar's fourth career blast against Wakefield in just 30 at-bats — the most home runs he has against any pitcher. That's surprising, given Millar's reputation as a fastball hitter who struggles with off-speed stuff, but Kevin Millar is a man of contradictions.

Millar is the quintessential asset in the clubhouse, widely credited with bringing the winning attitude that propelled the Red Sox to the 2004 World Series championship. He coined the team's "cowboy up" slogan, and was at the heart of the self-styled "idiots" — guys too busy having fun to worry about a century-old curse. Millar talks to anything that moves, and exudes positive vibes. Indeed, with Toronto in first place early in the season, many cited his leadership as a reason for the team's unexpected success. With all that in mind, it seems almost inconceivable that Millar began his big league career as a replacement player during the 1995 players' strike. Given the contempt that major leaguers have for "scabs," how could he escape pariah status, let alone become a locker room stalwart, a player's player? Perhaps it's no more improbable than a pure fastball hitter going yard against Tim Wakefield every eight at-bats.

Carlos Zambrano

On June 5, the Cubs hurler returned from a six-game suspension in style, pitching seven shutout innings for his 100th career victory and blasting a decisive home run for good measure. But all is not well with the Cubs hurler, who earned the suspension with a prolonged tantrum culminating in the destruction of the dugout Gatorade machine. After the milestone win, Zambrano was asked if he has his sights set on 300 career wins. No, he explained, because he plans to retire in a few years so he can spend Mother's Day at home. His home run today came with the switch-hitter batting right-handed against a right-handed pitcher for the first time in his career. Why the switch? A combination of a sore left hand and ignorance of the fact that the left hand is the power hand for a right-handed batter.

CHAPTER 7

Miscellany Matters

On more than a few occasions, something happened during the 2009 season that triggered thoughts — comic, tragic, entertaining, edifying — united only by this: they reflect baseball's fascination in ways that have nothing to do with statistics, and thereby illustrate what's lost when baseball is regarded as a vehicle for data analysis.

The Forgotten Hero

On April 15, all players in both leagues wore # 42, celebrating Jackie Robinson Day. (In a mildly pleasing coincidence, the Red Sox's 42-year-old knuckleballer Tim Wakefield took a no-hitter into the eighth inning of a complete game victory.) You could fill libraries with books about Robinson, and he deserves every bit of commemoration. But how many books have been written about Larry Doby? Any idea what number *he* wore? History's treatment of Doby as an afterthought is partially puzzling and wholly shameful. The American League's first African American player, and the Major League's second, he debuted for Cleveland less than three months after Robinson broke the color barrier. He endured the same death threats, beanballs, and verbal abuse. He, too, was a gallant man and superb player — a seven-time all-star and probably Robinson's equal. Yet, for all that, he wasn't inducted into the Hall of Fame until 1998, four decades after his retirement, and there are no Larry Doby Days around baseball.

Robinson and Doby parallel Charles Darwin and Alfred Russel Wallace, the men who independently and simultaneously founded evolutionary theory. History has rendered Darwin a scientist for the ages and Wallace a footnote. History is an ass.

Fans, Stands, and Baseballs

On April 20, Red Sox pitcher Justin Masterson's pickoff attempt at second brained the Orioles' Ryan Freel, who lay motionless for several minutes and needed assistance off the field. That frightening episode wasn't the game's only occurrence involving a dangerous thrown ball on something other than a pitch to the plate. In the eighth inning, after a foul ball into the crowd, a fan threw the ball back onto the field and it landed uncomfortably close to Red Sox reliever Javier Lopez. That random act of stupidity served as reminder of a curious change in the attitude toward the baseball as souvenir. A few decades ago, part of the thrill of going to a game was the possibility, however remote, of a foul ball coming your way. But at some point the custom developed at some ballparks of throwing the ball back on the field after a home run by the visiting team. This strange custom has tribal overtones, as if the ball, complicit in the enemy's success, is contaminated. Or maybe returning a valued emblem is a form of sacrifice made necessary by the home team's sin of yielding a home run. Whatever its meaning, this custom still jars those of us who remember the days when relinquishing an in-game souvenir would have been unthinkable.

This isn't the only attitude change that has taken place with respect to fans and baseballs. Moises Alou's tantrum aimed at poor Steve Bartman during the 2003 NLCS ushered in a new concept: fans are seen as obliged to sacrifice their souvenir so a player can record an out. Bartman dared to go for a ball in the stands that Alou might otherwise have caught. When the non-catch helped sustain a Marlins rally, and the Cubs lost the game and the next game and thus the series, Bartman became the scapegoat. Amazingly, much of the media bought into the idea that a fan in the stands cost the Cubs the pennant.

Two Red Sox games in 2009 showcased this same dubious thinking. On May 3, with two outs in the ninth inning, Jacoby Ellsbury launched a foul ball into the seats near third. The Rays' Evan Longoria reached into the crowd but the ball was snared by a large man wearing a Rays t-shirt. Longoria stared the man down and delivered an X-rated diatribe. Fortunately, Tampa Bay is not Chicago (and half the Tropicana Park crowd roots for the Red Sox anyway), so this man did not need an escort from the stadium and entrance into the Witness Protection Program. Indeed, undaunted by Longoria's invective, he proudly displayed his souvenir. Good for him. This new-fangled notion of the fan as extension of the team needs to be re-thought. Bartman (who happens to be a devout Cubs fan, poor fellow) was under no obligation to root for the Cubs, much less to decide that an eighth-inning out mattered more than the thrill of catching a fly ball at a major league game.

But Red Sox fans don't see it that way. On July 3, during the Sox-Mariners game, a fan not only outfought Kevin Youkilis for Ryan Langerhans' foul ball, but made the catch with a baseball cap. In the pre–Bartman world, he'd have received an ovation. The Fenway crowd booed lustily. When Langerhans doubled, they chanted "all your fault" at the offending fan. After another Mariners double and a home run, the booing and chanting grew louder. The fans weren't razzing Tim Wakefield, whose hanging knuckleballs were getting smoked, but a guy in blue jeans who did what fans have been doing since the days of Alexander Cartwright — treating the stands as his own.

The *Boston Globe*'s account of the game the next day focused not on base hits and defensive gems but on the fan who outfought Youkilis. The man, who refused to identify himself, going by the faux name "Zupa," expressed regret. The *Globe* also quoted another fan, seated ten rows behind Zupa, who spoke for the masses. "You've got to be aware. If any [Red Sox] player has a play on the ball, you have to give him a chance to make a play. I'm just shocked he's not a Mariners fan." Someone should explain to Red Sox fans that Zupa is not on the Red Sox payroll. Au contraire, Zupa paid good money for his seat.

The Perils of Paranoia

On April 21, paranoid Cubs fans (redundancy noted) were abuzz over events in the fourth inning of the team's 7–2 win over the Reds at Wrigley

Field. First, a cat ran on the field. That's not a huge deal to the rest of us, but Cubs fans aren't like the rest of us. They immediately thought back to 1969, when a black cat found its way onto the field at Shea Stadium in a game against the Mets and, according to Cubs lore, either caused or symbolized the Cubs' collapse down the stretch. Today's cat wasn't black, but paranoiacs don't dwell on details. Lo and behold, in the same inning as the non-black cat made its appearance, a pop foul by the stands in shallow left might have been caught by Cubs left fielder Alfonso Soriano but for the interference of a fan. As Cubs fans duly noted, the ball was in almost the identical spot where Steve Bartman achieved infamy during the 2003 NLCS.

To non-nuts this was meaningless amusement, but you don't have to be superstitious to believe in self-fulfilling prophecies. Tom Boswell wrote a terrific essay about the Red Sox's collapse in 1978, arguing that the Sox were indeed whipped by the ghosts of their past, or at least the demons of their imagination. Haunted by the Sox's storied collapses, manager Don Zimmer never felt safe. Even with a double-digit lead in the standings, he wouldn't rest players who desperately needed it, including several who nursed injuries. Zimmer's shortsightedness, not some supernatural curse, did the Sox in, but you can't completely separate the two. Chicago's obsession with billy goats, cats, Steve Bartman and other juvenile jinxes may have some subtle effect on the team.

Near-Perfection

There've been books written chronicling baseball's perfect games; one ought to be written about near misses. On April 30, pitcher Matt Garza's bid for immortality was thwarted in the worst way — Jacoby Ellsbury's flimsy infield hit to start the seventh. It gets worse. Ellsbury's squibbler came up the middle. Garza falls off the mound toward first after each delivery. If he did so a bit less forcefully, Ellsbury's little nothing would have fallen into his glove. As it was, it breezed by tantalizingly close — Garza desperately waved at the ball, missing by inches. Garza may have trouble shedding the fleeting image of the ball just beyond his glove. And when that image imposes itself, the ball will be easy to grasp and it will seem inexplicable that he failed to extend his arm just a little further or faster. Such is the toll exacted by flirtation with perfection, a brush with baseball cruelty that fittingly occurred on the last day of April.

Give Us Your Tired and Lame

On May 7, the Red Sox scored 12 runs in the sixth inning before the Indians recorded an out, tying a record set by Jackie Robinson's Brooklyn Dodgers 55 years earlier. The Sox's key hit, if you can say that about a 12-run inning, was a two-run single by Rocco Baldelli that broke a tie and opened the floodgates. Baldelli also made a spectacular catch in center and registered an outfield assist. (He threw out Ben Francisco attempting to stretch a single into a double with his team down 13–2, a baserunning gaffe that may have set some sort of record as well.) Baldelli was one of the season's feel-good stories, coming back from a mysterious illness that sidelined him for most of last year. He suffered something akin to what used to be called Chronic Fatigue Syndrome, where even the slightest exertion left him exhausted though no underlying clinical condition could be ascertained. Eventually he was diagnosed with a version of channelopathy, an immune system dysfunction which can be treated by medication and nutritional supplements.

Even so, Baldelli couldn't possibly handle the stresses of, say, football or basketball. Baseball, far more than any other major sport, has been decorated by players with disabilities. Pitchers Mordecai Brown, who won 239 games with three fingers on his pitching hand, and Jim Abbott, who won 87 without a non-pitching hand, lead a long list. Indeed, an entire book is devoted to the subject of baseball players with disabilities,* chronicling the careers of more than 20 players (several of whom are in the Hall of Fame) with missing or partially missing limbs or extremities, diseased limbs, impaired organ function, and other disorders. The sport demands off-the-charts coordination and reflexes while somehow not disqualifying people with serious ailments.

*Rick Swain, *Beating the Breaks: Major League Ballplayers Who Overcame Disabilities* (2004).

Kill the Ump

On May 26, the Sox's last gasp in a 5–2 defeat was a seventh-inning rally that put runners on first and third with one out. J.D. Drew grounded into what looked like a routine double play, but the throw to first went astray, allowing a run to score and seemingly putting Drew into scoring position. Except, as Drew headed towards second, he ran into the first base umpire, slowing him down enough so that he was thrown out. His team's rally snuffed out by an out-of-position umpire, a livid Terry Francona came out to protest. Was he arguing umpire interference? "No, I just wanted to yell at him because he got in the way," Francona explained after the game. "It's just hard to watch."

On the surface, most arguments with umpires are not just futile but insane. A trained, impartial arbiter makes a call, often correct or too close to judge even with the benefit of slow-motion replay, and someone with a weaker view and partisan perspective runs out and screams at him, sometimes viciously and profanely, though it can't do any good and delays the game. But a tradition that has survived this long must serve some function. Francona's candid admission that he "just wanted to yell" at the umpire points to the purpose: catharsis. Baseball can be an accumulation of frustrations, and giving the umpire hell, especially when he contributes to your frustration, amounts to letting off steam — for the manager, and vicariously for his team and its fans.

High Hopes

On May 29, Baltimore fans experienced the long-awaited debut of highly-touted prospect Matt Wieters. Wieters is a commanding presence behind the plate and tore up the minors. He went 0–4 in his debut, but the crowd treated him to repeated ovations. The cellar-dwelling Orioles were averaging roughly 20,000 fans a game. For Wieters' debut, they more than doubled that. This is a city starved for baseball success. The last thing they had to cheer about was Cal Ripken putting on his uniform every day.

But O's fans had better be careful not to get too giddy about

Wieters — the baseball gods have a way of mocking great expectations. In a sobering coincidence, Wieters' debut occurred on the same day the Rockies fired their manager. Clint Hurdle. Three decades ago, rookie Hurdle was celebrated on the cover of *Sports Illustrated* as a can't-miss superstar, maybe even a once-in-a-generation player. He played two seasons as a regular and eight as a bench-warmer, amassing all of 32 home runs and a career batting average of .259.

Pretty Please, Ump?

On June 4, Detroit's starting pitcher against the Red Sox was Dontrelle Willis, attempting a comeback that history suggests will not succeed. (Pitchers rarely recover from Steve Blass Disease.*) The flamboyant left-hander enjoyed a sensational season in 2005, winning 22 games and posting an ERA of 2.63. The next two seasons he struggled, losing more games than he won. He was traded to Detroit before the 2008 season; the Tigers hoped that a change of scenery would revive Willis. Instead, the wheels came off. In eight games last year, Willis had an ERA of 9.38 and walked 35 batters in 24 innings. He started this season in the minors, made some progress, was recently called up, and had a few decent starts. His start against Boston marked a step backward.

Even Red Sox fans found the third inning painful to watch. Willis walked four batters and hit another before he was mercifully removed. He ended up with an almost surreal pitching line: two innings, no hits, five earned runs. Many of Willis's pitches were wild, but several just missed the outside corner, and Willis made no effort to conceal his displeasure with the umpire. (Neither did his manager, Jim Leyland, who was ejected for protesting balls and strikes when he came out to remove Willis.) The scene evoked one of those baseball stories that is really a life story.

As legend has it, the Yankees' wild flamethrower Ryne Duren was

*For the uninitiated, Blass was the ace pitcher who overnight lost his control. In 1973, Blass, who won 19 games the year before, suddenly walked and hit batters like the worst pitcher on a junior high school staff. For years he and the Pirates tried to diagnose and cure his mysterious affliction, but never managed to.

walking batter after batter on pitches close to the strike zone. Finally, after a particularly close pitch, Duren barked at the umpire, "Where was that?" The ump motioned shoulder high. "Up here," he said. "A little high." Duren thought it over, then snapped, "Goddamn it, I got to have that pitch."

One Pitch, One Out

In a June game against the Rangers, hard-throwing Red Sox rookie Daniel Bard was summoned from the bullpen with runners on second and third and two outs. He promptly bounced a fastball in front of the plate that rocketed to the backstop on one hop. The ball shot back to Jason Varitek so fast that the catcher's flip to Bard caught Marlon Byrd at the plate. Bard threw one terrible pitch and killed Texas's rally, his performance calling to mind that of Don Liddle in the 1954 World Series. Liddle was called in to face Vic Wertz, who greeted him with a mortar shot that traveled over 400 feet before Willie Mays tracked it down with his famous over-the-shoulder catch. Liddle was immediately removed from the game and promptly declared, "Well, I got my man."

Style Points

The Braves' closer, Mike "Cobra" Gonzalez, has a pitching style that defies description. Perhaps the best attempt was by a sportswriter who referred to the pitcher's "trippy, rocking, swaying, tension-building, batter-mesmerizing, back-and-forth motion." Gonzalez's wild style suggests an unusual feature of baseball rarely remarked — many players' idiosyncratic approach. For instance, before each pitch Kevin Youkilis maintains a split grip on the bat — his top hand a foot above the bottom hand, its fingers tapping the bat. As the pitcher delivers, he brings his hands together.

Enough batters have a distinct stance or swing that some enterprising fellow named Gar Ryness has a popular gig on YouTube imitating them. You have to go back more than a decade to Barry Sanders to find an NFL player with a truly distinct running style, and few if any quarterbacks have a memorable or distinct throwing motion. Ditto in the NBA, where virtually all players shoot, pass, and dribble roughly the same way. By contrast, baseball has hackers and slappers, short swings and long, and an endless range of stances and preparatory routines. Similarly, pitchers have high kicks, low kicks and no kicks, an overhand motion, side-arm, and submarine, with variations of each. Other sports have exceptions, of course, players with strange form, but they are just that — exceptions to an established norm. In baseball, idiosyncrasy *is* the norm.

Get a Grip

On June 25, the story was John Smoltz making his first appearance in over a year and first ever as a Red Sox. The Nationals touched Smoltz for five runs in five innings, but the remarkable aspect of his performance is that there even was one. At the age of 41, with nothing to prove (he'd won a Cy Young Award and a World Series) and Cooperstown waiting, Smoltz underwent shoulder surgery, followed by a year of painful rehab, so he could pitch another year or two. To Smoltz, this isn't remotely unusual. "I love to pitch and I love to compete, and I would come back throwing sidearm, throwing a knuckleball, whatever it would take to continue," he explained. Even apart from the reference to the knuckleball, the pitch used by Jim Bouton to wage the comeback at the heart of *Ball Four*, Smoltz evokes the ending of that classic book, where Bouton observes, "You spend a good piece of your life gripping a baseball and in the end it turns out that it was the other way around all the time."

Heresy: Willie Mays' Overrated Catch

In a game against the Orioles in June, J.D. Drew's home run to right-center, equidistant between Orioles right fielder Nick Markakis and center fielder Adam Jones, caused both outfielders to give chase and simultaneously, a few feet apart from one another, make the identical attempt to climb the fence. The comical sight, suggestive of a new Olympic event (synchronized wall climbing?), illustrates a serious point: the athleticism of today's outfielders. Historically, the most famous catches (Gionfriddo, Amoros, Mays, Swoboda) involved running or diving, not scaling walls. The latter was rare. These days, with Torii Hunter in the vanguard, the running, leaping, home run theft is almost commonplace, and one expects the attempt — hence two Orioles on a single play desperately climbing the wall. It was mere warm-up for Jones. Later in the game he scaled the center field wall to take a home run away from Kevin Youkilis.

These amazing catches suggest baseball folklore's resistance to reality. If you asked knowledgeable fans to name the greatest catch in baseball history, by far the leading choice would be Willie Mays' over-the-shoulder grab in deep center field in the Polo Grounds to rob Vic Wertz in Game 1 of the 1954 World Series. (You know, the one where Don Liddle got his man.) Mays' play has received such iconic status that it is sometimes referred to simply as "The Catch."

But we have seen the play dozens of times and are left scratching our heads. While Mays traveled a great distance to make a fine play, it sure looks less difficult than the many times Hunter climbed a wall to prevent a home run, far less difficult than Jim Edmonds' uphill, full-out dive in Houston, less impressive than many catches over the years. Mark Twain quipped that Wagner's music is better than it sounds. Could Mays' catch somehow be better than it looks?

Significantly, at the time, the catch was *not* regarded with universal shock and awe. In the locker room after the game, manager Leo Durocher barked at reporters who asked if it was Mays' greatest catch. "He's made catches like that all year. Where you been?" Indians outfielder Al Smith gave an even more ho-hum assessment. "Personally, I thought Mays had time to run the ball down and turn around to catch it, but Willie liked making dramatic catches like that." Sour grapes from a player on the losing team? Then consider the description by Mays' teammate Monte Irvin. "The ball was hit pretty high but on a line, and Willie left at the crack of the bat and caught the ball with not that much difficulty.... I've seen Willie make better catches."

The *New York Times* front page story on the game the next day was titled "Giants Win in 10 From Indians 5–2 on Rhodes Homer." The third subtitle (underneath "Grissom is Victor in Relief") notes "Mays' Catch Saves Triumph," but the actual article does not mention the catch until the 35th paragraph. The *Times* sports section did devote two three-paragraph articles to the catch, but these belie any notion that it was regarded as *the catch*. One article, "Reminder of Gionfriddo," relates Joe DiMaggio's opinion that Al Gionfriddo's catch in the 1947 World Series (robbing DiMaggio) was better than Mays' catch. The other, "Mays Catch Appraised," is subtitled, "Better Play Made By Willie in Brooklyn, Giants Scout Says," and in the article Giants chief scout Tom Sheehan reels off several catches by Mays that he considers better. Notice that the *Times* asked only whether it was Mays' personal best, with no suggestion that it was the greatest catch ever.

Some years later, the notion of Mays' catch as preeminent took root. Odder still, the myth has only grown rather than receded over time, even as numerous catches have surpassed it. This calls to mind the wry observation (reported in *Ball Four*) by Johnny Sain at an Old-Timer's Day. "There sure is a lot of bullshit going on about these old-timers. The older they get, the better they were when they were young."

Could it be that Mays' catch became mega-hyped because it came in a World Series? Catches become immortalized because of the moment as much as the catch itself. But there has never been a shortage of great World Series catches. The 1912 World Series featured a pair (one by Fred Snodgrass on the very next play following his immortal muff), and in a single game in the 1952 World Series the Dodgers outfield made three sensational plays, two robbing Yankees batters of home runs. Ron Swoboda's astounding catch in 1969 was in a World Series, and Joe Rudi made a half-dozen sparklers in the 1972–74 World Series, a few of which surpass Mays' on the difficulty scale. Ditto Devon White's eye-defying catch in the 1992 World Series when he won a collision with the center field wall. Endy Chavez's wall-climber for the Mets in 2007 was in Game 7 of a League Championship Series, as close to a World Series as you can get.

In all likelihood, the reason Mays' catch has been over-hyped is the reason so much is misremembered and mischaracterized: the Bowie-Buckner phenomenon discussed in Chapter One. We need our heroes and goats and love our stories tidy and dramatic. Unlike poor Bill Buckner, Mays falls on the right side of the hero/goat fence. What could be more satisfying than telling our grandchildren, and ourselves, that the Say Hey Kid made the most amazing play in baseball history?

Life Imitates Art

With rain falling increasingly hard, the fifth inning of the Marlins–Red Sox game on June 18 took on special urgency — the Marlins, leading 2–1, needed three outs to make the game official and the Red Sox desperately needed a run. David Ortiz hit a ball a mile high near second base, flung his bat in disgust, and jogged to first. Third baseman Emilio Bonifacio (playing near second on the Ortiz Shift) and second baseman Dan Uggla zig-zagged in pursuit of the wind-tossed ball, arrived simultaneously, and collided. The ball fell. Ortiz, who should have made second easily, stood at first. In each dugout, a manager fumed.

One out later, Jacoby Ellsbury chopped the ball to first baseman Wes Helms. Helms threw to second for the force, but there was no doubling the speedy Ellsbury at first. Had Helms stepped on first and then thrown to second, he'd have gotten the slow-footed Ortiz easily for an inning-ending double play. With the rain threatening to end the game before it became official, the Marlins had twice given away an out. But Jason Varitek struck out to end the inning and it was instantly the Red Sox's turn to agonize about the weather.

Sure enough, the rain picked up and the umps halted the game two batters into the sixth. The downpour never relented, and a few hours later the game was called. What's worse than losing a one-run ballgame? Losing a five-inning one-run ballgame. At the Hall of Fame in Cooperstown hangs the famous Norman Rockwell painting "Bottom of the Sixth" (where one manager needles another during a rain delay, while the umps look at the sky deciding whether the game can resume), which captures the angst that accompanies rain in a game half-played. In the painting the score is 1–0, not 2–1, and in the bottom of the sixth, not the top, but life can only come so close to imitating art. Meanwhile, in the sport famous for the absence of a clock, the Marlins won ... by a few minutes.

False Folklore

With the Red Sox and Braves tied 4–4 in the seventh inning on June 21, the Sox had George Kottaras on second and J.D. Drew at the plate. Eric O'Flaherty delivered a fastball near the middle of the plate. Expecting something else, Drew took the pitch, but umpire Bill Hohn must have been fooled too; he called it a ball. Drew drove the next pitch off the wall, plating Kottaras with the go-ahead run. O'Flaherty berated Hohn and was ejected. No big deal; he's replaceable. Braves manager Bobby Cox flipped out and got himself ejected, which the Braves are used to; it was Cox's 145th ejection, the most in baseball history. But then third baseman Chipper Jones, the Braves' best player, flipped out and got *himself* ejected — the last thing the Braves needed in the late innings of a close game.

So, wouldn't you know it, Jones' replacement, weak-hitting Kelly Johnson, doubled to lead off the eighth, and came around to score the tying run. However, the Braves could not long enjoy the law of unintended consequences. On the first pitch of the ninth inning, Nick Green hit a walk-off home run just inside the right field foul pole — the famous "Pesky Pole" — all of 300 feet away.

The game focused attention on a delicious piece of baseball lore that, like much baseball lore, is false. The casual Red Sox fan believes the Pesky Pole is so-called because Johnny Pesky, a slap-hitting shortstop in the 1940s–50s, managed many cheap home runs near Fenway's right field pole. In fact, only six of Pesky's 17 career home runs even came at Fenway. The more serious fan knows that the name was conferred by pitcher-turned-broadcaster Mel Parnell based on Pesky's opening day "blast" in 1946 that won Parnell a game. That, at any rate, is Pesky's explanation, memorialized by the *Boston Globe* in 2002 and repeated on the official Red Sox website. Just one problem: it's not true. Pesky hit only one Fenway home run in a game pitched by Parnell, and it was in the first inning of a game the Red Sox lost.

Lucky Lobber

On July 4, the 70th anniversary of Lou Gehrig's gallant "luckiest man on the face of the Earth" speech, a candidate for the luckiest man in baseball today took the mound in Philadelphia. At the age of 46, Jamie Moyer was pitching in his 24th season in the big leagues though he'd already been released three times by the age of 30 and his fastball has never reached 90 mph. These days it tops out at 85, yet he's in the starting rotation for the defending World Champions. On this day he pitched against the Mets, which is lucky for anybody. The sixth inning epitomized the Mets' folly-filled season. Paul Bako lofted a pop in foul territory, where David Wright camped under it and then, at the last second, pulled away and let it drop. (Apparently he thought he heard shortstop Alex Cora call him off.) Bako walked. No harm done, because with two outs Shane Victorino popped a foul ball to catcher Omar Santos ... who dropped it. Victorino singled in Bako. Moyer won his 253rd game. Not bad for a guy whose "fastball" has high school velocity.

Risk Aversion

On August 13, Victor Martinez stole a base. That's an item? Yes, because in Martinez's seven-year career, spanning over 800 games, he had one previous steal. *One.* Martinez looks fit, does not appear ridiculously slow, and players steal the occasional base just by showing up. Consider that Bengie Molina, who lays a legitimate claim to being the slowest player in baseball history, has three career thefts and Prince Fielder, who resembles a sumo wrestler, has 13. Martinez's theft put him one up on another catcher, Gus Triandos, who stole a single base in a career spanning 13 seasons and 1,206 games. His only theft came on the last game of the 1958 season, with his team trailing 6–3 in the ninth inning. Risky, but this guy knew what he was doing on the bases; in his long career he was never once caught stealing.

There's a delightful story about the voter who told a reporter he planned to vote against Barry Goldwater because Goldwater wanted to abolish TV. "No," the reporter explained. "Not TV. TVA — the Tennessee Valley Authority." The man thought it over, then replied, "I'm not taking any chances." He and Gus Triandos.

Strange Career Arcs

On August 26, the Red Sox won despite sliding catches by the White Sox's Carlos Quentin in consecutive innings — with a runner in scoring position in the seventh, and keeping the speedy Jacoby Ellsbury from reaching base to lead off the eighth. Quentin exemplifies a career arc unique (or nearly so) to baseball: the one-year wonder. His first two seasons he batted .230 with little power, before exploding last season, hitting .288 with 36 home runs and 100 RBIs. This year he's returned to earlier form — low batting average, reduced power.

If Quentin doesn't turn things around, he'll join a surprisingly long list of players who shined for a single season but couldn't bottle the magic — Mark Fidrych, Joe Charboneau, Davey Johnson, and Steve Stone, to name a few. Rookies of the Year include players you probably never heard of (Jason Jennings, Todd Hollandsworth, Harry Byrd, Bob Hamelin, Marty Cordora, Pat Listach, Jerome Walton, anyone?) and the ranks of MVPs include many who only received from zero to two Hall of Fame votes (Ken Caminiti, Ken Burroughs, Zoilo Versalles, Jim Konstanty, Willie Hernandez and Kevin Mitchell). Baseball also features players who had superb careers but never returned to the heights they reached in their first or second year — Al Kaline, Fernando Valenzuela, Vida Blue, Fred Lynn, and Dwight Gooden, among others. And baseball has players who completely lose their skills overnight — the dreaded Steve Blass Disease. More happily, some players turn back the clock at an advanced age. A 37-year-old Carlton Fisk blasted 37 homers, by far his career high. At the age of 39, Rickey Henderson stole more bases than he had in nine years. Mike Mussina won 20 games for the first time in his 18th season, at the age of 39. The extreme malleability of performance from year to year is one of baseball's many distinguishing features, and fits with the game's profound unpredictability.

Outside the Box

The cookie-cutter treatment of closers we've called LaRussaization is part of a larger phenomenon: managing by the numbers. But the 2009 season offered a few (all too few) examples of managing way outside the box. On July 12, with the Cubs trailing the Cards 4–2 in the ninth, Cubs left-hander Sean Marshall issued a walk to load the bases with no outs. Lou Piniella, trying to keep the game close, faced a dilemma; he wanted a right-handed pitcher to pitch to the right-handed Brendan Ryan, but he wanted Marshall, his only lefty reliever, to pitch to the two left-handed batters to follow. So he summoned Aaron Heilman to replace Marshall, but kept Marshall in the game — in left field. The move worked to perfection. Heilman whiffed Ryan, then Marshall returned to the mound and retired two batters to end the threat. (In the bottom of the ninth, Cards closer Ryan Franklin struck out the side — all looking — to make Piniella's maneuver moot.)

A few months later, in the decisive eighth inning of a Red Sox–Rays game, Rays manager Joe Maddon showed some original thinking. Slow-footed catcher Dioner Navarro was on first base, the potential tying run. He stayed there for 17 pitches. But when the count reached 3–2 on Carl Crawford, Maddon sent in Gabe Kapler to pinch-run. Maddon was reluctant to take out his catcher in a close game, but with two outs and a 3–2 count, the runner would be moving on the pitch, and a fast runner like Kapler might be able to score on a long single or double. That tipped the balance in favor of a pinch-runner. (Crawford flied out. What's that they say about the best laid plans of mice and managers?)

Manny and the Head-Hunter

In the Dodgers' feisty victory over Arizona on September 7, Manny Ramirez hit a towering home run in the second inning and was ejected in the third — Manny being Manny squared. The next inning, Diamondbacks pitcher Max Scherzer drilled Russell Martin between the numbers, and umpire Doug Eddings issued warnings to both teams. After the game, players on both teams expressed surprise at the warnings (even Martin acknowledged he wasn't being thrown at), but Eddings knew exactly what he was doing. The Dodgers pitcher was Vicente Padilla, who needs little excuse to throw at batters. When Texas released Padilla a month earlier, Rangers players expressed delight. "About time," said Marlon Byrd. Ian Kinsler shook the hand of General Manager Jon Daniels in front of the media and beamed "Congrats!" The Rangers were tired of getting thrown at in retaliation for Padilla's head-hunting.

Life Goes On

The role of the 2001 World Series in re-establishing normalcy and buoying the American spirit post–9/11 has been much remarked. The Angels–Red Sox game on April 10 was a microcosm. The game was preceded by a ceremony honoring Nick Adenhart, the Angels' promising 22-year-old pitcher killed by a hit-and-run driver the day before. Life goes on, but it seemed cruel to make the Angels play ball right after an intolerably sad tribute to their fallen teammate culminating in Torii Hunter and John Lackey holding Adenhart's jersey aloft at the mound. How do you hit major league pitching while in the throes of grief? How could pitcher Jered Weaver face major league hitters when, as he admitted after the game, he thought about Adenhart between pitches throughout the game?

Never underestimate human resiliency. Someone tuning in five minutes late wouldn't have noticed anything amiss, and would never believe that the game was played in the shadow of tragedy. The players played, the crowd cheered and booed. Displaying their usual gusto (including four stolen bases), the Angels defeated the Red Sox, 6–3. Distracted though he may have been, Weaver pitched well. For the Angels, and to a lesser extent the entire baseball world, the week encapsulated the human condition: the unbearable fragility of life and the consolation that we somehow cope. We do so, in part, by returning to routine and indulging life's daily pleasures, the gifts that keep on giving through it all.

Conclusion

In the course of discussing Matt Garza's near perfect game in Chapter Seven, we wrote, "There've been books written chronicling baseball's perfect games: One ought to be written about near misses." That sentence, written before Jim Joyce's infamous bad call cost the Tigers' Armando Galarraga a perfect game on June 2, 2010, may have been prescient. Somewhere today, we suspect, someone is writing if not exactly that book, then perhaps one dealing solely with the Galarraga-Joyce game and its aftermath.

If such a book is written, it will surely be a celebration of baseball and the human spirit, a feel-good story about a monumental screw-up that ended up elevating both the culprit and the victim. In the immediate aftermath of the game, everyone assumed that the botched call cost Galarraga baseball immortality and earned it for Joyce in the worst possible way. Two reactions tended to dominate: sympathy for Galarraga, and a mixture of anger and sympathy towards Joyce. Galarraga was deprived of a perfect game through no fault of his own — that was unambiguous. Joyce's situation was more complicated. On the one hand, he *did* mess up royally. On the other hand, who wants to see someone's life ruined by an innocent mistake? Bill Buckner was banished to Idaho and became synonymous with World Series goat because of a single error. Surely a similar fate awaited Jim Joyce. Meanwhile Galarraga, on the verge of joining the short list of pitchers immortalized for achieving perfection, would instead join the long list of unremembered pitchers who came close.

Then, of course, the twist ending. It started immediately with Galarraga's Zen-like response to the call that cheated him out of immortality, his enigmatic smile at first base. In a sport where players routinely abuse umpires over garden variety mistakes (and even good calls the players *think* are mistakes), Galarraga didn't so much as scowl or mutter an expletive. Joyce's reaction was less surprising but equally endearing; he stepped up to the plate and took full responsibility for the screw-up. He didn't just admit he had blown the call, but he emphasized its importance and out-rageousness. "It was the biggest call of my career, and I kicked the shit out of it." He seemed sincerely sorry, and not for himself—for Galarraga. As the saying goes, "If you're going to fall on the sword, fall on it completely." Joyce plunged the sword through his heart, and thus won over a society accustomed to evasions of responsibility from politicians and others in the limelight.

The next day brought another unlikely grace note. Tigers manager Jim Leyland, the epitome of a macho tobacco-spitting baseball lifer, did more than just publicly forgive Joyce (which would have been enough). He tapped into his inner Oprah and concocted a feel-good plan, sending Galarraga out to home plate with the line-up card, which the pitcher would hand to the man who happened to be umpiring the plate: Jim Joyce. The pitcher and umpire, already joined at the hip in baseball lore, exchanged affectionate pats, Tigers fans responded with more cheers than boos, and the new narrative had already written itself—in 24 hours, tragedy trans-lated into an uplifting tale for the ages.

That day Galarraga received a car from General Motors, and he never stopped receiving gushing compliments from fans, media, and fellow play-ers. Far be it from a forgotten flirtation with perfection, his effort will go down as the second-most famous perfect game in baseball history. The asterisk next to it will denote not that it wasn't really a perfect game, but rather that the pitcher distinguished himself for exemplary sportsmanship after an erroneous call, and then bore down to retire the next batter—a unique 28-batter perfect game. Joyce? Within weeks of the incident, play-ers voted him the best umpire in baseball. Needless to say, that made head-lines. Not only was he hailed for his manly comportment in the aftermath of the game, but he received long-overdue recognition for a career of dis-tinguished work. It's doubtful that the players would have voted for him were it not for the publicity surrounding the blown call. (He'd never received such recognition before.) Certainly, but for that call, no one would have paid much attention to the survey results. How many umpires can you name who were voted best umpire by the players?

Of course, the basic plot line described above has been much remarked — the morphing of a depressing story into a feel-good story literally overnight. But in all the celebration, something important has been overlooked; the twist ending post-game mirrored the twist ending in the game itself. Consider that, when in the ninth inning ESPN switched from coverage of its original game to Detroit to catch the possible history-making ending, scenarios raced through the minds of viewers. On each batter, fans were pulling for Galaragga to throw a first-pitch strike. If he fell behind, he'd have to be concerned about a walk and might groove a pitch. And especially when he retired the first two batters, and Cleveland's Jason Donald strode to the plate, who didn't think of those poor infielders (and to a lesser extent outfielders), imagining the heart-stopping pressure they would feel on a ball hit to them? The baseball history buff might even have thought about the home plate umpire. He, too, must be feeling extraordinary pressure. Would he expand his strike zone? After all, the last pitch of Don Larsen's World Series perfect game in 1956 was probably a ball, but Babe Pinelli, the home plate umpire working his last Series before retirement, and perhaps eager for a cameo in the history books, called it strike three (against a batter, Dale Mitchell, who almost never struck out). Thoughts of every kind raced through the minds of everyone watching. Yet one thing probably never crossed anyone's mind: what if the batter is clearly out at first and the umpire calls him safe?

That's exactly what happened. Except it isn't! It only seems that way, on account of a bizarre oversight. Donald was *not* clearly out at first. He appears clearly out from the reply angle usually shown, with Galarraga's back to the viewer, but from the camera angle showing Galarraga catching the ball, one discerns a slight but unmistakable juggle when the pitcher receives the toss from first baseman Miguel Cabrera. Donald may well have been safe. Certainly, with the bobble taken into account, it was a bang-bang call that could have gone either way. That inconvenient truth muddies the tidy tale, but it adds an element of texture. Joyce probably never saw the juggle — he never mentioned it — but that merely renders the play stranger still. He may have made the right call for the wrong reason.

There's also a small postscript to the story that adds a little more spice, an almost eerie element of déjà vu. The next day, in the Indians-Tigers contest played in the shadow of Galarraga's quasi-perfect game, Jason Donald was again credited with an infield hit on a play where he was clearly (from all camera angles this time) out. It's not quite true to say you can't make this stuff up. You can, it's just that no one would believe you. No one, that is, except one well-versed in baseball's capacious imagination.

If a book is indeed written about the Galaragga-Joyce game, ideally it will probe all of the parts of the story we've discussed: the improbable ending, Galarraga's almost surreal reaction and Joyce's admirable acceptance of responsibility, the crusty Leyland going soft against type, the overlooked fact that Donald may indeed have been safe, the fact that this would have been the third perfect game of the young 2010 season (unprecedented and inexplicable), and that nothing in Galarraga's brief career heralded perfection — in short, all of the things that make this a quintessential baseball story, featuring one unpredictable event after another, even after the final out of the game was recorded.

We can also imagine a different kind of book written about the game. Imagine this book written by a sabermetrician. Not Bill James, who appreciates the game's majesty and mystery, but one of the dyed-in-the-wool third-wave sabermetricians who buries himself in esoteric formulae. This hypothetical book would analyze all perfect games and locate factors that run through them — most of the pitchers had winning records the previous month, were pitching against sub–.500 teams in ballparks where the run per game average was in the bottom quintile for the league that year. These and countless other data would be used to create a formula called Perfect Game Likelihood Matrix (PGLM), and it might turn out that Galarraga's pre-game PGLM was .0021. While that would superficially suggest that the odds of his perfection were remote, such a conclusion overlooks the fact that the average PGLM is an even more microscopic .0014. Thus, Galarraga was actually more likely than most pitchers to pitch a perfect game that day. Not to rain on your parade, Armando, you did a great job, it's just that this quasi-perfect game was actually among the less remarkable.

Which book would you rather read — the one that seeks to capture the story's magic or the one that treats the too-strange-for-fiction story as fodder for a mathematical probe?

In an earlier draft of this book, we included the following discussion (since taken out, for obvious reasons) about a Blue Jays–Red Sox game in 2009:

> Lyle Overbay's seventh-inning single may have prevented history from being made. No, it wasn't the Blue Jays' first hit. It was their second, at least officially. The first was an infield single by Kevin Millar resulting from an unambiguously bad call. (Replays showed Millar to be out by a half-step.) Has an umpire ever cost a pitcher a no-no?

The Galarraga-Joyce game rendered our hypothetical question not just moot, but terribly tame. After all, Joyce's call didn't just cost Galarraga a no-hitter, but a perfect game. And it wasn't at any old point in the game, but on the last batter.

As always, baseball showed more imagination than we ever could. And infinitely more imagination than those who would reduce it to numbers.

Selected Bibliography

Albert, Jim, and Bennett James. *Curve Ball: Baseball, Statistics, and the Role of Chance in the Game.* New York: Copernicus, 2001.

Barra, Allen. *Brushbacks and Knockdowns: The Greatest Baseball Debates of Two Centuries.* New York: St. Martin's, 2004.

Bizzinger, H.G. *Three Nights in August: Strategy, Heartbreak and Joy Inside the Mind of a Manager.* New York: Mariner, 2006.

Boswell, Thomas. *The Heart of the Order.* New York: Penguin, 1990.

Bouton, Jim. *Ball Four.* New York: World, 1970.

Bronson, Eric. *Baseball and Philosophy: Thinking Outside the Batter's Box.* Chicago: Open Court, 2004.

Costa, Gabriel B., Michael R. Huber, and John T. Saccoman. *Practicing Sabermetrics: Putting the Science of Baseball Statistics to Work.* Jefferson, NC: McFarland, 2009.

_____, _____, and _____. *Understanding Sabermetrics: An Introduction to the Science of Baseball Statistics.* Jefferson, NC: McFarland, 2007.

Felber, Bill. *The Book on the Book: A Landmark Inquiry into Which Strategies in the Modern Game Actually Work.* New York: Dunne Books, 2005.

Goldman, Steve. *It Ain't Over Till It's Over: The Baseball Prospectus Pennant Race Book.* New York: Basic Books, 2007.

_____. *Mind Game: How the Boston Red Sox Got Smart, Won a World Series, and Created a New Blueprint for Winning.* New York: Workman, 2005.

Gould, Stephen Jay. *Triumph and Tragedy in Mudville.* New York: W.W. Norton, 2003.

Grey, Scott. *The Mind of Bill James.* New York: Doubleday, 2006.

Hample, Zack. *Watching Baseball Smarter: A Professional Fan's Guide for Beginners, Semi-Experts, and Deeply Serious Geeks.* New York: Vintage, 2007.

Honig, Donald. *Baseball When the Grass Was Real: Baseball from the Twenties to the Forties, Told by the Men Who Played It.* Lincoln: University of Nebraska Press, 1993.

James Bill. *The Bill James Baseball Abstract.* New York: Ballantine, annual editions, 1977–1988.

_____. *The Bill James Gold Mine.* Skokie, IL: ACTA Sports, 2010.

_____. *The New Bill James Historical*

Baseball Abstract. New York: Free Press, 2003.

_____, and James Henzler. *Win Shares.* Morton Grove, IL: STATS, 2002.

Keri, Jonah, ed. *Baseball Between the Numbers: Why Everything You Know About the Game Is Wrong.* New York: Basic Books, 2006.

Klein, Alan. *Growing the Game: The Globalization of Major League Baseball.* New Haven: Yale University Press, 2008.

Kurjikan, Tim. *Is This a Great Game or What? From A-Rod's Head to Zim's Heart—My 25 Years in Baseball.* New York: St. Martin's, 2007.

Lewis, Michael. *Moneyball: The Art of Winning an Unfair Game.* New York: W.W. Norton, 2004.

McCarver, Tim. *Baseball for Brain Surgeons and Other Fans.* New York: Villard, 1998.

Neyer, Rob. *Rob Neyer's Big Book of Baseball Blunders: A Complete Guide to the Worst Decisions and Stupidest Moments in Baseball History.* New York: Fireside, 2006.

Olney, Buster. *The Last Night of the Yankee Dynasty.* New York: HarperCollins, 2004.

Paulos, John Allen. *Innumeracy, Mathematical Illiteracy and its Consequences.* New York: Hill & Wang, 2001.

Perry, Dayn. *Winners: How Good Teams Become Great Ones (and It's Not the Way You Think).* Hoboken, NJ: John Wiley, 2006.

Pierce, Gregory F. Augustine, ed. *How Bill James Changed Our View of Baseball.* Skokie, IL: ACTA Sports, 2007.

Ross, Ken. *A Mathematician at the Ballpark: Odds and Probabilities for Baseball Fans.* New York: Plume, 2007.

Schwarz, Alan. *The Numbers Game: Baseball's Lifelong Fascination with Statistics.* New York: St. Martin's, 2004.

Swaine, Rick. *Beating the Breaks: Major League Ballplayers Who Overcame Disabilities.* Jefferson, NC: McFarland, 2004.

Tango, Tom, Mitchel Licthman, and Andrew Dolphin. *The Book: Playing the Percentages in Baseball.* Washington, DC: Potomac Books, 2007.

Torre, Joe, and Tom Verducci. *The Yankee Years.* New York: Anchor, 2010.

Thorn, John, and Pete Palmer. *The Hidden Game of Baseball: A Revolutionary Approach to Baseball and Its Statistics.* New York: Doubleday, 2005.

_____, _____, Michael Gershman, and Matthew Silverman, eds. *Total Baseball: The Official Encyclopedia of Major League Baseball.* Kingston, NY: Total Sports, 2001.

Walker, Eric. *The Sinister First Baseman and Other Observations.* Millbrae, CA: Celestial Arts, 1982.

Will, George. *Men at Work: The Craft of Baseball.* New York: HarperCollins, 1990.

Wright, Craig, and Tom House. *The Diamond Appraised: A World-Class Theorist and a Major-League Coach Square Off on Timeless Topics in the Game of Baseball.* New York: Simon & Schuster, 1990.

Index

199

Index

Index

Index

205

Index